the
honor
was
mine

the
honor
was
mine

*A Look Inside
the Struggles of
Military Veterans*

ELIZABETH
HEANEY, MA, LPC

Published by Grand Harbor Press, Grand Haven, MI

www.brilliancepublishing.com

Amazon, the Amazon logo, and Grand Harbor Press are trademarks of Amazon.com, Inc., or its affiliates.

ISBN-13: 9781503935747
ISBN-10: 1503935744

Cover design by Kimberly Glyder

Printed in the United States of America

Table of Contents

AUTHOR'S NOTE

Names, ranks, and physical descriptions have been changed to protect privacy. Changes were made to details—such as how many times I talked to the soldier, where the soldiers came from, their ethnic backgrounds, if they had deployed, whether they were married or had children—as long as doing so wouldn't alter the underlying nature of the actual exchange, the crux of the conversation, or the essence of the soldier's concerns. Some interactions described represent an amalgamation of conversations I had with many different service members. It's likely *many* soldiers could imagine a described scene is about them, but I have taken precautions to make sure individuals are not otherwise identifiable. In order to further preserve privacy, specific bases and base locations are not named.

Members of the United States Marine Corps are officially called Marines; members of the Air Force are airmen; Navy service members are sailors; Coast Guard members are coasties; and those who serve in the Army are soldiers.

For the purposes of this book, the term "soldiers" is used generically, although service members from each of these branches of the United States military, except for the Coast Guard, are represented in these stories. Because the Army is the largest branch of the armed services, the language used is Army-referenced for simplicity's sake, since the military terms and colloquialisms can vary widely from one branch to another.

MILITARY RANKS, ABBREVIATIONS, AND TERMS

RANKS

Captain (CPT)
Command Sergeant Major (CSM)
Corporal (CPL)
First Lieutenant (1LT)
Lieutenant Colonel (LTC)
Major (MAJ)
Private (PVT)
Private First Class (PFC)
Second Lieutenant (2LT)
Specialist (SPC)
Staff Sergeant (SSG)

ABBREVIATIONS

15N (military occupational specialty of avionic mechanic)
CAO (casualty assistance officer)
DFAC (dining facility)
FOB (forward operating base)
IED (improvised explosive device)
MOS (military occupational specialty)
NCO (noncommissioned officer)
PCS (permanent change of station)
PT (physical training)
PX (post exchange)
SOF (special operations forces)

TERMS

block leave: when most or all of the unit takes leave at the same time, which commonly occurs before and after deployments or during the summer and Christmas holidays
class A: dress uniform
downrange: soldiers' term for combat overseas
in-process: a regular procedural practice soldiers must undergo when they return from deployment
outside the wire: beyond the boundaries of the base of operations
re-up: reenlist for a specified number of years
tasked (to do something): assigned to do it

PROLOGUE

"Here's how it was: if something moved, I had to shoot." Corporal Springer's face is ashen; all the color drains out as he remembers deploying into Iraq at the very beginning when the killing was crazy and out of control. "You understand? *If it moves, I shoot.*"

"I understand, corporal. If it moves, you shoot." I keep my voice and my gaze steady, direct.

Springer is out of the Army now; he came to the base for counseling when his symptoms began to be too much to manage. He doesn't like having to interact with people, so he works as a landscaper, spending his workdays alone and silent. He has just started seeing me.

"Everything was so damned hyped up." As he speaks, his body becomes agitated, his hands flailing. "We were clearing buildings, moving through the worst parts of the city—dangerous, *dangerous* neighborhoods. If something moved, I couldn't take the time to figure out what it was. If I hesitated, I'd be dead."

I look at him and nod, but I stay quiet, wanting him to keep telling the tales he can't bear to hold inside anymore. He tells me he and his buddies were fighting hard, never knowing who the enemy really was. Someone who looked like an innocent shopkeeper might be carrying a bomb; a young woman leaning against a doorway might be spying on troop movements.

"It was insanity. I shot at anything that moved. Could've been a sniper or a dog or even a little kid. You understand?"

This battle-ravaged soldier wrings his hands and then runs them back and forth across his buzz-cut blond hair. His square jaw is set, his face like stone. He sits on the edge of the worn gray couch in my counseling office at the battalion building, not looking out the window, not glancing around the room. When he's not looking intently at me, he's gazing downward at the cloud patterns in the linoleum floor.

"When I went over there, I was nineteen. I thought I was hot shit, all gung ho, *let's do this!* I thought I was *prepared*, you know? But when I got there, it wasn't anything at all like what we'd been told in the training . . ." His voice trails off and he shudders.

"My buddies were dropping like flies. I lost count after the first week or two. I thought I would be next—every minute, every single day. Then it became so simple: just keep shooting. Shoot at everything. Shoot *first*. It was gonna be me or them, and I had to make sure it was them. That was the deal. By the end of my first month, I felt like a goddamn monster; I still had a whole year left in my deployment."

Springer studies the linoleum floor as if it holds answers; his body is frozen in the memory of how it felt to be on high alert, fearing for his life and taking the lives of others. As we talk, there are times when Springer gets anxious and looks like he's going to bolt out of the room. He tells me it's extremely difficult to suppress the urge to run. In those moments, he goes quiet and sits statue-still, forcing himself to stay seated until the urge to flee has passed. At other times, he speaks so fast and so frankly, I can hardly keep up with his words.

This fast/slow rhythm mirrors the jolting pace of his out-of-control nervous system.

His voice drops. "Here's the thing, ma'am. Sometimes, when the fighting was close-up, I saw the guy's face. Just before I pulled the trigger, we would look at each other. I remember their faces. I *remember* them, ma'am. And now I keep wondering, 'What will God think of me?' I know I had to shoot. But *what will God think of me?* I was raised Catholic. I used to go to church. Now I don't know if God will even look at me."

Springer's voice is nearly a whisper. He's barely breathing.

"That's what you're trying to sort out, right? 'What kind of person am I if I did all these things?'"

Springer nods and we sit in silence. After a while, he looks up and says there's more he wants to tell me, but that's enough for today. He tells me he'll stop by soon to talk some more, and I shake his hand as he leaves.

When he shows up at my office again a few days later, Springer begins with a statement: "I'm not crazy, ma'am."

He comes back to this phrase again and again as he tells me the things he feels compelled to do: He checks his refrigerator a hundred times a day, even though he knows exactly what's in it. While driving through his quiet neighborhood, he scans the side of the road for bombs or hidden enemies. He feels instant, raging frustration if he has to wait in line for any reason at all, so he avoids grocery stores and home improvement stores. Since crowds make him nervous, he usually skips going to movies or to the mall. Stadiums or arenas are out of the question.

After confessing each of these difficulties, Springer looks at me with his piercing blue eyes and repeats, "I'm not crazy, ma'am."

I assure him: he's not crazy. He's doing the things soldiers do when PTSD is scrambling their inner world. He's trying to find ways to feel safe while his neurological system is telling him danger is immense and immediate.

Even though it's been seven years since he returned from Baghdad, Springer still wakes up every night, screaming and sobbing, from heart-splitting nightmares of the things he saw and did. He lives by himself. "That way, ma'am, no one hears me scream; no one will think I'm crazy."

Springer stays quiet for a while and I watch him as he stares downward, swimming in his fears and memories, trying to piece together what's happened to him. I sit quietly, knowing he needs these silent moments to gather himself before we wade further into the turmoil. A few minutes pass before Springer looks up, fixes his gaze on me, and says, "I don't fit in real life anymore."

With this statement, it's as if all the air has been sucked out of the room. He's stating one thing no one ever wants to admit: *I don't fit*. He's not talking metaphorically or figuratively. He's not saying he *feels* like he doesn't fit. He's admitting a clear, straightforward knowing that resides like a scalding ember in his core.

At this point in our conversation, Springer looks particularly stressed. He scoots up to the very edge of the couch and leans forward intently, as if he's getting ready to jump right off the edge of it. His body is like a tight spring, coiled and tensed.

"Ma'am, I have to tell you something."

I nod.

"Ma'am, when I came back, I was glad to be home and out of that hell over there, but life didn't make sense anymore. It seemed like I was supposed to just go along as if nothing had happened and nothing had changed. But I wasn't the same person at all, and I had all kinds of weird things going on inside me. I tried to act like I was OK, but I could tell people thought I was fucked-up. I wasn't myself and everyone knew it, no matter how much I tried to fake it.

"After a couple of months, my enlistment was up. I left the Army and went back to Montana to stay with my parents. You know, I just didn't know what else to do. My family there, they kept telling me, 'You're different. You've really changed.' But I couldn't help it."

His eyes well up and he tucks his hands under his thighs, willing himself to stay on the couch's edge. There's a kind of pleading in his eyes.

"Ma'am, I . . . I . . ." He keeps his eyes on me like he needs ballast for the next part of the story to come forward. Finally, he blurts out, "Sometimes I hide in my closet. I can't help it. I know I'm a grown man, but I can't help it."

"It's OK," I tell him, "I know you can't help it. You're just trying to not be so scared."

"Yeah." His voice is very faint as he slips into the image of himself in the closet. "I get way back in the corner. Sometimes I pile clothes on top of me. I pull things off hangers and try to cover myself up with them. It's dark and quiet in there."

"Right," I say. "It's quiet and nothing happens. You're safe for a while, aren't you?"

Springer's face flushes. He nods and takes in huge gulps of air, tears streaming down his face.

"But I have to tell you something else."

I nod.

"One day, when I'm in my closet, I hear my dad calling my name. He's walking through the house, calling me and looking in different rooms trying to find me. I know it's him. I mean, I know it's my dad. But I can't get myself to move. I hear him getting closer. He walks into my room to see if I'm in there. He starts to leave, but then I can hear him walk over to the closet and he turns the door-knob. He sticks his head in and sees me, and for a long time we just look at each other.

"Then my dad gets down on his knees, crawls into the closet, pulls me into his arms, and he starts crying. He just holds on to me real tight and we both cry like babies."

Springer breaks down and sobs; his body shakes violently.

"I'm glad you have a dad like that," I say quietly.

When he looks up, his hard stare has weakened ever so slightly, and his gaze holds a tiny hint of vulnerability that wasn't there before. He's finally beginning the long journey home.

CHAPTER 1

As the wars in Iraq and Afghanistan dragged on, military leaders began to recognize the impact of multiple deployments on combat veterans and their families. To help soldiers and families cope with the enormous stress of lengthy separations, war injuries, and death, the Department of Defense initiated a program on military bases that offered soldiers free counseling that was strictly confidential. To implement this program, civilian counselors were hired to work on military bases all over the world.

As a counselor with little knowledge of the military, I was surprised and impressed when a few of my colleagues became part of this new program, signing up to work on bases where soldiers were getting ready to deploy into combat or just returning from combat deployments. When I first learned of their new jobs I thought about the possibility of joining them, but I relished the freedom of my private practice work and enjoyed the wide variety of clients who came to see me. Working for a company that would send me to one base after another—and working with just one population of clients—seemed limiting and unappealing to me, so I dismissed the opportunity.

A year or so later, however, circumstances changed my mind. I was in my midfifties, single and childless, and for a couple of years I'd been grappling with a strong inner urge to make big changes in my life. As the months passed, the urge to change became more and more forceful and persistent. The feeling was also confounding: Where would I live? What would I do for work? Why should I leave the place I had loved and enjoyed? As the urge grew, my pleasantly settled life began to shift underneath my feet, without my assent. I began to feel *pushed* out of all that was familiar, and I sensed that this inner demand for change simply would not be ignored.

As the ensuing upheaval rolled through my life, it was as if Tucson withdrew from the embrace I had felt during the twenty-six years I had lived there. I spent my last two years in Tucson grappling with a cascade of losses unlike anything I had ever experienced before. The experience of driving along Campbell Avenue, River Road, or Speedway, streets that had been my daily routes, felt "flat"—the roads suddenly seeming foreign and unknown. My favorite cafés, book-stores, and shops—Bentley's, The Cup Café, Antigone Books, Feast, and Beyond Bread—no longer held any appeal for me. All the lovely threads that had been holding me closely entwined with my city were cut, one after the other. I might as well have been in Morocco or Tanzania, for I felt no sense of connection to Tucson at all. I was stunned, and I felt uprooted as other unwelcome changes took my life apart.

During these months of dismantling, my house was broken into. Twice. The first time it happened, I walked into my ransacked house to find my grandmother's marcasite watch from the early nineteen hundreds; the delicate gold and miniature-pearl necklace I'd been given for my First Communion; an antique gold necklace my parents purchased at an estate sale; and "junk" jewelry given to me by my grandparents—pieces that sparkled with blues, greens, and purples in fanciful detail—all gone. The intruders also had taken the TV, the stereo, the microwave, and any furniture that could be easily carried. I found my dog cowering underneath an end table, traumatized by the break-in.

During the second burglary, the thieves took my computer *and* the computer's backup system, along with my cell phone, the printer, and some of my clothing. By taking my computer's backup system, the burglars effectively wiped out my entire electronic history. I lost all my music, all my photos, fifteen years' worth of notes, outlines, handouts, and tests from classes and workshops, and twenty years of essays and other writing. For months, I couldn't think of the loss without crying.

One night shortly after the second break-in, I woke to find myself standing in the middle of my bedroom, half-crouched, heart pounding, my hands out in front of me, ready for a fight. In my startled-awake state, I didn't know what had propelled me, still asleep, into the middle of the room. I must have heard a noise while I was sleeping and leapt into a "defensive position" before I was even fully awake.

Over the twenty-six years I'd been in private practice in Tucson, I'd built a good reputation and had a steady stream of clients. I often had a waiting list of folks who wanted to work with me as soon as I had an opening in my schedule. As this chapter of upheaval in my life unfolded, however, the phone literally stopped ringing. Without any logical reason that I could think of, my appointment book became page after page of barren time slots. I now had only a few sessions scheduled per week, and a slew of empty days in which I wasn't sure what to do with myself.

Floundering emotionally, I took long hikes by myself in the Catalina Mountains, spent a lot of time at the branch library two blocks from my house, and watched TV with vacant eyes. I fought off a sense of panic over the fact that I couldn't stop the destruction of my comfortable life. The losses moved through one area of my life after another, and I began to slip into days filled with struggle and fear. I had the distinct experience that the changes were happening *to* me, as opposed to seeing things I was doing that might lead to the shifts.

Close friends wondered aloud what the heck was going on with my life. They had always known me to be a steady, grounded person whose life lacked drama or upheaval.

"I'm sorry. I don't get it," said Terry, after I called and told her of the latest calamity to befall me.

I'd gone for a hike in the nearby mountains to burn off some stress, and while I was on the trail, someone threw a large rock through my car window and then stole my wallet, including my credit cards, and all the tools in my trunk. This happened the week after I had taken my car in for a very minor repair that had ended up costing me several hundred dollars. It seemed as though every time I spoke with Terry, I had new hardships to report.

"This isn't like you," Terry said. It felt like a rebuke.

"Well, it's like me *now*," I told her sadly—and a little defensively.

In her eyes, I had become someone who called up to talk about one sad drama after another. In the past, we had laughed and shared our lives with pretty consistent optimism. Now, my voice was flat, I struggled to see anything good in what was happening, and my sense of humor was completely gone.

She seemed to think I should hold it together better, that I should keep myself in a more positive frame of mind. I felt like Terry didn't understand at all. As she began to sound vaguely impatient with my reports, I felt like I'd worn her out with my tales of hardship and suffering. She seemed frustrated with my failure to *do* something that would reverse my string of misfortunes. Eventually, her frustration and her inability to grasp my helplessness in the face of mounting losses led to the end of our twenty-five year friendship, and I grieved yet another loss.

Other friendships ended, too. I dropped out of touch because I couldn't manage to return phone calls or answer emails. At times, I was too weary from the difficulties to keep up the effort of being sociable. I began to feel more and more alone.

One friend, Jonathan, had been a brother to my heart for twenty-five years. I'd spent countless Christmases, Easters, and Thanksgivings with him, his wife, and his family. I'd gone to family weddings with them, and we'd camped and hiked all over the Southwest together. Our bond felt as solid as the earth beneath my feet. One morning, out of his New Age perspective on life, Jonathan gently shared that he felt I was "creating" the difficulties I was grappling with. That hurt. If a person had been through this sort of tsunami of loss, he would grasp that no one would choose to "create" this kind of trauma.

I had known for many years that Jonathan sincerely embraced the paradigm that we all create our experiences in life. While I didn't always share that perspective, it had never resulted in a conflict between us. Now, however, in his view, I had to be doing *something* to create all of the catastrophes I was experiencing. I knew with every cell of my being I wasn't causing all these things to happen. After that, an unbridgeable gap opened between us, and we stopped communicating—and I spent even more time alone, wondering how to get through the storm.

Some friends showed great compassion toward me, but even with them, I heard baffled helplessness in their voices as they listened to my ever-evolving tale of struggle and loss. One friend said it was my "Saturn return" (an astrological construct for huge life-shifts). Another believed it was a midlife crisis, while yet another framed it as an "identity crisis." Whatever it was, as time went by and the losses continued, I wondered whether it was even worth trying to share these experiences with others. My friendships seemed to have become a one-sided tale of woes.

Morning after morning, I dressed as soon as I woke up and headed out on long, rambling walks to stave off anxiety. I felt slightly frantic and on guard, wondering which thread of my life would come unraveled next. I began to live in fear of the next unexplainable event, the next unexpected loss. If I didn't begin walking as soon as I woke up, the anxiety and dread would get a foothold and my body would start trembling. Tucson streets are laid out in a simple east-west/north-south grid. I'd walk east toward the dawn and watch as the sun rose over the mountains, then I'd turn around and walk home.

During the second year of unraveling, my sixteen-year-old dog died, and my heart stumbled with fresh grief. I had found Ojito tossed out on a dirt road when she was a tiny, five-week-old pup. She had been a source of true joy and companionship all through those years, but now she was gone, too. My dad ended up in the hospital after a bad fall; my sister faced cancer.

I thought, *Good Lord, I'd better leave here, or I'm not going to have anything left.* My life was being stripped down to the studs. Or more accurately, down to the foundation. The process felt relentless and brutal, but it also felt very *purposeful*; there was an almost surgical precision to the way my life was being dismantled. Something important was unfolding, and while I wasn't yet privy to the exact purpose, I could intuitively feel the pristine intentionality of it. Strangely, it was in the darkest moments that I tapped into this intuition about the process. Waking in the middle of the night, shaky with fear, I would quiet my breathing and slowly dive deep down inside to steady myself. In the inner depths, I began to find the feeling that there was a sense to all this, even if I didn't understand what it might be. Whenever I felt panicky, I'd whisper to myself, "Shh . . . something important is taking place. See if you can hang in there."

Nothing had happened in my life to start all this; no event had triggered the landslide of loss. Still, every day of the last two years I lived in Tucson, the disorienting process of change led me to feel like I was wearing clothes that didn't fit. *I* didn't fit in that life anymore. In the end, moving away and starting again seemed like the only option.

As I struggled to imagine my future, I remembered the military job and realized it would buy me some time. I didn't take the job out of any dedication to helping service members. I simply figured it would give me steady work while I sorted out what to do next, and it would move me around the country so I could explore new places to live.

And so, on an already-hot June morning in Tucson, I slammed my trunk lid down with a solid thunk and walked around to the driver's side door. I leaned against the side of my twenty-year-old Honda Accord and took a long last look back at my house. The front porch I had once filled with pots of bright-blooming flowers was bare. The windows that once held sweet lace curtains were dark and vacant. The tin roof that had often thrummed so beautifully beneath monsoon storms was silent.

I had spent the past several weeks sorting out what to put in storage and what to pack into the car as I began my new life as a roving counselor. I couldn't take much, so I chose small comfort items—my favorite pillow, a few cherished photos, a cozy comforter that was threadbare from use. I made room for Ojito's sweetly worn-out dog collar, a few books that would carry me until I landed near a library, and the road atlas that would soon be tattered with wear. I took basic living items, too—kitchen utensils, laundry needs, work files, and office supplies.

I stood in the shade of a hundred-year-old eucalyptus tree, listening to the cicadas' loud chirring and contemplating the threshold I was about to cross. I tend toward teariness in poignant moments, but this moment was much more than poignant, and too complicated for tears. It was relieving and freeing and frightening and sad and overwhelming to be leaving. What I felt was a kaleidoscope of strong feelings. I was turning away from the place where I had lived for most of my adult life, had developed my career, and had come to understand how to navigate the ins and outs of daily life. With my car packed and house emptied, I now made the final surrender to change.

Turning out of my driveway, I didn't look back. I drove across town and got on the interstate, aiming for a military base in the Deep

South—a part of the country I'd never been to before. My new life was, at that moment, not at all clear to me; all I knew was where I needed to report in a couple of weeks.

I had no idea then of the journey I was about to begin. If I'd had any inkling, I might have put my belongings back in the house and clung to what was familiar.

As a therapist, I was skilled enough to work comfortably with clients whose lives were different from mine, so I had no concern about the actual counseling I would be doing with soldiers. I was capable of rolling up my sleeves and giving them the support they needed. But as I drove across the country to my first assignment, I mulled over the vague, uninformed notions I had about the military and about service members.

Back then, I thought I'd be dealing with a bunch of war-obsessed people who mindlessly followed orders; I thought I'd get bored because the counseling conversations would be about post-traumatic stress disorder (PTSD), all day, every day—as if that were the only issue any service member ever struggled with; I thought every soldier would be a cookie-cutter repeat of every other soldier, all individuality having been stomped out of them in boot camp. I never thought about the soldiers' families. They weren't in my consciousness at all, as if soldiers floated around in disconnected islands of squads and platoons, without loved ones to embrace them and miss them.

As I approached the eastern edge of Albuquerque, New Mexico, I pulled to the side of the road at the top of a rise, got out of the car, and looked back across the vast Rio Grande valley down below. Clouds were scudding across a wide blazing-blue sky, and I felt like I could see the edge of the world, out there to the far west. I said good-bye to my beloved Southwest, not knowing when or if I would ever come back. I knew that once I drove past these mountains, I would drop down onto the plains of Middle America, and "home" would fade from the rearview mirror.

LEAVING

Leaving is an integral part of soldiers' lives: they leave their homes, their families, and all that's familiar to join the military. They leave on deployments that take them to the other side of the world, and, over the course of their military careers, they repeatedly leave for new assignments on distant bases where they are assigned new duties and new roles, once again leaving the familiar behind. Eventually, they leave the military to rejoin civilian life.

At any given time, service members are deployed to one hundred fifty countries around the globe, for a variety of reasons—including combat missions, peacekeeping, and humanitarian or security missions.[1] According to Defense Department data, about 2.5 million service members deployed during the Afghanistan and Iraq wars. More than a third deployed more than once, and nearly thirty-seven thousand Americans deployed more than five times.[2]

In combat deployments, soldiers leave families, spouses, and loved ones. They leave daily routines and responsibilities. They leave safety and ease. Many combat veterans told me they acted like leaving was OK—their parting gift to loved ones was walking away strong and assured. But in quiet conversations, they talk about how those leave-takings *really* feel: the grief over missing children's birthdays, holidays, and special occasions back home. A son's first baseball game, a daughter's first steps, a wedding anniversary. They grapple with the loneliness of being a world away from spouses, parents, dear ones. They feel the anger that can come with the pressures of war and the loss of warrior friends. They stare down the fear of never coming home.

Even coming home entails a very complicated kind of leaving for the soldier. Warriors who return from deployment get to rejoin their families, but that also means leaving their battle buddies, who in turn rejoin their own families. They've spent every day in extremely close quarters for months on end, and they've bonded with each other intensely in the service of saving one another's lives. They've seen each other scared or wounded or brave or hysterical. When they come home, they greet loved ones, drive across the base, and leave behind their shared experience to live separate lives.

"It feels weird to leave them," the soldiers tell me. "I just can't get used to it."

Leaving is a part of a military career, right up through the conclusion of it. When they end their careers, many soldiers lose the sense of purpose and honor they lived with during their military years. Most say they struggle to find deep purpose in civilian life. And their years of military professionalism and achievement might count for nothing in the civilian world. One service member—a thirty-year veteran—said to me, "You know, I achieved so much. I worked hard to get to this rank. I gained a lot of respect and helped a lot of soldiers on the way up. But the day after I retire from the military, I'm nothing."

Before I started working with soldiers, I didn't have any idea how much leaving they faced. Perhaps because I had just left so much behind, I had "new eyes" that allowed me to see the ways leaving is woven through military lives, bringing with it everything from fresh starts and new successes to true sadness and aching grief.

CHAPTER 2

In my new job, assignments were to last anywhere from one month to six months. My first assignment was a sprawling base of tens of thousands of soldiers, where I was to work for three months. Small installations might have only one or two counselors assigned to them; massive bases (like the one where I started) might be assigned twenty-five counselors or more. My job description stated that it was my duty to offer support to soldiers, spouses, and civilian employees. I was expected to interact with them in facilities all over the base: offices, dining facilities, motor pools, common areas, base stores and libraries, family gatherings, staff briefings, and various troop celebrations.

The prospect of arriving at, and acclimating to, my first military base was as unnerving and mysterious to me as the idea of landing in the wilds of Borneo and trying to sort out how to relate to the local tribe. When I pulled up to the guardhouse and presented my paperwork to the guard, my posture changed: my back stiffened and straightened, as if the act of ordering my body upright would help me fit in. I looked at the guard—taking in his uniform, his curt politeness, his stiff instructions to put this paper *here* and that I.D. *there*—and I thought, *Here we go.* I tucked the paperwork above my car visor and pulled forward.

In that moment, my relationship with the military world began.

That small distance—fifty yards, from *off base* to *on base*—felt like a monumental transition from one world into another. This feeling of marked transition occurred every time I drove onto a base, throughout the years I worked with soldiers.

As I pulled onto the base, I slowed to twenty-five miles per hour— the posted speed limit on this and most bases—and searched for the brigade building where I was to report. I passed manicured lawns and trim, orderly landscaping. Groups of soldiers walked along sidewalks with an air of purpose. Every building was signed or numbered with a large plaque on the front facade: "Housing Services," "Chaplaincy Office," "Wounded Warrior Unit," "Bldg. 17-S." The area where I was going to work had been developed more recently than the rest of the base. The modern cube-shaped buildings were two stories high, painted a bland shade of tan on the outside, and squares of dark tinted windows striped the sides. I could tell the land had been scraped bare before construction of the buildings had begun because the landscaping remained sparse. The way the buildings were arranged around massive parking lots reminded me of a community college campus.

Driving at the lower speed limit was a striking experience for me— no rushing, darting, honking craziness here. The slower pace, the clear signage, and the meticulously ordered buildings created an atmosphere that was calm and serene.

I had imagined the base environment would feel rigid and harsh, but it actually felt somewhat calming, even pleasant. The palpable difference between this ordered calm and the more chaotic, jumbled, jacked-up civilian world made me wonder how it was going to feel to navigate the gap between the two every day. I also wondered how soldiers felt as they navigated this split between the military world and the civilian world.

When I found the brigade headquarters, I pulled my car into a nearby parking space and walked up the wide sidewalk to the glass front doors. Off to the right of the entrance, a gigantic old black cannon stood on display. A huge concrete sign proclaimed the name of the brigade, and beneath the name, bold script quoted a proud phrase for which the brigade was known. (I would soon learn, as I moved from base to base, that most brigades and battalions had these proud phrases.) Apache helicopters skimmed by overhead en route to training areas, the rotors' deep *whopp-whopp-whopp* reverberating through my body. Mortar rounds exploded in distant woods, where armored troops were practicing field exercises. The flood of new stimuli served to remind me just how far I was from my familiar environs.

Inside the brigade headquarters, I made my way to the conference room where my colleagues and I were to participate in a counselors' orientation meeting with one of the brigade commanders. I took a seat at the huge U-shaped conference table and opened my notebook, ready to take notes.

The commander walked in and strode to the front of the room just after I was seated, followed closely by two soldiers. The atmosphere changed immediately—tension blanketed the room as if a freezing wind had just blown in. I don't remember the commander's name or rank, but I remember her intensity and bearing. She had close-cropped dark hair and held herself as tightly wound as my most basic soldier preconceptions would dictate. Her uniform couldn't have been more pristinely clean and crisp, although she was wearing the same digitally patterned camouflage uniform that all the other soldiers wore. She turned toward us with a precisely executed step-and-stop movement. She was all business.

The room fell silent. As she made eye contact with every single counselor in the room, her face remained stoic and serious. She definitely had our attention.

Twenty-five of us counselors looked back at her from around the faux mahogany table. The room's off-white walls were covered with framed photos of past commanders and complicated battalion insignias made up of swords, cannons, guns, and unfurled wings.

"You're all adults," the commander stated, looking again at each and every one of us. "You are capable of getting yourselves where you need to be on time, are you not?"

A few folks murmured, "Yes."

"That would be 'Yes, ma'am.'"

"Yes, ma'am."

I looked at the clock on the wall behind her. What was she talking about: "on time"? The minute hand was straight up, nine o'clock on the dot: exactly the time our orientation had been scheduled to start. I had always considered it part of my professional duty to be very conscientious about showing up on time, beginning and ending sessions on time, etc. Her tone was unnerving, and I felt like I had failed a very basic part of my duty. People shifted in their seats, not sure where this exchange was going.

"OK. Then you should understand that in my military, being on time means you're here and ready to start at least fifteen minutes before the scheduled time. Fifteen minutes. While you're working in this brigade, that's the expectation. Any questions?"

I avoided eye contact with her but studied her face any time she looked at the colleagues on the other side of the conference table. Not a hair out of place, no flinch in her gaze, no relaxation in her ramrod straight bearing. I felt like a teenager who had brought home bad grades, sweating and wondering what my pissed-off parents were going to do when they lowered the boom at the end of the talking-to. It had been a long time since I felt so out of place and intimidated.

"If you're going to work in my brigade," she continued, "you're going to have to step up and perform. If you can't do that, we don't need you to be here. I want you on time. I want you in the battalion building you're assigned to. I want you supporting our soldiers and spouses. I don't want to hear about any of you slacking off or performing poorly. Is that clear?"

"Yes, ma'am," the entire group chorused.

"We've not had counselors in this brigade before. And I'm not sure if we really need you here. So, we're going to see how this goes. In other words, we'll be watching you. Do we understand each other?"

"Yes, ma'am," we chorused again.

I squirmed inwardly—though not outwardly. I wasn't going to show my discomfort in front of her. Less than five minutes into the job, and I had already screwed up a simple cultural norm. I took a lot of pride in handling my professional duties well, so this was an unusual situation for me. My heart rate was up, the tension was palpable, and I saw a few colleagues shifting in their seats. My eyes were riveted to the commander's face; I wasn't going to miss another cue. (Nor would I make that mistake again. For the next two and a half years, I was at least fifteen minutes early for every meeting I was asked to attend, no matter which base I was working on. Very often, the soldier I was to meet with was already there when I arrived.)

"You'll each be assigned to a battalion, and there will be someone to escort you to your assigned office. Captain Dodge, do you have that list?"

"Yes, ma'am," Dodge responded, his eyes riveted to her, too.

"Any questions?" she asked the group.

Not willing to hazard a rough encounter, we all stayed silent.

"All right. I'm going to turn things over to Captain Dodge. He will go over your assignments and the protocols you'll need to follow. I will just say again that I expect more from you than what I saw today. Thank you."

Her thank-you was more a curt dismissal than an expression of gratitude. She turned and walked out, followed by the two soldiers who shadowed her.

As Captain Dodge moved to the front of the room to take over the discussion, dread flooded through me: what had I gotten myself into? I'd left a private practice where I was in control of my every decision, and where I'd felt extremely competent and clear about how to handle my duties as a counselor. Now, expectations were razor-sharp, and I'd already gotten myself thoroughly scolded. Captain Dodge read out the list of assignments, pointing to the soldier who would take each counselor to his or her assigned office. Soon he called my name and read out the name of my assigned battalion, a jumble of numbers and letters that meant nothing to me.

A young officer approached me. "Ma'am? I'm assigned to escort you to the battalion building. It's a couple of blocks away. Do you have everything you need?"

I wasn't sure anymore what I might need, but I nodded my head and followed him outside, where he pointed in the direction of the building and gave me quick driving directions. He was waiting for me at the entrance after I'd parked and walked up to the front doors. Slight of build with closely shorn blond hair, my baby-faced escort didn't smile or wave as I walked up the steps. He looked to be about fifteen or sixteen and clearly wasn't there to chat. As I reached the top of the stairs, he turned and opened the door for me, executing his assigned duty with polite precision.

He led the way down a long hallway and turned into an open doorway on the left-hand side. "Here you are, ma'am. This is the office I was to show you. The key is there on the desk. You have a good day, ma'am."

With that, he turned and disappeared down the hall.

My "counseling office" was a shockingly barren beige-painted concrete-block room with a desk, an old and tattered swivel chair, and three folding chairs.

I stood in the middle of the room and turned around a couple of times. A wave of panic rolled through me as the morning's changes hit critical mass. I felt like I might burst into tears as I reckoned with the choice I'd made: I'd gone from the polished wood floors, French doors, and soft lighting of my private practice to this drab room with dirty, cracked windows and harsh fluorescents hanging from the ceiling. Ratty old blinds hung crookedly across the windows, and there were little bits of dust in all the corners of the room. I couldn't imagine anyone wanting to come into this room for counseling. I hadn't yet learned that most soldiers barely noticed their surroundings, that they're used to adapting and making any situation work, and that bare walls and a scuffed linoleum floor wouldn't even register for them. Eventually, a coworker and I would spruce up the room with thrift store finds, making the space a little more pleasant for both the soldiers and myself. But that day, all I felt was the starkness of my situation.

I pushed the desk and chairs around, trying to make the space more inviting and trying to let my distress ebb a bit. Soldiers walked by and glanced into my office, but not a single one of them entered the room. The only exchanges I had came in the form of a very formal, clipped "Good morning, ma'am" from one or two. These soldiers had never had a counselor assigned to their battalion before. I was as foreign to them as an exotic animal.

DUTY

The word "duty" comes from the Latin word *debere*—literally, "to owe." Duty means offering what is proper and just, what is owed; doing what is required or obligated by one's position; the binding or obligatory force of doing what is right.

Soldiers can draw on the clarity of duty when faced with the enormous pressures of combat, focusing tightly on their obligations to their comrades and commanders. Their sense of duty helps them navigate the subtle bindings of daily life in the military structure; each service member has a duty to relate to an officer in a certain way, to perform his or her job to a certain standard, to respect the chain of command, and so on.

There are nearly thirty different ranks represented in each branch of the armed forces; duty guides the relationships and communications between each of those ranks. There are hundreds of military occupational specialties, or jobs; duty informs and saturates the performance of every one of them. Every year, more than one hundred eighty thousand people join the military, and nearly twenty thousand more become officers.[3] Duty aligns each of those service members with his or her mission, whether that's the cook in the dining hall, the supply clerk in the warehouse, the sapper clearing minefields, the pilot in the bomber, or the general commanding vast numbers of soldiers. In each branch of service, duty is defined and anchored in the creed that soldiers, airmen, Marines, sailors, and coasties commit to when they join up.

One combat veteran told me, "I always considered duty to be my promise, my contract to my fellow soldier to protect him first, before myself; to have his back in whatever situation we found ourselves, *especially* in a combat environment. Ultimately, that's who you fight for—your buddy, your fellow soldier—not flag or country or ideology. My duty first is to him, and I know his is to me. It's what makes a guy take several rounds and still drag his buddy half a mile to safety. It's what makes a medic jump out of a helicopter to save his fellow soldiers. He may be hit with sniper fire, but he still saves the lives of those other soldiers. It's the sense of *duty*, of doing your job no matter the cost to yourself. By taking your duty seriously, you pay what you owe to them."

As I began working on bases, I used my sense of duty as an organizing principle for the work I was doing, too. What did I *owe* these combat veterans I was trying to help? What duty did I have to them? In a very basic way, I had a duty to show up on time, to reach out as best I could to those in need, to stay present in the face of their troubles. Through this lens of duty, I also saw what I owed them on a deeper level: to understand them, their lives, their values, and their service in the deepest way possible. Coming to understand their bedrock sense of duty was perhaps the key to understanding their world, and orienting to my own sense of duty took me deeper into myself and my work.

CHAPTER 3

On my second morning, I walked down the hallway toward the main battalion offices to introduce myself to the commander and his officers. Full of nerves and uncertain about how to conduct myself, I perceived the long fluorescently lit hallway as being a mile long. I wore my assured professional demeanor like a cloak of competency I used to mask my cluelessness about how to navigate within this setting.

The battalion building's main hallway was made up of standard beige concrete-block walls. Dark green doors lined both sides. Inside those offices, soldiers tracked the schedules, needs, and movements of nearly nine hundred battalion soldiers. At the end of the hallway, the staff duty desk and a waiting area sat in a large open space. The entrance to the commander's office was through a doorway at the back of the large area. I introduced myself to a soldier seated at one of the first desks I came to, and he called for someone to escort me to the commander.

The battalion commander, Lieutenant Colonel (LTC) O'Malley, stood up behind his desk as his command sergeant major (CSM) walked me through his doorway. He offered me a firm, quick handshake and gestured toward the chair in front of his desk. His brown hair was cut "high and tight," buzzed nearly bald on the side, and only slightly longer on the top. O'Malley's face looked like the weathered, chiseled face of the Marlboro man, and his sheer physicality implied he could lead his troops through intensive physical training (PT) several times a day with ease.

"You're the counselor who's going to be here for a while?"

"Yes, sir. I'll be here to support your troops over the next few months."

He nodded. "You've been shown to your office?"

"Yes, sir."

"If there's anything else you need, just let someone know and we'll take care of it."

I nodded and thanked him. His manner was professionally appropriate, but I wouldn't say it was warm or particularly welcoming.

"Is there anything you want me to know as I get started?" I hoped for some direction. I thought he might tell me about issues he'd like me to keep an eye on or soldiers he might want me to work with.

He shook his head. "Not really. I'll let you do your job. Appreciate you being here." He stood up.

We were done.

I had hoped LTC O'Malley would say, "Well, we'd like you to do *this* and track *that* and make sure you talk to *this person* and please show up for *these briefings*." Something clear and definite, a road map into this work. Instead, I was on my own and, once again, the pressure felt enormous. Over time, I would find out that—for the most part—I was responsible for filling my days; there were a few tasks and meetings and briefings I was expected to attend, but my daily schedule was pretty much up to me.

I stepped out of LTC O'Malley's office and back into the beehive of activity in the surrounding offices. All the soldiers were busy: phones were ringing, computer keys clicking, papers shuffling. Whiteboards were overfilled with lists of names and codes and tasking details. I walked around, saying hello, introducing myself, and shaking hands as I worked my way through the maze of desks. I was greeted with polite puzzlement and an air of quiet welcome. As I shook hands through many layers of commanders, officers, and company leaders, I soon found my mind swirling with the names and job descriptions that made up the complicated structure of the battalion.

The tsunami of acronyms and ranks, protocols and directives overwhelmed me very quickly. Although I'd spent time before I arrived at the base studying the handbook my company provided, including its pictures of rank insignias, the flood of new faces and names left me incapable of keeping everyone straight in my memory. I had no grasp of military rank and how it would shape every one of my interactions.

I walked back into my office and closed the door. I felt like I might cry from frustration—and I did *not* want any of the soldiers to see my reaction. I sat in the broken office chair behind the desk, steadied myself as it wobbled and threatened to tip, and gazed around my barren room. I was in a new setting, with new people all around me, within a system I didn't understand—and I was somehow supposed to figure out what to do. Literally: What was I supposed to do *right now*? I knew I was supposed to "support soldiers and spouses"—but I was as lost as I could be when it came to knowing what that meant I was to *do* in that moment.

The insignias were the most basic code I needed to learn in order to relate correctly with others. I would have to learn the difference between two stripes and three; a diamond vs. a star vs. a star with a wreath; gold vs. silver; gold vs. black. (Later, when I moved to a different base, I would have to learn everything all over again, as each branch of military service uses different rank titles and insignias. For example, a private first class in the Army was equivalent to a seaman in the Navy, a lance corporal in the Marine Corps, and an airman first class in the Air Force, yet their insignias differed, despite their equal status.)

I not only needed to learn these, I also needed to be able to read them at a glance in order to instantly ascertain who I was speaking to and where that person fell in the chain of command. This system of rank and status—the bedrock of military interactions—came at me constantly like an instant-recognition exam I couldn't afford to fail. Eventually, I learned to glance at the insignia even before looking at the name tag, because the insignias cued me in to the appropriate way to interact.

In those first days, I misread an insignia and addressed a command sergeant major as "First Sergeant." I could feel the air bristle with his reaction. Basically, I'd just insulted him. He was good-natured but *very* direct when he said, "Ma'am, it's been a long time since I was a first sergeant." His hard stare and pointed silence made sure I got the distinction. I was on thin ice with that mistake.

On another day, during an encounter with a couple of battalion officers, I deferred to one officer, only to turn around and realize I should have deferred to the other.

Later that first week, I stood in a reception area waiting to meet with yet another commander. This one was in charge of scheduling the briefings I was to give to returning soldiers. As I stood in an open area surrounded by the usual innumerable doors, I noticed a display of photos of fallen battalion soldiers on the wall next to me and wondered: *Am I allowed to stand here?* I looked to my right and left, concentrating on the placement of the staff duty desk, the commander's doorway, and the display of photos. I sought some indication of what was correct. I found none—or at least nothing I was able to read as an indication—but very shortly after I had the thought, a soldier came up and graciously said, "Ma'am, do you think you might like to wait right over there?" He pointed to an area just a couple of feet away from where I was standing.

I moved.

The abbreviations of military-speak left me feeling just as lost. One day just after lunch, I bumped into an earnest young private first class who had a few moments to chat before he had to report for work. As we stood in the hallway, he told me he came from a farm up in Nebraska. His enthusiasm for military life was apparent. With his big green eyes, ready smile, and clean-cut appearance, he exuded excitement and eagerness even as he casually leaned against the wall and rolled his cap in his hands.

"Yeah," he told me. "I want to change my MOS so I can PCS out of here."

I had no idea what he had just said. He smiled at me and waited expectantly.

I scrambled for a response, finally sputtering, "Uh . . . well . . . how's that going?"

"Oh, pretty good. My wife wants to go to Aviano, but no one gets in there, you know? I'm probably going to switch to a 15N. I think that'll give us the best shot. Or maybe Richardson. They've got Airborne up there."

I smiled. I tried to process what he had said, and tried to sort out what to say in return. Aviano? 15N? Richardson?

In the end, I said, "Well, I really hope that works out for you guys."

He smiled and walked off down the hall toward his afternoon duties.

In my hotel room at the end of the day, I dropped onto the bed and looked up the acronyms in my handbook. He wanted to change his job, or military occupational specialty (MOS), so he could move to a different base, referred to as a permanent change of station (PCS). The handbook contained page upon page of acronyms and my heart sank as I despaired of ever understanding what the soldiers were saying.

How could I be any kind of help to soldiers or spouses if I didn't even understand their language?

The small, subtle ways I stumbled were innumerable. When a soldier asked to meet with me, I confirmed we'd meet at "6:30." His look of confusion cued me in to the fact that if I didn't intend to meet with him at 6:30 in the morning, I should have said "1830."

One day I saw a husky, dark-haired specialist I had been looking for and launched into an avid response to his question from the previous day, an issue I had needed to research before answering. After I had carefully detailed the process he had inquired about and relayed the information I had thoroughly researched, I suddenly realized I was talking to the wrong soldier. Such a rookie mistake. I awkwardly offered my apologies. The fact that all the soldiers wore the same clothing and had the same basic hairstyle meant that I needed to push myself to attune to them in more specific, attentive ways.

I was usually the only person dressed in civilian clothes in the battalion offices or motor pools, so I was highly visible as I tripped through faux pas after faux pas: willing to learn but finding the base as confounding as the wilds of Borneo.

Though these mistakes were small, they piled up day after day. I was mindful of the soldiers' precision and of why they were trained to avoid mistakes at all costs: getting information wrong in the heat of battle could have disastrous—even fatal—consequences. Failing to understand a simple acronym could cause chaos at the worst possible time. I didn't have that kind of pressure on me during the performance of my job. Still, the military's strict expectation of perfection weighed heavily on me—particularly when I made such incredibly basic mistakes.

My colleagues were willing to help when they could. But we were all assigned to different battalions in widely separated areas of the base and we were all adjusting to our assignments, so we rarely saw each other. Sometimes, I turned to a couple of the more experienced counselors for help with job protocols I didn't grasp; they'd already worked on several different bases and had a better sense of the job.

Occasionally, I got to work alongside a coworker, but for the most part I was on my own.

I was beginning to understand, though, how crucial it was for me to wade through my fears and show up to get the job done. I was beginning to understand that I was on a mission, too—a mission to be of help to those who had sacrificed so much—and that understanding them was key to fulfilling my mission in the deepest possible way.

MISSION

In military terms, a "mission" is the task assigned to an individual or a unit, as well as the purpose of the task. In Iraq and Afghanistan, for example, soldiers were tasked with a wide variety of missions. Those deployed into combat included infantry, field artillery, helicopter pilots, bomb specialists, and snipers, along with many others, all of whom had missions that made their daily purpose supremely clear—whether that was detonating IEDs (improvised exploding devices) or maintaining surveillance on a nearby village.

Those deployed in noncombat positions included dentists, doctors, lawyers, chaplains, supply and mail clerks, radio operators, and cooks. These, too, had specific missions with a clearly defined purpose. Being part of a non-combat mission didn't mean that one was out of harm's way; a "safe" base could come under attack at any time, and if your mission required travel, there was a high likelihood you would be exposed to IEDs or enemy fire. Whether or not one was assigned to front lines, each soldier's mission was defined by his or her unit and chain of command.

Most veterans told me that their idea of combat changed abruptly when they went on their first combat mission. As they left the forward operating base (FOB), their adrenaline would spike and everything would become surreal. They remember becoming hyperaware of the ground they were walking on, the terrain in front of them, the position of each of their fellow warriors, the sound of the wind whistling in nearby scrub brush. Many said they could hear their own breathing or suddenly feel their heartbeat in a hyperfocused way. Every single soldier remembers his or her first combat mission. No matter how they adapt and adjust in later missions, that first combat mission remains burned into memory with remarkable clarity.

Those carrying out missions grew rapidly in number: in 2002, there were seven thousand troops in Afghanistan[4]; by 2007, that number had climbed to twenty-three thousand.[5] The number of American troops reached 101,000 in June 2011—the peak of the U.S. military presence in the war—according to Pentagon figures. In January 2014, thirty-eight thousand troops remained there.[6]

As of June 2016, 6,699 U.S. service members have died while on missions in Iraq and Afghanistan. (7)

Civilians

Major (MAJ) Buchanan walks into my office and pulls the chair a little farther away from my desk before he settles into it. He's been retired from the Air Force for several years and now works as a consultant on the base. His body is developing that late-in-life paunch, and his close-cut gray hair only grows on the side and back of his head. He wears clothes that look off-the-rack from Sears: polyester pants in a variety of grays and browns, plaid shirts with button-down collars, and a pair of shiny shoes in a reddish shade of brown that doesn't go with most of his outfits.

"There's something I need to talk about, and I honestly don't know how to say it." He says this as soon as he walks in, as if he's been giving a lot of thought to this exchange. His manner is strikingly sincere. He leans back in his chair and physically relaxes, and his gaze is open and earnest.

He looks at me for direction, so I suggest, "Well, you can just tell me what's on your mind."

He's starting to squirm a bit and starting to look less relaxed. "I don't know how to say this. It might seem pretty offensive."

"You know, in here you can say anything you need to say. It'll stay between you and me. Take your time." I put my elbows on the desk and lean forward, trying to give the impression that we can take all the time we need to discuss things.

"OK," he says. "I guess I'll just dive in."

Buchanan hitches his pants up at the knees to ease the pull on his legs as he crosses them. "Here's what I came to talk about: I've been noticing something for a long time and I really wasn't going to do anything about it. But then I heard you folks were here on base, so I figured I'd stop by and get some input."

Buchanan says all this as if he's getting ready to discuss an engineering concern and this is a collegial consultation about a technical glitch.

I nod and wait.

"Here's the thing. I . . . well, I . . ." He fidgets, then stutters a bit as he tries to begin again. "To be honest with you . . . it's just that . . ." He uncrosses his legs and leans forward in his chair. "Well, I have to say, *I can't stand civilians.*"

Buchanan looks over at me as if he's waiting for some condemnation or dismissive response. I simply nod. "OK. Tell me more about that."

"I spent twenty-two years in uniform. I gave up holidays with my family, spent months at a time overseas. I missed birthdays and anniversaries, soccer games and graduations. I kept my body trained and learned how to take responsibility for every assignment." Warming up to the topic, Buchanan jabs his finger at the top of my desk with each point he makes.

"And then there's accountability. It's a military thing. I know that if I'm talking to a military man, and I ask them to do something, it's as good as done. It's understood. It'll get handled, and I don't have to give it another thought. Civilians don't have that kind of account-ability. I'm sorry to say it, but they don't. They don't step up in the same way."

Buchanan's on a roll. He waves his arms around as if his points are visible in the room. His face reddens a bit, and his breathing is rapid in between sentences as he pulls air into his lungs to launch the next disappointment on his list.

"To be honest, they seem lazy and irresponsible. I mean, they com-plain about everything! They expect everything to be handed to them; they act so goddamn entitled. I'm sorry, but they're whiny and spoiled. I'm embarrassed to admit all this, but it bothers me enough that I figured I'd better talk to someone about it." He shrugs his shoulders and waves a hand dismissively in the air, like he's pushing all the lazy civilians out of his world.

Now that he's gotten himself started, he keeps going. "When I go into Walmart or Home Depot, I look around at the civilians, and I think—" Here, his voice takes on a tone of sarcastic disdain. "What did *you* do? How did *you* contribute? Because I know they didn't. They didn't do their part. They didn't carry their share of the burden. They sat back and watched TV and lived their safe little lives while the rest of us were taking care of business."

Buchanan pauses and nods to himself as he grasps the last point he needs to make. "To be honest with you, I feel disgusted. I don't want to feel that way, but I can't help it. *Disgusted.*"

I've heard soldiers discuss similar sentiments before, though in much milder tones.

"So how do I go about fixing this?" Again, he sounds like we're discussing a simple technical difficulty.

We begin to talk about what his time in the Air Force has meant to him and about all the things he has accomplished. We have a thorough conversation about his relationship to serving his country, and we air out all the costs of that service to him and his family. I encourage him to find similarities—*bridges*—between himself and civilians, but those don't exist for Buchanan. He hates the feeling of being "trapped" in the civilian world in the years since he retired, and worries he just won't be able to overcome his disgust.

Before he leaves my office, Buchanan makes a second appointment with me for the next week, saying he wants to keep wrestling with his concerns. Later, he cancels the appointment because his work schedule changes. He never calls to reschedule.

Puzzling over his absence, I speak to a colleague about the work I'd done with Buchanan. I wonder aloud if there were details I might have missed, clues that might have aided in making my responses more useful or helpful, if only I had seen them.

My very savvy coworker—also a Navy veteran, with a thorough background in both the military and counseling worlds—grins. "Well, you missed the one big factor."

"What's that?" I'm completely baffled.

"*You're a civilian.* How's a guy who hates civilians supposed to open up to one of them?"

She's right. I had completely missed that factor. As much as I might have understood Buchanan's feelings, and as much as I had encouraged him to talk and open up, I had failed to notice and acknowledge the one thing that could have been a barrier between us.

I never saw Buchanan again. But from that point forward, I had a much clearer awareness of the substantial gap between myself and my military clients.

A Different Kind of Front Line

Darrell is a slightly stooped retired Air Force officer who looks much older than his fifty-eight years. His hair is mostly gray; his arms and hands, spotted and wrinkled. Although he looks like someone who might have kept very fit once upon a time, his body is softening with age.

Darrell works at the base's education center, sitting at the information desk for hours on end, giving directions to classroom locations, offering up brochures, and chatting with service members and family members who have come to the center to take classes or attend trainings. Because Darrell seems like a take-charge kind of person—incredibly sharp-minded and motivated—the low-key job strikes me as an odd fit for him.

"Darrell, how'd you come to work here?" I ask one day as I make my rounds through the building.

He laughs, as if he guesses what I'm getting at. "Well, I tell you. I've been here for many years. I wanted to go into law enforcement when I retired from the Air Force. I was looking at becoming a detective, but I got injured, hurt my back. That ended the whole detective idea. I got to thinking, the only other thing I'd want to do was something that let me stay involved with the military. This job was open, and even though you might think it's a little beneath me, I don't think that way at all. Not for a minute. I get to help soldiers all day every day. What's important is that I'm helping the troops that come in here."

Roy chuckles and tilts back and forth in his cushioned chair. "Look, I know I don't need to be here. I don't *need* to be working. I've got my pension and my disability. But it's not about the bank account. It's about being with soldiers."

He shakes his head slightly and then looks me square in the eyes and says with conviction, "Put it this way: it's my way of giving back. That's all I can say. I believe in every single one of these service members. They're making the greatest sacrifice. For me, this is like standing and saluting each and every one of them, every day."

Darrell clears his throat and drums his fingers on the arms of his chair. "If you were in the military, you'd understand. There's just a code, among all of us. We're in it together. And while I'm doing this work, I feel like I'm still on the team, still moving the mission forward. It's a different kind of front line, and I want to be here with these soldiers and airmen, marines and sailors. Right here. Front line."

Centimeters and Millimeters

I walk up and down the hallway of the battalion building, glancing into offices, trying to get a finger on the pulse of how soldiers are grappling with the news. Most offices are empty—desks bare, chairs askew, lights off. Soldiers have congregated elsewhere to sort out what they've heard.

As word of Corporal (CPL) Tompkins death in Afghanistan spreads among the soldiers, I hear the same phrase over and over: "It was just a few centimeters." The story ripples through the battalion offices like a fast-spreading virus: "He was parallel parked and couldn't get his Humvee out. He backed up a few centimeters—*just a few goddamn centimeters*—and his tire hit the IED." These remarks are always followed by a shocked silence, a shake of the head, a look of stunned disbelief. Their buddy is gone.

Near the end of the hallway, I look into an office and see a big broad-shouldered staff sergeant who's standing at the end of his desk, intently focused on a dark blue uniform laid lengthwise on the desktop. He's the very picture of brute strength and tough soldiering.

I pause to watch from the doorway as he leans over the desk and places a narrow silver pin on the chest of the uniform. Before he attaches the pin, he checks its placement in all four directions with a small measuring device that calculates precise millimeters. Once he's attached the pin perfectly, he begins to check the placement of the shiny brass buttons down the front of the uniform. With each button, the placement is painstakingly measured in those same perfect millimeters.

His face is set; he's absorbed in the task. Even from a distance, I can tell his eyes are steadily focused on the measurements he's taking. He's wearing delicately thin white gloves on his huge hands, which touch the uniform gently, reverently. I feel as if I'm watching a prayer.

Before this, the only time I'd seen soldiers preparing their dress uniforms was when they were preparing to go before the board for promotion or getting ready for the battalion ball. I'd watched them fuss a little to make sure they had everything in place. But this was different. I'd never seen this kind of meticulous care, or felt this sense of devotion.

"That's going to look nice," I say quietly from the doorway. "Are you going up for promotion?"

"No, ma'am." He glances at me and then looks back at his task. "I'm escorting Tompkins's body back to his family in Iowa."

A long silence follows.

"I'm so sorry you have to do that." I wait a beat before adding, "And I'm grateful you're here to do that." I'm deeply touched by his respect for his buddy.

"I wouldn't have it any other way, ma'am. He was my soldier."

"He was your soldier?"

"Yes, ma'am. I trained him. I was his sergeant while he was here on base. I'd say I knew him as well as anyone."

There is a slight pause.

"He was a fine soldier, ma'am."

His eyes never leave the uniform. His hands never stop moving, measuring.

I don't want to intrude, so I tell him to take care on the trip. "I'll see you when you get back."

He thanks me, and I move on down the hallway.

My days since have been filled with thoughts of the courage it must have taken for the sergeant to make that particular journey. I realize his blessed attention to every minute detail was a tribute to his comrade, to their shared lives as soldiers—lives that are sometimes calibrated in just a few centimeters.

And in tiny, precious millimeters.

CHAPTER 4

During the years I spent working on various bases, my "home" was one hotel room or another. The first hotel room I landed in was decent enough: a large bed, a stiff-cushioned couch, a kitchenette, and a wide-open view of the ugly parking lot down below. The room was decorated in rich earth tones of warm brown, gold, and rust. The curtains were thick and lush in a paisley print of various browns tinted with gold. But it was still a hotel room. It looked like it had been rolled off an assembly line. If it was going to be home for the next few challenging months, I had to make it cozier and more emotionally nourishing as an antidote to the weariness caused by my daily challenges.

I went back to my car and brought in the few things I had carefully packed to help me feel more at home during my wandering work. My favorite pillow with a soft flannel pillowcase that I loved, and a deep-red patterned quilt from home went on the bed. The shiny, stiff polyester one from the hotel went into the back of the closet. I set a large photograph of dear ones on top of the dresser. When I'd put my things in storage, I decided to keep a blue pottery cup and plate with me, so that something as simple as the cup I drank out of would stay steady and familiar. I put them in the kitchenette's cupboard. I taped favorite poems and quotes onto the edges of the gigantic mirror that covered one whole wall of the dressing area, and I cooked familiar food in my tiny kitchenette each evening, creating for myself as much of a feeling of home as I could. (After a few assignments, I learned to ask for a room on an upper floor on the back side of the building—much quieter. I also learned to make friends quickly with the hotel staff; they would be my logistical support system for the next few months, helping me with mail, cleaning, and suggestions for local shops. I learned, too, to take the slider locks off the window frames so I could open the windows wide for fresh air.)

During this first assignment, some of my colleagues were staying at the same hotel, but we rarely crossed paths. We were all weary by the end of the day and had different ways of winding down: some went out to eat, some holed up in their rooms, some took long runs or worked out in the hotel gym. At times, some of us had to work into the evenings. For all of these reasons, even though they were staying right down the hall, I didn't see my colleagues very often at the hotel.

At the end of my long days, I'd lean back against the wall of the elevator, feeling weary from work and wanting to get back to the sanctuary of my room as quickly as possible. Sliding the key card along the slot in the door handle, I waited for that tiny green light and solid click that meant I was off duty at last. After the heavy spring-loaded door slammed shut behind me, I tossed my book bag on the dresser, kicked off my shoes, and removed my name tag. I couldn't get out of my work clothes fast enough. This habit was a holdover from the days when I'd worn a uniform during elementary and middle school: taking off day-clothes and shrugging myself into jeans and T-shirts meant my personal downtime had officially begun.

My hotel room became the refuge where I stepped back from the steep learning curve and tried to gather myself for the onslaught of the next day. Sometimes I felt like I had been holding my breath all day, so utterly determined was I to overcome the steep learning curve that seemed to be besting me.

As daylight faded outside my window, I sat cross-legged on the bed and turned on the adjustable light mounted on the wall next to the bed. I opened up my laptop and pushed myself to file the paperwork I had to complete on my day's work. I wanted to shut down. I wanted to watch TV or call a friend or linger over my late dinner. Instead, I had to fill out a form on every soldier I had talked to during the day.

Since I wasn't allowed computer access on the base (unless I went to the base library, which I rarely had time to do), I kept a small folded piece of paper in my pocket during the day and wrote down a running tab of each and every conversation. No identifying information: just some small thing that would help me remember the conversation so I could fill out the form. "Red-haired spouse, divorce; sergeant, staff problems; Texas accent, deployment; waiting-room guy, family; motor pool lieutenant, med board; wife in coffee shop, parenting; major, depressed." On and on, notation after notation, my tiny folded paper walked me back through my day.

No music, no emails or phone calls with friends filled my evenings; there was just this thorough review of the details of my day. It exhausted me. Even after a day filled with all the new patterns, words, systems, and individuals I had to grapple with and understand, I still couldn't shut down and rest. If I left the forms until later in the evening, I would be even more tired when I did them. I knew the next day would be just as overwhelming as this one, so I didn't want to let any work carry over. No matter how brain-dead I felt, I filled out the forms.

Although I needed to unwind, I found it impossible to read a book or watch television. I didn't have any attention left to follow one more story line; I had been tracking story lines all day. My days were incredibly busy, the pressure to find ways to relate was immense, and the chronic sense of not fitting in was stressful. By the time I turned out the light and lay down to sleep, my overstimulated brain had difficulty drifting off.

I sometimes found myself thinking back to my time in Tucson. I thought of my sweet backyard and the fresh desert air that drifted into my bedroom in the evenings. I thought about the vast, clear sky there, and the bright stars I could see nearly every night. Now, superbright security lights washed out the sky, blocking the stars from view, and the night smelled like exhaust from the parking lot instead of fresh desert air.

I missed ease. I missed things being familiar. I missed feeling capable and competent.

During those early weeks, when I wasn't attending a meeting or briefing, I'd sit alone in my barren office and stare at the empty parade ground just outside my window, listening to the constant buzz of activity in the offices around me. When soldiers saw me, they kept up their formal "Good morning, ma'am" greetings, but anything beyond that exchange was rare.

I was having very little success at interacting with the soldiers. I didn't feel like I was being of any use to them. I showed up each day, making sure soldiers saw me in my office or in the hallways. But my presence and availability didn't lead to any substantial interactions that would help the soldiers. I attended meetings about educational changes on the base or the scheduling for troops' return, and I tried to participate even though I felt out of my element. I went to the motor pool on my assigned days and said hello to a soldier here or there. But aside from my very brief exchanges with MAJ Buchanan and Darrell, the conversations didn't move past pleasantries. A few weeks into my assignment, I'd only had one official session with a soldier—a surly private first class (PFC) who told me he had to see me because his platoon leader required it. He had no interest in counseling and no interest in changing his bad attitude.

I had to change my approach.

After nearly thirty years of clients showing up in my office eager to talk openly and freely, I now found myself in the position of needing to figure out how to reach across the formidable divide between the soldiers and me. If they were ever going to see me as a useful resource, I had to find a way to bridge the gap.

The program I was working for was a remarkable opportunity for soldiers. For the first time, they could get support from a counselor without the information going into their personnel files, where it might put an end to their promotions. In the past, they had to ask their chain of command for permission to seek help; now, they could get counseling without anyone knowing about it. The program was such a big change in military policy that I needed to *convince* the soldiers that anything they said to me truly was confidential. Clearly, I needed to be more involved with them in order to get this point across.

One morning, I decided that just getting soldiers to talk with me—helping them get to know me—would be a good first step. I pushed back from my desk and walked out the building's side door to the wide concrete stoop where soldiers took their cigarette breaks. Six or seven privates and specialists were scattered up and down the cracked concrete steps, each leaning against the step higher than the one they sat on, or hunched forward, elbows on knees. An old, worn-out elm tree arched next to the stairs, covering them in shade.

I recognized most of the men as ones I'd passed in the hallways: the shy, skinny private from Montana; the boisterous guy who bragged constantly about his skills on the firing range; the Southern boy with skin so dark it shone; the red-haired specialist who now ducked his head and studiously ignored me, as if he could make the counselor go away by refusing to acknowledge her presence. They were sharing lighters, grousing about sharing cigarettes, and complaining about the PT run they'd done that morning. As I walked toward them, I heard, "Ten miles! What the hell was he thinking? Too damn hot for that shit."

The conversation stopped when I drew near; the soldiers looked at each other.

"Can I help you, ma'am?" There was unmistakable distance in the boisterous one's voice.

"Oh no . . . I just thought I'd get some fresh air." I spoke with a casualness I didn't feel. I didn't sit down—that would have been too presumptuous in the face of their reaction. Instead, I walked down the steps and then turned to look back up at them. "So, what are you guys up to? Don't you all belong in some office somewhere?"

They laughed and began to complain about their jobs and workloads. After that, I started joining them on the stoop regularly, and conversations began to flow. Nothing to do with counseling: just me getting to know them and them getting to check out this counselor creature in their midst. We spent that first break on the steps talking about the finer points of buying a new pickup truck. For a good thirty minutes, they talked about which ones they wanted, who already had a pickup, which features they would get (oversized tires were a big draw; custom paint jobs were popular), and how much the trucks would probably cost. It was a fine conversation. I learned a lot about trucks, and they began to see I might be OK to talk with.

After I'd hung out with the soldiers on the stoop several times, one of them got brave enough to say, "I don't mean to be rude, ma'am, but what exactly do you do here?"

I didn't take offense. Soldiers just couldn't "place" me in their world. They were becoming comfortable enough to chat with me, but they still couldn't figure out what a counselor was doing in their midst. They never saw anyone come to my office for counseling, and they honestly thought my services were unnecessary in their tightly structured world where emotions didn't have a place. In those early weeks, more than one soldier told me (without any harshness), "No one's going to come see you, ma'am."

"Well, I'm here to help you guys adjust to being back home," I said. "I mean, it doesn't have to be anything about combat, really. We might talk about how things are at home or how you're doing with work—or we could just chat. You know, just someone to talk with."

The soldier eyed me with bemused patience, and the two other soldiers standing with him nodded slightly as if to say, *OK. I guess that's all right.* I tried to make it sound like talking to me was no big deal. We didn't have to do an official "session," and they didn't have to have huge problems.

Once I knew some of the soldiers and could relate to them on a more personal level, I stopped to talk whenever I ran into them on the sidewalks. I visited with them in the hallways. I chatted with them over lunch in the dining facility. At briefings I attended, I'd stand near the doorway, casually chatting with people before and after the programs. Rather than positioning myself as the counselor who knew so much, I let my ignorance show: asking for directions, asking what the different patches on their uniforms meant, asking about their military jobs and their training.

"How did you get the 'fun' job?" I asked one soldier who was walking back and forth in tight repetitive lines across the grass in front of the battalion building, picking up cigarette butts and tiny bits of litter.

Shaking his head like a scolded schoolboy, he chuckled and said he had shown up late for PT, so the cigarette butt task was his punishment from his "favorite" sergeant. We chatted for a while, and every time he saw me after that, we shared a conspiratorial smile.

One soldier at a time, I started to connect. At lunch in one of the fast-food places located on base, I ended up at a table next to one of the soldiers from the battalion. With eight hundred soldiers in the battalion, it was natural for me to sometimes run into them even when we weren't in the battalion building where we worked. The soldier and I nodded at each other, and I was going to leave it at that. But then I said, "So what's new with you?" and he began to tell me about the specialized training he was getting to do: learning all about a particular tracking system. His face lit up and his voice sounded full of enthusiasm. Each time I saw him after that brief exchange, I made sure to ask him how his training was going. Small victories, one soldier at a time. By the end of my first month, things were beginning to warm up between the soldiers and me.

Day after day, I kept reaching out, asking them about where they were from, or what they had eaten for their first meal after their year-long deployment to Iraq. I asked about their spouses or children. I chatted with them about how difficult it was to be a single soldier and how they tried their best to find a girlfriend or boyfriend. I talked more about guns and trucks and sports teams than I ever would have dreamed. I was given detailed tours of their tattoos. I got used to the vivid swear words that peppered their conversations. In fact, I felt it was a sign of progress when they stopped watching their language and let the curses fly while I was in their midst.

I also weathered curt dismissals from soldiers who didn't trust me, and downright disdain from those who saw no point in having a counselor in their battalion. Some commanders were glad I was in their midst; others refused to even acknowledge me when we passed in the halls. One commander asked me what he could do to support my work with his troops. I told him, "Speak to me in front of your soldiers. Show them it's OK to talk to me. Let them see you interacting with me. That will have a huge effect on their comfort in seeking my help."

Slowly, I started to find the rhythm of their military lives. I felt like I had finally found the right bandwidth for the radio station I had been searching for. I would never be one of them, but I could become familiar with what it *meant* to be one of them.

In trying to connect, however, I made some ridiculous mistakes.

"Good grief, it's hot out here!" I commented late one summer after-noon while chatting with four soldiers on their cigarette break. The temperature was in the upper nineties and the humidity was extremely high. The air felt dense and heavy, and being outside for just a few minutes caused me to feel sleepy and my skin to feel sticky. The soldiers and I were standing in the shade, but heat radiated off the sidewalk and the battalion building. Having come from Arizona, I knew heat—but this muggy heat was stifling and unbearable.

After my remark, there was a long, awkward silence. None of the soldiers looked at me or at each other. PFC Hudson, someone I'd often talked with in the hallways, finally glanced at me from underneath the low brim of his patrol cap and said steadily, "Ma'am, I hate to tell you, but this is *nothing*. In Iraq, we sat in armored vehicles—with all our gear on—in the blazing sun. If we were on a mission, we might sit in there all day long. It was over a hundred and twenty degrees outside. Who knows what the temperature was inside those damn things. I'm just sayin': this doesn't really qualify as 'hot,' ma'am."

I felt instantly embarrassed. My remark showed my true ignorance of what their combat days might have been like. It showed the unconscious privilege I came from, the distance between me and the combat experiences and daily hardships they had faced.

"Wow. I can hardly imagine that." It was all I knew to say.

I never complained about the heat—or any other physical discomfort—to a soldier again.

These casual conversations weren't mindless, useless exchanges; they were rich with the intricacies of the soldiers' world. They were helping me tune in to who they were, and I absorbed as much detail as I could, slowly finding my way closer to the core of their world. We discussed what they liked about being in the military and what they didn't like. I had long conversations about different weapons they used *downrange* (their term for combat overseas). I learned about breaching walls, driving tanks, and what it took to become a sniper or a scout.

One day I was walking between buildings, heading back to my office after a weekly counselors' meeting. I passed a shaded picnic table near the motor pool where soldiers often gathered to smoke or take a break. I saw that the soldiers sitting at the table were from the battalion I'd been working with, so I stopped to talk. I asked them what they planned to do when they got out of the military.

"I'm headed to Dallas," said PFC Wong. "My uncle has a garage— you know, working on big semitrucks. He's got a mechanic job waiting for me, and that's exactly what I got trained to do while I was here. I worked on Humvees, supply trucks, and armored vehicles. I'll be all set." He pushed his geeky thick glasses back up on the bridge of his nose and reached for the Mountain Dew can on the table in front of him. I knew from previous conversations that he was from a tiny town in East Texas, so I imagined he was looking forward to moving to the big city.

Specialist (SPC) Roth stood a little taller when he spoke. "I'm aiming for the White House."

I turned toward him with a puzzled look. "I want to join the Secret Service," he elaborated, "and get on the detail that protects the president. I've been thinking about that for a long time. I mean, I know it's a long shot, but that's what I'd really like to do."

Roth was a tall, strikingly handsome young man with dark hair, dark eyes, and a penchant for aviator sunglasses. His body was uberfit, and his precise, focused dedication to his mission was noticeable. I could easily imagine him in the ranks of the Secret Service, speaking into a microphone in his sleeve and taking his responsibilities very seriously. We talked about the things Roth thought he might have to do in order make his dream happen, such as keeping his service record clean and getting certain security clearances.

PFC Sherman was proud of his training in avionics technology. "You know I can make six figures as a contractor overseas?"

"No—I had no idea," I admitted.

"Oh yeah. I got a buddy that's already over there." Sherman pushed the cap back on his head and raised his eyebrows with eagerness. He shrugged his shoulders and lifted his hands, palms up, as if he was talking about the easiest thing in the world. "He got out, and now he's making over three hundred thousand a year, with a month off every year to come back home. I can do it for a few years, save up, then come back and buy any house I want."

"Sounds like a plan." I gave Sherman a high five as they all stood up, stretched their legs, and began to walk back toward the motor pool buildings. These were young men finding their way into adulthood.

In those early weeks, I met soldiers who seemed tough and locked down, but whom I eventually found to be deeply sensitive and thoughtful, spouses who exhibited a kind of commitment and grace that was remarkable, and civilian support staff who took great pride in helping the troops get the services they needed. My vague stereotypes were falling by the wayside as I let myself see who soldiers *really* were, beyond the narrow imaginings that had come to mind while driving across the country.

Every day, I found myself immersed in the work, dismantling my previous methods for connecting with people, and allowing soldiers to show me new and different paths.

One morning, my colleague Rita and I approached a group of soldiers in the paved training area behind the battalion's company buildings. The two-story buildings that housed company offices were arranged as three tan buildings on one side of the concrete, lined up across from three identical tan buildings on the other side of the concrete. (The buildings were such exact replicas of each other, in fact, that later that afternoon, Rita and I unknowingly walked back into the same building we'd been in an hour earlier as we made the rounds to introduce ourselves to various company commanders. We didn't realize our mistake until a commander we'd already met walked out to greet us . . . for the second time. I don't know who was more surprised: us or him!) On this muggy morning, a hundred soldiers were scattered throughout the training area, gathered in small groups to be trained on different weapons, tactical gear, and logistics. Rita and I stood on the edge of a group of fifteen soldiers who were packing and repacking parachutes. They studiously folded chutes and cords, packed them into contraptions that looked like backpacks, then got their work checked and tested before taking it all apart and repacking the parachutes again. Rita and I chatted and passed out business cards while they worked.

As the conversation warmed up, the soldiers invited us to try our hand at packing a parachute, and to this day I'm sorry I didn't. It would have been a great moment of bonding with them, and I'm sure our clumsy civilian attempts at parachute packing would have given them some good laughs. But at that point, my uncertainties about relating to them kept me feeling a bit shy. I wasn't sure if we would be in the way or if it was against protocol for us to join them. Given the same opportunity during later assignments, after I'd gotten more comfortable in their world, I would have jumped at the chance to participate.

Our outreach with them that day was still effective, however. Less than an hour after we walked away, one of those soldiers privately dialed the number on the card and asked for help with his wife who hadn't been very happy with him since he returned from deployment.

"Uh, ma'am? I was in that group you were talking to this morning? I'm wondering if you could talk to my wife. Ever since I got back, she says I'm spending too much time with my buddies and not enough time with her. Do you think you could talk to her?"

We set up a time to meet the next day, and he brought his wife in so they could talk. This was a common scenario: returning soldiers often felt more comfortable and more bonded with their combat buddies than with their families. They'd spent a year in very intense situations, had relied on each other daily, maybe even kept each other alive. After coming home, it was easier for many to rely on the tight bond with their buddies than it was to reconnect with spouses or families. It usually took some time for the issue to resolve, and I saw many marriages falter or fail before such resolution could occur.

A couple of weeks later, Rita and I were scheduled to work on a distant part of the base to do outreach with a different battalion. As we walked to the training area behind the battalion building, we kept ourselves in the shade of the vast oaks that lined the sidewalk. The heat was cranking up again. Once the line of trees ended, we moved over next to the building so we could walk in its shade.

Rita and I chatted as we walked, talking about recent challenges in our work and discussing our plan for working our way through the battalion offices that day. When we rounded the back corner of the building, I happened to be looking down. Rita reached over and put her hand on my arm to stop me.

Not knowing why she had stopped me, I looked up to see a company of soldiers in the training area practicing the military funeral ceremony, complete with a makeshift casket stand and an empty casket-shaped box draped with the American flag. We stood still for several minutes, watching their crisp movements and their quiet, focused attention. The atmosphere was solemn and nearly silent.

We weren't sure whether our presence would be welcome and didn't know if moving closer would be perceived as intrusive. But one of the company officers motioned Rita and I closer, so we joined the company as they continued practicing the ceremony. We watched, mesmerized, for nearly an hour as they tirelessly repeated each meticulous move: marching forward and turning sharply with the casket level and steady between them, placing it on the stand, folding the flag, stepping back from the casket, and crisply marching away. They counted out their steps as their boots thudded in time, the lead soldier called out commands, and their movements got tighter and tighter. The soldiers were dressed in their everyday uniforms, but given the precision moves and their somber attention, I could picture them in their dress blues. The company commander gave his critique after each run-through, and then they'd go through the ritual again, with corrections.

Rita and I chatted with the soldiers during their breaks and handed out business cards.

"It's poignant to watch you do this," I said to the captain directing the group.

"Well, this company is on call for funerals for the next month. If anyone needs a military funeral on the base or in a nearby community, this team would be responsible for the ceremony. We need to get it right."

Soldiers laughed and talked during the break, but when it was time to return to their practice, their faces grew solemn and they focused on the absolute perfection they were aiming for.

"What if it was me in that casket, or my dad or mom? They both served. I'd want someone to give this kind of attention to their ceremony," said a tall, skinny corporal with a pure Boston accent. "It's an honor, and I couldn't be more serious about that."

As I talked with soldiers about their work, their dreams, and their interests, I was outgrowing my notions that soldiers were all about war, or were cookie-cutter repeats of each other. The simplistic stereotypes I'd made up simply didn't fit anymore, like a container that had become too small, as my experiences and understandings expanded.

As a therapist, I knew people often used stereotypes to avoid grappling with the real complexity a group of people might embody. Back when I didn't know much about service members, it had been simpler to paint them with a broad brush of presumptions. As I came to understand the nuances of soldiers' lives, their commitments and motivations, those assumptions were replaced with an abiding respect—and curiosity.

I came to understand that a lot of soldiers were as wary of me as I had been of them. Many soldiers feel misunderstood by civilians. They were polite to me in our interactions, but I could see that many of them didn't trust me. As I settled into the rhythm of my military work, I began to feel touched by the lives they lived. Many young adults go to college or move forward in other ways, but these men and women had signed up to serve. In them, I saw dedication, focus, and a clear sense of purpose—qualities I knew civilians often lived without. The orderliness of the soldiers' world supported them and gave them a kind of steady, clear structure many had not had earlier in their lives. They forged a kind of bond with one another I'd rarely seen in civilian life. They shared experiences that catapulted them far, far beyond the range of normal life, and they could never truly communicate what that was like to civilians.

In order to join up and enter this world of clear purpose and tight bonds, they'd had to make huge sacrifices in their lives—leaving loved ones, enduring daunting physical training, pushing themselves to their limit physically and mentally. I was hoping the sacrifices I had made in leaving Tucson would take me into similar territory in my own life: a chapter of deeper purpose and bonding. Until that happened, all I could do was honor the experiences and the bonds that existed for them.

Just weeks after entering their world, I was surrendering the most basic of my stereotypes. These weren't cookie-cutter soldiers at all. They were a million shades of struggling hearts and human yearning.

Drinking Buddy

SPC Tolson is a remarkably handsome African American soldier. He's got deep-brown eyes, ebony skin, and a face that marries perfectly balanced features with a seemingly permanent look of kindness. He moves with a fluid grace, and his friendly personality matches the benevolence in his face. He can usually be found talking quietly with his buddies or listening carefully to someone who's venting about the inherent lack of fairness in the company duties. He seems like he never gets ruffled, never gets charged up or reactive.

In the quiet hour after lunchtime, Tolson stands in the doorway of my office—not willing to come in all the way and sit down but clearly reaching out in his own way for some support.

"How are things, Tolson?"

"Yeah. Good. You know? Well, sort of."

"What's the 'sort of' part?"

"Jackson. You heard about that?"

I'm reading between the lines. I know Jackson was one of the battalion soldiers killed in their recent deployment to Afghanistan. I never met him, but several soldiers have told me stories about him. I know his death has hit all of them hard. The company has been back for a month now, and they still get somber whenever his name is mentioned.

Tolson steps gingerly into the office and sits down. I step around my desk, close the door, and then sit down in the chair right across from him. I know to keep things casual; this needs to feel like a conversation and not a "session," or Tolson might bolt.

"Yeah, me and Jackson were tight. He was my drinking buddy. Lived next door to me in the barracks when I was single. We were really good friends, you know?" Tolson leans back in his chair, seeming to relax a bit into some memories of good times with his friend. He's even got a smile on his face.

Then his face takes on a sad, serious look. "Anyway, that day downrange, I knew his unit was out on the road. We'd set up an outpost about seven klicks (kilometers) from the FOB, and his unit was bringing us our mail. We got the call that they were under fire. That was nothing. Happened every day. If you went outside the wire, you were going to be taking fire. I didn't think anything of it."

Tolson is tense now. He's sitting toward the front of the chair, his elbows on the chair arms, and is leaning forward as he talks.

"But then the call came in that they'd been hit, and I felt like I lost my mind."

His face floods with raw grief, and he stops talking. I watch his face carefully, and every time I see a fresh wave of sadness pass across it, I gently ask, "What are you thinking?" He tells me more about that fateful mission.

"I had to go out with Sarge and bring his body back. I had to identify the body."

Tolson gazes at me with such a bland, neutral expression that I realize he goes into shock whenever he remembers the awful task.

"I couldn't even tell it was him. He died a hundred times right then—right before me, he died a hundred times—again and again. That was the worst day of my life. Oh God. He was just trying to bring us our mail." Tolson shakes his head slowly.

"I'm so sorry, Tolson. I'm really sorry." He looks up at me and stares silently for a moment.

"They shouldn't have been on that road. They shouldn't have been outside the wire. They were a supply company, not a combat company. They shouldn't have been sent, just to bring us our goddamn mail." His voice is still calm, but his eyes begin to look red around the edges.

"Who gives a shit about the damn mail?"

For Mom

I walk toward the battalion building and see SPC Cassano smoking a cigarette on the front steps. Noticing he looks a little glum, I stop to say hello.

"How's it going, Specialist?"

"Going fine." There's so little enthusiasm in his voice, it's as if he's just found out he's getting shipped to the worst post on the planet. He's a compact Italian American guy with olive skin and dark eyes, originally from Detroit or Pittsburgh—one of the cities up north where the economy has tanked. We've chatted on several occasions when he was with a group of his buddies, but this is the first time I've encountered him alone. He's never been very talkative, but it's unusual to see him this somber.

"So, what's up?" My words offer him an invitation to tell me what's making him so unhappy.

He glances over at me and takes a long drag on his cigarette, buying time and also weighing whether or not he's going to say more. He shrugs, as if deciding it's not a big deal to say what's on his mind.

"I don't really like the Army. It's not what I thought it would be. I'm not even sure what I thought it would be, but I'm really not happy here. I'm supposed to re-up in the next few weeks, so I guess it's weighing on me."

"You thinking about getting out?"

He shakes his head. "Nah. This is it, for me. For a while, anyway."

"Really? What do you mean?"

"It's for my mom, ma'am. She doesn't have anyone to take care of her." He flicks the butt of his cigarette to the ground, smashes it with his foot, then bends over, picks up the butt, and puts it in his pocket.

He looks off into the distance. "My dad was never in the picture. He took off before I was born, so it's always been just me and my mom. I joined up to make sure my mom was taken care of. There's no jobs back home, and my mom, she's not doing too good. She's sick a lot. If I don't help her out, there's no one else who will. I send her part of my pay every couple of weeks, and . . . you know . . . it makes things a little easier for her."

Moved by his dedication to his mom, I tell him, "You should be proud of yourself, Cassano. Not too many twenty-two-year-old guys would do what you're doing."

"I know." His gaze is still focused off into the distance. "I know."

I want to talk more, but his face has closed now, and the look in his eyes tells me he's very far away.

Melting

As I scan the auditorium full of recently returned soldiers, my attention keeps returning to a soldier in the front row, slouched low, his face a sea of anguish. He keeps rubbing the side of his head, and looks out with flat, dead eyes. He shifts in his seat, then slides low again. He fidgets, blinks, looks around like he doesn't know where to focus. He picks at spots on his palms as if there are scabs scattered there, but I don't see any.

When the briefing is over, I casually walk over near his seat, and I ask if he's doing OK. He says he is, but I don't believe him. He knows I'm a counselor because I introduced myself to the group during the morning briefing. I nod when he says he's fine, and I move away toward the front of the room. I act like I'm just hanging around chatting with other soldiers, but I'm tracking him. I stay in his line of sight, so he knows I'm still around. The crowd dwindles as soldiers file out. I keep chatting with a few at the front until they leave, too. Sure enough, once the auditorium is empty and all his buddies are gone, he pushes himself up out of the seat and walks over to me.

"Hey, can I talk to you?"

I nod, and we decide to meet in my office, a couple of buildings away.

He arrives at my office five minutes later, tears coursing down his cheeks before I even get the door closed. He's a big, handsome guy who looks like the perfect model for a recruitment poster: chiseled features, sandy-blond hair, and a muscled body. But right now, his perfect body is crumpled into the chair, and that poster boy face is melting with pain. It doesn't occur to him to introduce himself, so I look at his name tag and see that I'm talking to SPC Higgins. He starts to talk immediately.

"I feel all fucked up, ma'am. My mind's all messed up, and I don't think I'm OK."

I ask him to tell me what's going on, and with tears still pouring down his face, he begins to tell me about his time downrange.

"I think I'm all fucked up. Over there, my job was scanning for IEDs buried in the roads, with the whole convoy following behind me. I was in this damn armored vehicle. It was about the size of a damn shoebox. I mean it. I'm six foot three, and the sides were *this* close." Higgins lifts his elbows about forty-five degrees from his sides. "I'm not kidding—this tight, side to side. And the front window was *here*." He holds his hand about eighteen inches in front of his face. I can't imagine someone as big as Higgins being folded into that small space, but I stay quiet so he'll keep talking.

"Here's the deal: it was up to me to make sure none of my buddies and none of the equipment got blown up. Nobody else was out front. Nobody else was scanning the road. No one. Just me. Every day. *Every goddamn day.* Sometimes I was in that thing for eighteen hours straight when we were doing maneuvers or I was waiting for the guys to clear things. And there was nothing to do. Just sit there and wait."

He leans down and fiddles with his boot strings. They're tied tight, but he needs to do something with his hands—and he needs to break eye contact with me before he bursts into tears. When he looks up, he's losing the fight against the sobs and his deep-blue eyes look like they're drowning. His voice breaks with his next words.

"All I had was a little radar screen to stare at all day long. I didn't have anyone to talk to. I thought I was going to lose my mind. I could talk to the guys behind me on the radio, but that sucked. Goddamn radio—scratchy and crackling. Forget it. I felt like I was in solitary confinement for the whole damn year." With that, he breaks down.

Sobs roll through his whole body, and he stops trying to manage them. He lets go and falls apart, and I sit in silence while he faces his pain.

Once he can speak again, Higgins tells me, "I was so scared, ma'am. I was so scared I was going to lose it. I couldn't take it. You're only supposed to be in that thing for three months, but I was good at it, and I was keeping everyone safe, so they left me in the damn thing. I begged my sergeant to give me a different job.

"Finally, my commander said, 'OK, we'll put Davis on it.' So he puts Davis in there, and we lose three trucks that day. The commander never said anything—he just looked at me real disgusted, like, 'See? See what happens when you decide you can't *handle* it?' The next day, I was back inside that damn box, and I stayed there for the rest of the tour."

He clears his throat. "Here, I'll show you."

He pulls his cell phone out of his pocket and taps on it a few times to find the photo he wants. He offers the phone to me.

I stare at a monstrous explosion: orange-yellow flames leap fifty, sixty feet into the air, black smoke billowing upward and outward from the flames. In the lower-left corner of the shot, I see a tiny tan-colored vehicle that looks like a miniature tank—the armor-plated sides are patterned with bolts and rivets, the bright flames are reflected in each tiny window. The explosion dwarfs the vehicle, and as I mentally process the image, he tells me the heat from the blasts could make the inside of it feel like an oven.

"Some days, while the guys did their thing, I lost track of time; I crashed in there. They were detonating bombs I'd found, or searching some village we were heading into. I didn't know what to do with myself. That's the truth, ma'am. I got to where I just didn't know what to do with myself, and I . . . I . . . I just really thought I was going to lose it."

He can hardly choke out his words, and while he's talking, he keeps glancing over at me to see if I'm still "there."

I keep my gaze steady: *I'm here, buddy . . . I'm here.*

I watch him fall into helpless despair. He's never talked to anybody about this—not even his platoon buddies. I encourage him to talk and talk and talk. I listen as he tells me about so many moments when he was scared or isolated or depressed.

"I'm so afraid I'll never feel normal again." His words come out through sobs.

I start to describe some of his symptoms to him, symptoms familiar to me as a therapist working with this kind of trauma. I hope if I can name some of his symptoms, it will help him know there's a regular pattern to trauma's hellish struggle. He'll know these symptoms are not random and that there isn't something wrong with him; it's a predictable pattern others have experienced, too.

"Are you waking up at night, freaked out?"

He nods.

"Having a hard time eating?"

He nods again.

"Pretty hard to talk to people, to follow conversations?"

Another nod.

"What about feeling jittery, edgy?"

He says quietly, "Every minute of every day."

I nod as if I understand every microscopic aspect of every morsel of the story he's sharing.

"I know it feels like it's never going to get better, but I promise you it doesn't stay this bad."

When he looks up at me, his eyes aren't dead anymore. They're full of grief and a vast, vast weariness.

CHAPTER 5

The practice of being curious and receptive toward soldiers began to pay off slowly, in increasingly substantial ways. Now, when I joined a group of soldiers outside during their break, I'd often find myself chatting casually with an individual soldier. Once soldiers noticed all their buddies had walked back into the offices, they might quietly mention an issue they were struggling with. They still would never come into my office for a session, but they asked for help when no one was looking: *How do I talk to my wife better? What do I do with my anger? How do I get along with my damn sergeant?* I was sincerely moved whenever they let the mask of capability slip just a little in order to reach for support.

During these exchanges, I was constantly "translating" conversations. I might be talking with a soldier about the sophisticated tracking equipment he used in Iraq, but what we were *really* talking about was his desperate need to know if all of his platoon buddies were OK out there on patrol. When one soldier started talking about not getting promoted, I thought we were going to talk about his sense of disappointment. Instead, we discussed how proud he was to stay a sergeant. He felt a real calling for training soldiers and was grateful to stay in that role. I had to slow down, give soldiers time, open myself up differently, translate adeptly. It was the only way to let *them* teach *me* how to relate to them.

A different sergeant, Masterson, talked about how much he loved the lush green foliage of the base, then segued into remembering how barren it was in Iraq. CPL Potter was complaining about the lunch fare one day, then drifted into reminiscing about how much he'd missed his wife's cooking while he was deployed. My attention had to be ready to slide with such changes in conversations in a much more agile way than it had with previous clients.

In my private practice, I'd been more familiar with the landscapes of my clients' emotional lives, which were usually a little more similar to mine. With soldiers, I was still learning, still a bit unsure of where the unspoken associations might lead or where the hints in their stories were heading. And getting it right felt more crucial with warriors: they were already hesitant to open up, so if I missed the cue or didn't quickly grasp the allusion or the cultural language, they might feel discouraged about asking for help. One of my first counseling mentors had spoken about how crucial it was to be "light-footed" in your work—to be able to shift topics, emotional tones, or focus, in order to stay closely connected to clients as they told their stories. Even after all the years I'd been in practice, I was learning to be light-footed in substantially new ways.

It wasn't easy to make this shift, especially after thirty years of working in a way that had been familiar and natural for me. I had to move past my usual word choices and therapeutic moves in order to let the soldiers offer their struggles in their own ways. Rather than pushing or prodding as I might have with previous clients, I learned to wait for the moment of courage when a soldier edged into the emotions he or she usually kept fenced off. I needed to work with more patience, more subtle nudging, more respect for how buttoned-up their world required them to be.

I'd said hello to SPC Perryman many times while the soldiers were sitting on the steps. Although we'd never talked, I sometimes saw him watching me and listening to the chatter that was happening around him. One day, while we were both walking back into the building, he and I found ourselves entering the doorway at the same time.

"How's it going these days?" I asked.

"Oh, it's OK."

Sensing a bit of strain in his voice, I decided to slow down and drop into step beside him. He paused in the hallway, and since no one else was around, I said, "Just *OK*?"

With past clients, I might have said something more pointed like, "You sound stressed—what are you really saying when you say *OK*?" But with soldiers, I'd found, this kind of casual invitation was more likely to pay off: *I'm listening if you want to talk.*

"Oh, nothing, really. I just feel like I'm supposed to be glad to be home, you know? But . . . I don't know. I feel just kind of blah about it."

I nodded. "Sounds hard."

Perryman nodded back and we stood there for a moment. Then he said, "I wasn't in combat over there, so I shouldn't even be having a hard time. But still, something changed in me."

Again, I just nodded and leaned against the wall, indicating that I had plenty of time to listen. No questions, no pressure.

"I don't feel like I can say anything since I wasn't in the actual fighting, but the FOB was targeted sometimes and I got kind of freaked, you know?"

"Hard to come back and just do normal life after that, right?"

Perryman nodded, said thanks, and walked off down the hallway.

This was another part of my new work—besides happening slowly, it sometimes happened in small increments. In private practice, the point was to open up emotional material and sort it out during that one conversation. But service members sometimes acknowledged a difficulty and then walked off. It might be days or weeks before we came back around to talking about the issue again. For this reason, I took extra care to remember these bits of conversation, filing them away in my memory to bring forward the next time I saw Perryman or others who had spoken briefly to me in the past.

Remembering all the stories was newly stressful, too. In private practice there was a clear regularity to seeing clients, so their stories stayed "intact." With soldiers, the story lines were left open, and it was up to me to retrieve the appropriate one quickly and sincerely when a soldier and I ended up in an empty hallway or sidewalk.

Also, when I worked with private clients, they tended to open up right away, while soldiers seemed to need more time. For this reason, I sometimes made distinctly less eye contact or feigned misunderstanding, in order to slow things down until a soldier who'd been drilled on the necessity of being tough could admit that he sometimes *wasn't*. If I looked away slightly, or seemed to misunderstand, the conversation's forward momentum could slow or pause—and thus seem less intense for a moment—and the soldier could get his or her bearings as we moved toward vulnerable topics. I found that I could easily miss the subtle openings they offered if I didn't pay deliberate, careful attention.

In this moment, for example, I had to notice how PFC Noonan's voice changed—ever so slightly—when he said, "My buddy Walters and I were in boot camp together. That's where I met him."

"Tell me about Walters."

Noonan was quiet, looked around, and took a deep breath. "He hit some bad times in Ramadi."

I fiddled with the strap of my book bag so I didn't look at him too intently. "Hmmm . . . what happened?"

"He got caught in a firefight. Probably won't regain the use of his hand. He's back in the States now, but I don't know how he's doing. He seems like he's having a rough time."

I had to fill in the blanks: how the two friends had become close in boot camp; how worried Noonan was about Walter's adjustments; how (maybe) they weren't in touch as much now that the "wound" was between them, making one the wounded warrior and leaving the other whole and fit for fighting. That kind of thing could make it hard to stay tight as friends, but all of this was between the lines of Noonan's minimal sentences, and I knew I needed to carefully offer Noonan the chance to tell me more. Each time he added one more sentence, we inched further into the story.

Casual remarks from a soldier were like soundings used to measure the depth of the ocean floor, searching out how I would react to the enormous burdens they carried. They wouldn't easily talk about losses or fears or regrets, so I had to stay still and let them test the waters to see if I would truly *hear* them.

I could relate to how hard it was to let expertise and buttoned-up toughness slide away for a while. My own mask of assured competency was continually slipping further from my reach as I built new patterns for myself.

Personal adjustments piled up on top of the work adjustments. I often stood at the window of my hotel room, gazing out at the parking lots below and wrestling with the cost of making such a huge change. I was very lonely for dear friends, for feeling—even in a tiny sense—as if I were home.

In moving from Arizona, I hadn't realized how disabling it was going to be to leave the places and the people I had known all my adult life.

One Saturday when I wasn't on call for work, I decided to explore the town where the base was located by going out to eat. I'd heard there was a little diner out near the highway that served good breakfasts, so I headed in that direction. I passed tacky strip malls filled with shops for tattoos, pizza, guns, Laundromats, sandwiches, and seamstresses. Dingy bars with names like "Gentlemen's Choice" or "The Rebel Yell" were tucked in there, too—the kinds of joints I would find near most military bases.

I walked into the Down Home Pantry and sat at a small table near the air-conditioning unit, hoping for some relief from the morning's mugginess. The table was covered with a plastic tablecloth that had seen better days, and the curtains on the window needed washing, but I could overlook all of that if the food was good. The place was empty, but I was an early riser, and I imagined the tables would fill soon.

"Hey, darlin'." I looked over at the window that opened into the kitchen and smiled at the waitress who seemed right out of Central Casting—beehive hairdo, a body as wide as the refrigerator, *Junie* stitched just above the left-hand pocket of her light-pink uniform blouse, and eyes full of Southern welcome. "You just get you a menu right there next to the napkin holder and I'll come by in a minute, hon."

I pulled out the plastic-encased menu and found a list that included grits, biscuits and gravy, pork chops and sausages, country cured ham, eggs, and more gravy. All of a sudden, I wasn't interested. I missed my favorite Tucson breakfast: *huevos rancheros* at Little Café Poca Cosa—tortillas, beans, eggs, and salsa served with music so loud you couldn't carry on a conversation. I missed their strong, flavorful Mexican coffee. I had never tried grits, but they didn't appeal to me. I wasn't a gravy lover, and pork chops and country ham didn't sound enticing at seven in the morning.

I looked around at the dingy white walls, linoleum floor, and metal chairs that tilted to one side or the other. Generic, cartoonlike drawings of kittens and puppies hung on the walls. As I took it all in, I missed the wild, saturated Mexican colors of Tucson cafés: hot pink, lime green, goldenrod yellow, and indigo blue. I missed Saltillo tile floors, stuccoed walls, arched doorways, and tin roofs. I barely touched my scrambled eggs and toast, sipped a little of the weak coffee, and drove back to the hotel feeling heartsick.

I couldn't keep up with all the subtle ways I felt uprooted. Something as simple as going out for breakfast only served to remind me how very far from "home" I felt. Finding familiar foods—like fresh Mexican spices or the amazing variety of produce choices so common back home—was a challenge. The flat, soggy landscape made me miss

Tucson's bold, craggy mountains. I ached to see just one warm, familiar face at the gas station, the movie theater, the coffee shop.

Although I sent many emails to friends, sharing the details of this new life I was living, none of them lived nearby; I couldn't show them what this new life was like. For all the phone calls I made to hear a friend's familiar voice on the other end, it wasn't the same as sharing a long, relaxed dinner or having an easy, comfortable conversation in each other's company. My hotel room stayed a little too spartan: a makeshift home that never felt truly warm or inviting. One of my friends told me it seemed I was on a "mini-deployment," on a mission far from home and loved ones. I completely agreed with him. My "deployment" didn't involve the danger and critical missions that soldiers faced. But the unrelenting sense of having been sent away from everything familiar while you tried to accomplish something important—that was shared.

Even the timing of my work was new and strange for me. In private practice, I'd had complete control over my work life: I chose who I worked with and how I worked with them and for how long. Every day had a different schedule. Sometimes I worked from late morning into the evening; sometimes I started early and finished early. Some days were heavily scheduled; other days were lighter.

Now my days were fairly regimented. I might see different soldiers from day to day or attend family support group meetings instead of seeing individual clients, but I was on duty at nine o'clock every morning (if not earlier) and didn't leave the base until five. I often attended family support meetings in the evenings. I was randomly on call during weekends, so I stuck close to the base in case something happened and there was an urgent need for a counselor. It wasn't so much that my hours had changed; it was the "feel" of my schedule and the degree of choice that shifted.

Even though I felt worn down with all the adjustments I was trying to make, I believed in the enormous changes I was navigating. An insistent and definite sense of urging had drawn me away from my comfort zone. The changes I was feeling in my heart, my growing capacity to care deeply about soldiers and their experiences, were what kept me on track. I stayed focused on my mission of forging a new life. In some kind of divine confluence, the vulnerability I felt at leaving my familiar life had left me vastly more open to being affected by the soldiers and their stories.

"So, where are *you* from?" a major's wife asked me as we ate lunch in the base clubhouse and waited for the commander's monthly briefing to start. She was dressed up in a navy blue suit, and her dark hair fell softly around her shoulders. Her bright-red lipstick matched the big red beads she wore around her neck. We'd talked on many occasions, and I enjoyed the sunny disposition she displayed in the face of military-life upheavals. She seemed like she'd seen it all during their years in the military, and her enthusiasm appeared to serve her well in the face of all the changes her family went through.

The ballroom was noisy as people milled about, finding places to sit and setting trays down on the tables they'd chosen. The commander was going to talk about an upcoming deployment, and wives of many of the soldiers I'd been working with were attending to get information. Even though the deployment was four months away, spouses and soldiers were nervous about the changes ahead.

The major's wife and I had been chatting about the different bases she and her husband had lived on during his eleven years in the service. Now, she was graciously extending the question back to me. This was a question I had started to dread, not because it was intrusive or unkind, but because answering it brought my situation into focus for me.

"I used to live in Tucson."

"Oh. Well, where do you live now?" she asked, picking up on the distinction I had made as she reached for her glass of sweet tea.

"I don't really have a home right now. I'm . . . uh . . . kind of in between places. I moved away from Tucson a couple of months ago, and

I'm not sure where I'm going to live next." I paused, embarrassed by my inept way of answering, then said, "I guess I'm from the Fairfield Inn."

We both chuckled, and the conversation moved on, but a version of this particular awkward exchange happened quite often. Sometimes it expanded into questions about why I'd left Tucson. I'd tell the person I had felt called to leave my life there, and more awkwardness would ensue. I didn't really have a clear way to speak about uprooting my life and starting a whole new chapter. I only knew there had been a very pressing inner prompting and my willingness to follow it.

I wondered how soldiers repeatedly moved to new places and began their lives over and over and over again. Although their moves had a direction and a structure that mine lacked, the shared experience of adjusting to new places was something I noticed.

To be honest, I found that working to establish connections with soldiers helped distract me from my own loneliness and sense of being lost. Like the soldiers, I could throw myself into the consuming intensity of my mission. This helped to distract my mind and heart from the shock of my recent uprooting and the challenges of understanding the military world.

CULTURE SHOCK

As soldiers shift from home to deployment, and from deployment to home, they can experience culture shock. Symptoms of culture shock have been well-researched and well-defined: extreme homesickness (or the opposite: longing for battle after one returns home), disorientation and isolation, depression, loneliness, sleeping and eating disturbances, loss of cognitive focus, irritability, inappropriate anger and hostility, and excessive drinking or drug use.

When troops deploy into foreign lands, they often find themselves feeling tremendously disoriented. From the moment they leave their home base, every aspect of their daily lives changes. They endure long travel days to get to their base downrange, and then face a geography that can seem strange and uninviting. They settle into a community and a base that is (at first) foreign and unknown. Their routines and daily rituals are impacted, even ones as simple as using the bathroom, eating meals, or taking a shower.

One female soldier related how difficult it was for her to make trips to the latrines. She was required to have someone accompany her, but others were often unavailable, and she was faced with either ignoring orders or scrambling for a "partner" so she could walk over to the section of the base where latrines were located. Other soldiers spoke of things they had to adjust to in downrange culture: cold showers, spending every single night for months on end in crowded quarters, unwashed clothing, food they didn't like.

Soldiers develop different coping skills for dealing with the culture shock of shifting from one existence to the other. One young man told me, "When I'm downrange, I don't think about home too much—well, I mean, I do. But I try not to. If I let myself remember home too much, it makes everything over there seem unreal, and I get too down. I try to focus on just being *here*. Everything else has to be pushed away."

Some warriors find it easier to simply avoid communicating with loved ones back home. Relating across the great divide between the two worlds is so difficult that they let long stretches of time open up between contact. "She tells me what's happening back home with the kids, but I can't do anything about it, so it just feels too hard. I'm in this crazy world of combat, and she wants to talk to me about the kids' soccer practice. I can't do it."

Other deployed soldiers try to keep home close, to help with the shift in cultures. They take small trinkets with them that represent home, threads of connection to the life they left behind. Some take favorite music or photos. One might bring a keychain his daughter made at church camp; another, a small carving of an elephant given to her by her dad. Or a soldier might keep a family rosary under his pillow or in her pocket. Each item helps the soldiers stay threaded to the faraway world of love, ease, and family.

Culture shock swings the other way, too. Once a soldier has adjusted to the world of combat, the landscape of home and family can feel foreign and difficult. Accustomed to being immersed in the pressures and clarity of purpose war requires, warriors who have returned home can feel restless, disoriented, frustrated, and distant. The purpose-fueled days of combat, the tight bonds of a tribe of warriors, and the sense of pride a soldier feels can all fade away after arriving home. During this transition, such culture-shock symptoms as anger, loneliness, irritation, and excessive drinking can arise. The result is emotional turmoil with loved ones—and relationships often crumble.

Containment

When PFC Barnard hustles back into the barracks to get another pack of cigarettes from his room, I'm left on the sidewalk with Sergeant (SGT) Gallagher. Although Barnard and I had been having a lively conversation about the upcoming change of command, an awkward silence falls like a curtain as soon as he steps way.

In the three weeks I've been assigned to this battalion, I've crossed paths with Gallagher many times—in hallways, in the offices, out on the steps where soldiers smoke. He has never acknowledged my presence, returned a greeting, or looked in my direction. This isn't unusual. There are soldiers on every base who want nothing to do with me because I'm a counselor, so I have let it be. Gallagher always looked particularly stern. I figured he just had a very somber approach to life, and I made sure to respect his preference for avoiding me.

Until now.

After Barnard trots off, Gallagher looks off toward the parade field and stays silent. He's very slight of build but has a tension to his body that could mean he works out pretty hard. He's one of those guys who looks like he might have a rough time in a yoga class because his muscles are so tight. He has dark close-cropped hair, dark eyes that are hidden behind his sunglasses, and his service cap is pulled down low over his brow so that I can hardly see his expressions.

"How are you doing, SGT Gallagher?"

"Fine, just fine."

"So, how long have you been with this battalion?"

"A couple of years."

I realize this bits-and-pieces kind of exchange isn't the best approach, so I shift into questions I hope will give him more room to talk. I begin to ask him where he's from, if he has a girlfriend, and what he likes to do on days off. These seem like things he might be willing to speak about, and I'm careful not to drill him for answers or pry into any deep topics that might make him uncomfortable. I'm simply chatting with him about his life beyond the battalion offices where I see him every day.

Gallagher begins to relax. He talks about playing flag football on the weekends and enjoying fishing in nearby rivers. He tells me about his pit bull mix and his fondness for barbecuing. When he mentions a new F-150 truck, I ask about it, and he launches into a long description of "The Beast." The subject matter stays light and Gallagher seems comfortable, and we end up talking for a good fifteen minutes before Barnard comes back out, saying he got delayed by a phone call. I excuse myself to go back inside and make it a point to shake Gallagher's hand before walking away. I think we've made some progress, but I don't realize how effectively I've broken through his natural reticence until the next afternoon.

Just after lunch the next day, Gallagher walks in and sits down in one of the chairs on the other side of my desk. I close the door and go back to my chair, keeping my tone as reserved as possible to match his style.

"Afternoon, ma'am."

"Afternoon, Gallagher. What's up?"

"Well, if it's OK, I want to talk to you."

I nod.

He pulls the chair closer and straightens it, so it's at a direct angle to the front of my desk. "I think my girlfriend's getting ready to leave me."

Gallagher leans forward, puts his elbows on his knees, and clasps his hands together like he's considering a detailed battle plan or an intricate play in a basketball game. His face shows no emotion, but his manner is deeply earnest as he talks about this painful turn of events. As a "68 Whiskey" (68W, combat medic), Gallagher tells me he learned not to share too much after three deployments downrange. He's dealt with horrific things: friends getting blown up or dying (or both), and innocent locals who were hurt, maimed, or killed by combat operations. He carries all those memories inside him.

The voice he uses to describe his work and his experiences is flat. He's learned very well how to contain his feelings. Watching him, I realize he doesn't even let *himself* know all the feelings he has. His eyes never leave mine, as if he's trained himself not to let his gaze turn away from anything.

Only when he begins to talk about the little children he tried to help in Iraq and Afghanistan do Gallagher's eyes shift ever so slightly. From that tiny shift, I can see it was the children that got to him the most.

"Anyway. No one needs to know about all that," he says. "My girlfriend keeps asking me why I don't talk about my work. Or she says she wants to know 'everything' about me. She doesn't need to know that stuff."

When I ask him what he *can* share with her, he looks at me with a blank face.

"I have no idea, ma'am."

So we spend the next hour talking about the kinds of things he might want to share with her: what he did at the office that day, conversations he had, who he ran into in the hallways, things he thought about during work. The small things that make up his day. Whenever I give him a suggestion, he says, "Roger," and nods his head definitively, as if I've just coached him on the next move in the basketball game. After the first couple of suggestions, he pulls a pen and a small notebook out of his pocket and begins writing down the list of ideas. "Roger." "Roger."

Gallagher says he'll let me know how it goes, and I find myself really hoping he finds a way to open the vault he's built in his heart.

Reunion

"I want a divorce."

This declaration begins almost every session I have with military spouses in the days before the troops return from their yearlong deployment in Afghanistan. Military husbands felt anxiety, too, but the wives felt anxious in a different way, and their nerves couldn't have been more on edge. Each one sits before me, jiggling her leg or twisting a Kleenex in her hands. Although she sits up straight in the chair, wanting to come across as certain and self-possessed, her demeanor is one of downhearted sadness. She's facing a gigantic cliff of unknowing, and her terror of what's about to happen fuels a tremendous urge to run away to familiar ground.

I ask her how she's come to her decision, and she starts to speak about recent struggles. There's usually been a rough phone conversation with her husband overseas. Maybe there've been several. She tells me he's been really unkind or bossy, controlling or mean. And now the wife sitting in front of me is so scared about who's coming home, she doesn't even want to wait and find out. Divorce. That's the solution. She can duck out, go back home to her family, and leave this crazy racing dread behind.

I start by listening to how awful her soldier-husband has been, how he's trying to control her from the other side of the world. I encourage her to tell me all the appalling details of the fights: the hanging up; the multiple screaming phone calls day after day. Her words tumble out fast as she tells me how unreasonable he's being. He's demanding her attention in a hundred ways, while she's trying to feed the kids or get to work. He gets jealous if she spends time with her friends and tries to tell her which ones he'll allow her to hang out with and which ones she should stay away from. If she doesn't answer his calls because she's just plain worn-out from the arguing, he gets wilder with fear and mistrust. He convinces himself she must be having an affair and harshly lays out what a terrible wife she is. She quietly speaks about the lack of gentleness in the long-distance talks she used to look forward to. Her frustration brims over like the tears now falling from her eyes.

I wait while she tells me how different he is from how he used to be. Or we talk about how much *she's* changed in the past year: "I don't need him anymore. I know I could raise the kids on my own if I have to. I've been doing it all year."

I listen as she fortifies herself with long lists of the reasons divorce looks to be the perfect option. Sometimes she starts to talk about who she can live with back home—her mom or a cousin or a best friend. She's already started to plan.

At some point in the session, I make sure she hears that I don't have an agenda about what she decides regarding her marriage. I tell her I only want to help her sort out all the pieces of how she arrived on the brink of ending a marriage, on the edge of being a single parent. We talk about ongoing issues that have never gotten resolved: countless moments of disappointment and anger, someone spending too much, someone not caring how the other one has to live, both feeling too tired to keep trying.

Eventually, we start to dip into her anxiety about the upcoming reunion. I ask her what she thinks it will be like to see him, and she struggles to imagine greeting this guy she doesn't know anymore. She's afraid they'll be awkward and distant with each other. Maybe they won't feel any love at all. They'll feel like strangers—or worse: people who don't even like each other. She used to imagine she'd fall into his arms with relief and joy, but the recent calls have blown that image apart. Now she's full of piercing doubt.

If she can tolerate the process—and most wives can, once we get her side of things aired out—we start to discuss how *he* might be feeling. I wonder aloud whether a young man might feel out of control on the other side of the world, not knowing what's going on at home, not feeling sure that he's still wanted or needed, not at all certain he has a place to return to. Out loud, I imagine him talking to his buddies as they get each other all jacked up and worried about what their wives might be doing while they're gone. I tell her that soldiers have spoken to me about their own feelings of helplessness and fear, their own disorientation in the midst of what is supposed to be a happy homecoming. I offer these things, hoping that such observations can help her start to ponder his side of this conundrum. All she sees right now is an angry, controlling bastard. I want to help her see they are really in the same boat: drenched in anxiety and enormously fragile.

By this time, the conversation has slowed. We're still unraveling the story line of what happened or what might occur, but now we're also puzzling over how complicated and scary this whole process is. We consider all the changes and adjustments "normal" married couples have to make their way through—new jobs, babies, moving to new cities or homes—all the things that test a once-steady intimacy. We puzzle over what happens when a couple doesn't know each other anymore.

We pause and marvel at how frightening it is to *not know* at such a basic level. At this point, she might start to get curious: How do other couples do it? What happens when a marriage is upended, seemingly broken and lost?

Sometimes, when we get to this point, the talking stops completely. We sit and stare at the paintings on the wall or gaze at each other throughout long minutes of silence. It's as if the powerful rationale train has pulled into a more contemplative station for a while.

I'm clear with her about how much courage it takes to hang on the brink of changing one's life story. I hope she can tolerate all the pressure that comes to bear when she sets aside the idea of a quick fix in order to wonder if things could work out. I hope she can begin to feel her vulnerability and fears, rather than hiding in false certainty about divorce.

So we sit together there on the edge, and she tells me she wants to think about it for a while, wants to go home and wrestle with her decision some more. Some of the couples will stay married, some won't. For now, it's all about the daunting task of sitting still while a tsunami of unknowns approaches from the other side of the world.

CHAPTER 6

By the time I was beginning my third month of my first assignment, I had started to shed my assumption that people joined the military because they wanted to go to war. In talking with soldiers, I heard a complex list of reasons that had drawn these men and women into service. Out of the thousands of soldiers I talked with over the years, I never heard anyone express a fondness for war. Let me be clear: soldiers loved doing their jobs and loved being exceptionally good at them. They were proud of the skills and training they had worked so hard to attain. They loved showing me what they knew about *this* technique or *that* piece of equipment, and they loved talking about trainings they'd completed. Some of them looked forward to combat because it was what they had trained for over many months. They were ready to step up and do their part. They looked forward to testing their skills and knowledge. The notion of war was a given part of the job, not something they aimed for or craved.

"I signed up after 9/11, ma'am. It just seemed like the right thing to do. I felt like my country needed me."

"I want to contribute, to do my part in protecting this country. I don't know why everyone doesn't feel that way, but I'm proud to carry my part of the load."

"There's no jobs back home. It's a steady paycheck, and if I work at it, I can keep getting promoted."

"Well, to be honest with you, I want my kids to go to college. I just re-upped so they'll have a college fund. I'm thinking ahead, trying to build something for them. My wife's in, too. We're both planning on staying in for twenty."

As we stood under a tree waiting for a training exercise to begin, one young private told me his parents had never given him any direction or attention growing up. While we talked, he kept bending down to pick up small sticks, and then would snap them into smaller and smaller pieces. "My folks really didn't care where I was or what I was doing," he said. "Even as a little kid, I was on my own. I just ran wild all the time. I thought maybe the military could show me how to be the kind of man I want to be."

"So, did it? Did it help you be the man you wanted to be?"

"Yes, ma'am, it did." He dropped the last stick and brushed his hands off on his uniform.

PFC King, a soldier from an inner-city neighborhood rife with crime and drugs, talked with me when we bumped into each other in an empty conference room. He was moving chairs out of the way for a meeting of company commanders that was to happen later that afternoon, during which plans would be discussed for upcoming field exercises.

King was muscling the chairs into stacks, then shoving the stacks into the edges of the room. I was checking to see if there were any erasers for the whiteboard I was using. He was of medium height and not too brawny, but his dark green, serious eyes and dark hair lent a kind of gravity to his demeanor, no matter what kind of conversation was happening. Today, as we talked, King confessed that he'd found himself unable to stop using drugs until he joined the military. As many times as he tried to get clean and sober, he had failed, again and again. He'd been in the service four years at that point, and he'd been sober every day of those four years. He told me he felt "damn weak" for not being able to stop on his own; I told him I admired the courage it took to join up and get it done. He picked up the last two chairs, gave me a nod, and walked out into the hallway.

Many soldiers were the second, third, or fourth generation in their family to join the military; they were carrying on a proud and honored family tradition. They might not be eager for war, but they were eager to be warriors, protectors, part of the vanguard.

As I waited in the dining facility (DFAC) line behind Captain (CPT) Wegman, he told me, "I love being of service, ma'am. I might be called to fight somewhere in the world, and I hope every person in this country feels a little bit safer because of what I do." He took his cap off his head and scratched the back of his head absentmindedly. "But there's more to it than that. I was sent to Haiti to help people there after the hurricane. And I've been sent to other places to help. I love that, ma'am. You can't believe how proud I feel to be an American at those moments when the trucks are rolling into some decimated town and you know you're the first people to show up and help."

"You think you'll stay in for twenty?" I asked, referencing the twenty years many soldiers aim for, the demarcation point at which his benefits would peak.

"Maybe more than twenty. This isn't what I do. It's who I *am*," said Wegman—more sincerely than I could have imagined.

In my own way, I could relate. I felt a calling to do my work, too. The soldiers' work took them into treacherous landscapes and into the heart of disasters. My work took me into emotionally difficult land-scapes where I sat with clients who were in distress, steadily facing down pain and suffering that I wished didn't exist in our world. Our work was in no way comparable, but I felt deeply called to contribute to others in the ways I knew to be of service.

Despite all that I was learning about soldiers and their culture, the learning curve I faced was incredibly steep. At times, I dropped the ball in key moments that I wished I could live over again, especially during those days before I had a clear grasp of what soldiers were carrying inside and the depth of response they sometimes needed from me.

One of those instances happened on a day when CPT Knox had come to talk to me. It was a day when I was working in an office in a little outbuilding, way out on the edge of the base. A couple of colleagues and I took turns working in this far corner of the base to serve soldiers who worked in the hangars nearby. Knox's unit didn't operate anywhere near this part of the base, so I later realized he had chosen to come to an office where no one in his unit was likely to see him. He had an accent I couldn't place, and as I showed him into my office, I asked where he was from.

"Egypt, ma'am. My family is from Egypt."

His clipped tone made it clear he wasn't up for chatting, so we settled into the chairs and I asked how I could help him.

Knox, a member of a unit that was in great demand during the wars, began to express his feelings of anguish and helpless rage. After his unit had deployed four times in rapid succession, his commanders had assured the unit they would remain home for at least a year. Instead, just six months after coming home, Knox had gotten word they were deploying again; right as he was finally feeling a bit settled into "normal" life, he was being sent back. There was no way to avoid going. He had three years left on his contract with the military, so he had no choice. His clear green eyes flashed.

"I don't even know my son anymore. My wife and I are just polite strangers. And now I'll be gone another year." His voice broke slightly, and his eyes dropped to stare at his boots.

Knox looked antsy as he talked—he scuffed his boots on the floor, he leaned on the right arm of the chair, then he leaned on the left—his body expressing the frustration and pent-up anger he was describing. He never used the word "grief," but I was sure this was another part of what he was feeling: a nearly intolerable mix of anger, grief, helplessness, and frustration.

"You can't imagine the things I've seen over there, and I'm not even going to go into all that. I want to serve. I would never, *ever* abandon my guys. But I don't want to lose my family, either. It feels like the military doesn't even care about that part of our lives. I can't take it."

In my desire to help, I jumped into therapist mode and tried offering him metaphors for his situation. I named the absolute powerlessness he was feeling in several different ways, scrambling to be useful. We talked about ways he might cope with the helplessness and anger: breathing techniques; upping his physical exercise to bleed off his rising tension; different ways to safely express his anger. We discussed options for dealing with his deployment.

At the end of the session, Knox politely shook my hand. But I had the sense he wasn't coming back for another session. I stood looking out the window, watching traffic buzz by on the street outside, and I knew I had missed the mark. My gut sense was strong and clear: I hadn't related to his story deeply enough. The sheer hopelessness of his situation had scared me. That was the truth. Rather than tolerating how helpless *I* felt, I'd offered trite solutions and emotional Band-Aids that would never fully cover the wounds of powerlessness and grief Knox was experiencing. I felt absolutely awful that I had covered over his anguish with my need to avoid the issue of how terribly helpless we both felt.

After I'd worked with soldiers for many more months, I often thought of Knox and wished our encounter had happened later in my exposure to the military. By then, I knew how to listen differently. I would have let more silence open up. "Yes," I would have said. "Tell me how hopeless this feels, this irresolvable tension between being accountable to your troops and saving your family." I would have listened and listened . . . and listened. I would have made much more room for his anguish to enter into the conversation. I would have heard more clearly the howling suffering of leaving loved ones behind, of being sent into a world he knew was going to exact an enormous toll on him, physically and emotionally.

Most importantly, I would have faced my own helplessness—the helplessness I felt in the presence of his. I would soon learn there was a *lot* soldiers had to talk about that left me feeling helpless. Unless I was willing to feel helpless as they shared their stories, I wasn't going to be able to tolerate the stories they needed to tell.

Part of being a skilled therapist is learning to fight off the perceived need to "fix" things for your clients. It's crucial to step away from the need to feel useful, smart, or helpful, in order to fully allow *their* needs to drive the process of therapy. It's a matter of learning to sit still while you deeply feel the grief or helplessness or anxiety the client is bringing forward. In this way, you "allow" the other person to share those emotions without getting pulled into them by your own reactions.

In Knox's case, I had let my fear drive things. I felt afraid of how truly powerless he was in his situation; I saw his pain and knew he didn't have any options. As I began to feel scared and helpless, I tried to avoid those feelings by jumping in quickly, trying to "make it better." In failing him, I'd learned that working with soldiers would require that I sit still in those roiling, painful layers of helplessness and grief they often carried. I needed to let those emotional waters wash over me, too, keeping myself steadily *beside* them as we found a way through the rapids. This was a powerful realization for me. I had tolerated depths of helpless pain in many clients in the past, but I was starting to understand that soldiers carried burdens that were in some ways heavier and more complex than those of the people I'd worked with before.

In contrast to this encounter of helpless frustration was a moment I experienced just two days later. At a battalion change-of-command ceremony, a colleague and I took our seats in the last row of plastic folding chairs that had been precisely lined up under a stiff white awning. This kind of ceremony was important in military culture. It marked the solemn change of leadership from one commander to the next; it typically meant a lot of changes would ripple through the entire battalion. In the front rows, twenty or thirty dignitaries waited for the ceremony to begin. Across a small parade ground, the battalion—about eight hundred soldiers—lined up in tight formations of platoons and companies that faced a podium placed in front of the awning, from which the new commander would address his soldiers for the first time.

Before the ceremony could begin, a torrential downpour suddenly moved in. Rain fell so heavily, troops just across the field looked like watery ghosts.

As it thundered, their CSM, who had been seated safe and dry under the protection of the awning, walked out into the rain and stood at attention next to the podium without saying a word. Instantly, he was thoroughly soaked; water poured off his face and shoulders, down his arms. His saturated uniform clung to his broad shoulders and puddles quickly formed around his feet. He didn't move. His action sent an unmistakable message to his troops: *I'm with you. Whatever you endure, I endure.*

I leaned over to my colleague and pointed toward the CSM.

"Yes," she said. "I guarantee you his troops will remember this exact moment when they're in combat with him."

Tears came to my eyes. I understood how powerful it was—in *any* context—to have someone say, *I'm here, no matter what. I've got your back.*

I was in a world where honor and integrity were guiding principles that were usually offered in silence. I was in a world where a father could drown in helpless frustration over having to leave his family far too often. This astounding range of experiences and feelings, from honor to heartbreak, made up my days. My heart had to stretch wide to make room for them.

The more complexity I learned to hold and the more vulnerable I became to my own feelings and changes, the more frequently soldiers turned to me with their concerns and stories. My new working methods pushed me out of my comfort zone, made me face new vulnerabilities as I worked—as in the case of stepping in too quickly when a situation felt helpless.

The fact that I was in new territory—geographically and metaphorically—meant that I needed to find new paths to follow. As I listened to unfamiliar stories of pain and struggle, I met my soldier-clients with less assurance, but with more heart. I'd been counseling for many years, but now I allowed myself to start anew.

I'd faced clients with helplessness and grief before. In the early years of my career, I worked with people with AIDS, back when that diagnosis was a death sentence. Later, I worked with mothers whose infants had died—a group so grief-stricken they seemed like they were barely on the planet anymore, moving through their days in a haze that kept them absent from their own lives. But this group—this valiant and wounded group—was different, their grief wrapped in stoic tolerance and aspirations of a warrior's invincibility. The challenge of unwrapping those wounds required of me new levels of patience, caring, and grace.

Although I still stumbled at times, I began to feel I could be useful to the soldiers, which was all I wanted. As I changed—finding and practicing more patience, and refining my attunement to their lives and stories—soldiers began to trust me. I developed more courage, so I became able to meet the courage it took them to ask for support.

They began to tell the stories that were so hard to speak.

HELPLESS

Soldiers sometimes spoke to me of the terrible helplessness they encountered during combat, moments when civilians were hurt, when they faced the deaths of innocent children, when they felt the mission had become untenable. They spoke of watching buddies suffer terrible wounds that would stay with them a lifetime, or of firefights that lasted "an eternity." And then there was the searing helplessness of watching a fellow warrior fall in battle.

Feelings of helplessness didn't usually arrive in the moments when soldiers' adrenaline ran high, making their attention laserlike and tightly focused on the battle. It washed in later, when the chaos had ebbed and they could feel things again.

Surrendering to the fact that they couldn't protect their combat brother was unbearable; they carry that helpless moment with them for the rest of their lives, reviewing over and over the instant when they couldn't act fast enough or couldn't find the sniper or failed to know the bomb was underneath the dirt.

All their training pointed them toward feeling capable—even invincible—in their combat duties. The *actual experience* of combat often turns them in the opposite direction, as the overwhelming reality of war pulls them into moments of immense and terrible helplessness.

When they come home, many soldiers feel helpless to navigate the return to normal life. They fear they will never be normal, never fit in, never find relief from the nightmares and memories and losses that torture their minds and hearts. In the face of that helplessness, they can numb themselves through drinking, popping pills, risk-taking, isolating themselves, or a hundred other ways, all of which drive those combat veterans further and further away from loved ones and friends. As their stress mounts, suicide sometimes comes to feel like the only option.

Admitting to feelings of helplessness is difficult in the close-knit, insular world of the military. Soldiers often worry that in doing so, they will lose honor, and they'll risk shame, stigmatization, and rejection. But I came to understand that soldiers sometimes needed to admit the moment helplessness first burned their soul—and I came to know how very difficult it was to sit with them and listen as they faced that moment. They are caught in an inherent paradox: they belong to a culture in which helplessness isn't allowed, yet that same culture places them in situations where profound helplessness is a given.

Over the years, I had learned to be deeply aware of the instances when I couldn't make a client's pain go away or change the profound struggle in which they were caught. Through the experience of helping soldiers come home, I realized something important: until we all grapple with our feelings of helplessness in the face of our veterans' struggles, they won't be able to unburden themselves of the heavy helplessness war brought to bear.

Do we wish all wars could stop? Surely. Do we know how to accomplish that in the face of current threats? Probably not. Helpless, aren't we? Do we wish every warrior was free of PTSD, injuries, and nightmares? Of course. Do we know how to do that, as they return, ravaged? We don't. Helpless again.

It's strange to imagine that as we tolerate the helplessness that arises within the complex world of war and warriors, we might find that we share with combat veterans bonds we never knew existed. If we can face how helpless we all sometimes feel about these things, we might share some of the crushing burden of all they carry home. Shared helplessness. What a strange bridge.

In recent years, civilians, too, have grappled with feelings of helplessness. Americans felt helpless in whole new ways on 9/11. Many soldiers volunteered for duty after that day to address that very feeling, to find a way to *do* something in response. Other Americans felt helpless, watching their nation get into long wars they simply couldn't believe in. And, more recently, we've felt helpless watching new horrors unfold across the globe.

When I offered a soldier "Band-Aids" of platitudes in order to avoid the helplessness they grappled with, I wasn't of use to them at all. Ironically, it wasn't until I could bear how helpless *I* felt that soldiers could unburden themselves of the particular helpless feelings that arise in war.

Stifled

PFC Anderson pulls out his phone and begins showing me photos of his three-year-old daughter. She's bright-blond with an impish smile and her dad's shining blue eyes. He tells me his little girl lives with his ex-wife several states away. He's sad about how little time he gets to spend with her, and he gazes at her photos with astounding pride and love. His face lights up as he tells me about their last visit—mornings spent coloring pictures of trees, and afternoons eating jelly sandwiches at the park. As he scrolls through the photos, Anderson softly admits the pictures were taken over a year ago, the last time he saw his little girl before being deployed.

We're standing out on the steps of the barracks, and the recently returned soldiers are scattered all up and down the wide stoop—some sitting on the concrete steps, others leaning against the metal pipe railing. While they fiddle with their cigarettes and puff out thin clouds of smoke, a few of the fatigue-clad guys tease one of their buddies about the atrocious dance moves he displayed the weekend before. Others grouse about being bored since coming back from overseas, with no new challenges to keep them busy, like in their days downrange. A specialist from California brags about how cool his hometown is, clearly eager to get back home during the upcoming leave.

I lean in toward Anderson's phone as he holds it out toward me, and I comment on how adorable his daughter is. A corporal standing nearby says, "You'd better not show those to my wife . . . she'll want to keep her."

I look at him with a puzzled expression, and as the group goes quiet, he explains he and his wife lost a baby boy just a few years ago.

Hearing the corporal say this, a third soldier stands up quickly and says, "*Jeez, dude.* Talk about an awkward moment." His words are filled with pure seething disdain, ending the conversation and silencing the man who had mentioned his son's death.

The soldier who had just spoken about his wife and baby is a tall, lean guy, a little older than most of the other soldiers. He's draped back against the railing with his foot propped up on the bar behind him. In the two weeks I've been working with this battalion, he and I have nodded to each other in passing, but I don't even know his name. I scan the patch above his right pocket: "Baxter." I make sure to remember it. Baxter looks away and studies the wall of the barracks like he's inspecting it for cracks.

The group on the steps gets jittery, as if some buzzing electric current has passed through them. They shift around, stand up, start dispersing into the barracks and to various offices they need to report to. Baxter saunters away, as neutral as a piece of glass.

The next day I see Baxter in the hallway when no one else is around. "I'm so sorry about your son. I was touched that you brought it up."

He glances at me warily. "Yeah . . . it's still tough."

There in that stark, dimly lit hallway, we talk for nearly an hour. We huddle against one side of the hall as if it's crowded with people passing—but it's just him and me, holding our own against waves of loss and sadness.

He speaks about his little boy's sudden death as an infant and the impact it has had on his marriage. His wife has never recovered from her grief. She's withdrawn from him, spending all her time on the computer, unable to leave the house. Going out into public makes her anxious; she can't tolerate seeing other families who still have their children.

She barely speaks to him, passing the weeks and months shrouded in a fog of grief he can't reach through.

His own grieving seems more settled, but his face drops into still-fresh loss when he describes the day he went to wake his baby son up from his nap and found him already gone. Without even realizing he's doing it, he keeps repeating himself: "He was already gone. He was already gone."

He falls silent, his face frozen. His eyes stare at the floor, but don't seem to see anything. I stand with him, also silent. Together we look into an abyss of loss and emptiness. Several minutes pass.

"I'm so sorry." My words are barely more than a whisper.

Baxter nods and stretches his neck in different directions, as if he can work out the kinks in his heart by rolling his head around.

After more long moments pass, Baxter pushes off from the wall and starts looking around as if he's waking from a dream. He shakes his head, blinks his eyes, and mumbles something about needing to get back to work. He begins to walk away, but turns after a few steps and says with a voice full of sincerity, "Thank you, ma'am. It means a lot to me, talking to you."

I watch Baxter walk away and I ponder how hard it must be to live in this world where raw grief makes others anxious, where his need to speak of his sorrow might very well get brutally stifled. I see him in passing a few times over the next several weeks. We nod and say hello. There's a knowing in his eyes that touches my heart.

Best Friend

PFC Canton and I are sitting at the picnic table outside of the battalion offices. He's not in a hurry to get anywhere, so we start chatting about his recent return from Afghanistan and how things have been since he got back. I ask him if he's happy to be home, and he shrugs. "I'd rather be over there. I asked them to extend my tour, but they wouldn't do it."

"Why would you want to extend? Most guys are glad to get back home."

Canton shrugs again. "Not much to come back to."

"Do you have family? You married?"

"Used to be." There's a hard edge in his voice.

"What happened?"

"I got divorced."

I'm not sure if Canton wants to say more, but it seems worth it to offer him an invitation. "Sounds like there's gotta be more to that story . . ."

He nods. "It's not a good story, I guess. I was married for about a year before we deployed. I loved my wife, thought we'd be together forever and all that. I was over there about seven months when my company ran into an ambush. I was injured—not too bad. I figured I'd call home to tell her I was OK. I didn't want her to hear about the ambush from someone else and be all worried and everything. And really, I just wanted to talk to her." Canton spins his cigarette lighter in his fingers as he talks.

"I stood in line for over an hour to get some time on a phone—it sucked trying to get phone time. Finally, a phone gets freed up. So there I am, standing in the middle of our little outpost, dialing her up and feeling pretty excited to hear her voice." He stops spinning the lighter, but starts to tap it on the side of his leg.

"My buddy Jake answered the phone. No big deal. That didn't surprise me at all. He was my best friend in college and we'd joined up together. His unit stayed back when we deployed, so he was at our house all the time—you know, fixing things for my wife or just helping her out. I considered it a big favor, to be honest with you. Like he was watching out for her while I was over here. I would've done the same for him.

"So anyway, he picks up the phone, and when I say, 'Let me talk to Diana,' he tells me she doesn't want to talk to me. I thought he was kidding around." As he says this, Canton drops his lighter onto the table and brushes his hands off on his leg, his tension clear in every brisk movement.

"I tell him, 'Seriously, man. Let me talk to my wife.'"

"He says again, 'She doesn't want to talk to you.'"

"I had no idea what he was talking about. I called him an asshole and told him to put Diana on the phone. He does this little half cough, like he's clearing his throat, and then he says, 'Listen, man. We need to talk. I mean it: she doesn't want to talk to you. In fact, she wants a divorce. Her and me are together now. I'm sorry, man.'" Canton stares hard as me as he says this, his eyes flashing with anger. He's so absorbed in the memory, it's as if he's directing the rage at me.

"I threw that goddamn phone down on the ground and walked away. I've never talked to either one of them since." He finishes with a bitter edge in his voice that could cut through the hardest granite.

"Oh no. I understand why you'd rather stay over there. So . . . how's it going?"

Canton lets his gaze slide away to the woods behind the battalion building. "It sucks. Once upon a time, I thought it would be such a great thing to be home. But it sucks."

He stands up abruptly and says politely, "Nice talking to you," but I hear the cold, dead flatness in his voice.

Stellar Soldier

When I walk into her work area, First Lieutenant (1LT) Sandario glances up at me. She registers that it's me, then looks back down to the log books lying open on the counter in front of her. Her pen moves line by line, making small check marks next to certain entries. The battalion has been in and out of the field for weeks, and she's checking the log that keeps track of the troops coming and going.

I stand a little off to the side of the wood-topped counter and fiddle with the ballpoint pen that's attached to the counter by a beady chain. Behind her, the office buzzes with activity; soldiers walk in and out, dropping off paperwork, checking in with officers, reaching for phones, and stopping to click away on keyboards. The whiteboards that line the wall to my right are full of notations that tell where each company is located out in the field, when they departed, when they'll return, and what their training will be. Soldiers with medical issues are listed in a column on the side; they're assigned to desk duty or other tasks while their units train.

"Hey, Lieutenant." I lean against the counter.

"Ma'am." Sandario keeps her eyes on the logs. Her voice sounds tight to me, without the warm, friendly tone I usually hear from her. I know the soldiers are beginning to hear about PFC Dawson's suicide. He killed himself while on leave, just after returning from his combat deployment, and the sad news is starting to trickle through the ranks today. Some of the soldiers are sad; some have become hardened from too many losses over the years and don't react much at all. Others are so angry about what he did, they're threatening to skip his on-base memorial service.

Since the people in the office are consumed with their tasks and aren't paying attention to my presence, I decided to check in with Sandario. "You've heard about Dawson?"

She nods, and her pen pauses in its checking of entries.

"Did you know him?"

"I didn't know him well, really." Her pen floats for another half beat. I can't quite read what's going on, but there's *something* in the way she's acting that makes me keep going.

"Sad news. How are you doing?"

"Can we talk about this later? I want to ask you something."

I tell her later is fine and let her know where she can find me the rest of the day. Sandario nods, and I move on to the rest of my rounds.

Sandario and I have chatted many times during my couple of months on base, typically while sitting in creaky old office chairs in a back room of the battalion offices. She's told me she always felt she had to do *more* as a female officer in order to be taken seriously. She grew up in a military family and had dreamed of becoming an officer since she was in the sixth grade. Her father was a noncommissioned officer with a twenty-seven-year military career, and Sandario had dedicated herself to making him proud of her. I admire the way she's faced the challenge of sexism in the military: she sees it, has noted it, and has been figuring out how to advance her career in spite of it.

She's only been in the military a few years, but there's a certain fierce pride in Sandario's commitment to serve. It's clear from the efficient way she moves that her body is tight and fit under her baggy uniform. Her dark brown hair is pulled back and tucked into a bun at the back of her head—not one stray hair escapes the neat pinning. I've seen her laugh and joke, but she's focused and responsible when she needs to be. She wants to be an exceptional soldier.

That afternoon, while I'm filing reports, Sandario walks into my office. She steps into the room so quietly, I only notice her presence when I hear the door click behind her. She sits down in the chair across from me, bringing her usual intensity to the conversation.

"Is this a good time?"

"Absolutely, Sandario." I set aside the reports. "What's up?"

"It's about Dawson, ma'am. He wasn't one of my soldiers, so I didn't know him well, but I knew who he was. I'm having a hard time wrapping my mind around what he did."

Sandario looks at me steadily and seems to know exactly what she wants to say, so I nod slightly to encourage her to keep talking.

"I know he was a stellar soldier, ma'am. I've seen his records: high marks across the board on all his tests—marksmanship, PT, trainings, promotion boards—all of that stuff. I heard he was valedictorian at his high school, star quarterback. One of his friends told me that when they deployed together, Dawson had written 'Never Quit' on the bottoms of his socks, just to keep himself right up against that edge of excellence."

She stares at me and presses her palms together. "I hear he used to share letters from his dad with some of his friends. His dad was so proud of him, always telling him what a great job he was doing. When he was downrange, his mom sent cards to him all the time and said she was praying for him. They both seemed so proud of him, all along the way, you know? From everything I've heard, they sound like a real close family."

Here, Sandario stops and looks at me with steady dark eyes. "You see what I'm saying, ma'am? You see what I mean?"

"Tell me, Sandario."

"I can't get my mind around it. How does someone with all that going for them decide to opt out? He was at the top of his game. Why does a guy like that decide to end it all?"

Sandario's deep-brown eyes are misty. I've seen earnestness in her face before, but in this moment it's more pressing, more *pure*. I wonder how closely Sandario is identifying with Dawson, how much she relates to his hunger for achievement, his pride and integrity, his drive.

"I think it's almost impossible for our minds to understand someone choosing suicide, right?"

"Yeah. I guess it is."

I very consciously aim my remarks for the place where I think Sandario might be seeing herself. "But imagine someone like him. Everyone thinks he's doing great; they think he's running all green lights, pretty much invincible. I'm just guessing here, but maybe all along, he *had* to be the guy who had it all together, you know? To fulfill their expectations, their image of him. That's a lot of pressure.

"If everyone saw you as being amazing, and perfect, and always on-target . . . and you were struggling, maybe tired or scared—who could you tell? What if you felt you weren't allowed to say, 'I'm not OK. I can't do this.' I mean, I wonder if it isn't impossible to break people's image of you when you're seen as some kind of superachiever. Seems it would be hard to tell them you're really down. I wonder about that."

Sandario stares at me, her dark eyes still moist and shiny with tears she holding back.

"Look," I say. "The hard thing is: we'll never know what was really going on below all that achievement and perfection. We can only guess there was more to his story, right?"

"Yeah. I guess. I guess that has to be true."

Because this has rattled her so much and because she's got some similar characteristics, I feel like I have to take the conversation a step further.

"Tell me this, Sandario: If you were really struggling and felt like you couldn't go on, who would you tell?"

She stares at me while the wall clock ticks its endless seconds.

"I'm not sure, ma'am." Her hands are still pressed together in front of her, but now she lowers them into her lap as she ponders the question. "I really don't know who I'd turn to."

"Would you turn to your dad?"

"We don't really talk like that."

"Got close friends?"

"Well, yeah. But it's not like that. We just hang out, and we're all . . . I guess, we're all trying to get ahead here."

"I know it's complicated, Sandario. I'm just trying to help you see how hard it might be to admit how dark things are getting. Give it some thought. Let's keep talking. See who you come up with—maybe a couple of folks you would talk to if things ever got too hard."

She nods and stands to leave. Just before she steps through the doorway, Sandario turns back to me. "This thing with Dawson scares me."

"Roger that."

Sandario smiles at my use of soldier language and says she'll see me around.

CHAPTER 7

Whenever I had worked my way through the endless stream of introductions and gotten myself oriented on each new base, I then turned my focus to figuring out what kind of outreach would work best. What worked at one base didn't necessarily translate to the next. At one base I spent a lot of time in the motor pools, talking with soldiers while they worked on the battalion vehicles. At the next base it was more effective to make my rounds through company offices and training areas. At another facility, I sat with soldiers and civilians while they cataloged belongings or mapped out shipments, pulling up a chair right next to them at their tables and talking for long stretches while they kept working. I might spend a lot of time with spouses at one base, and at the next, I wouldn't encounter too many of them. Figuring out the outreach method was a priority each time I moved. Some of my colleagues didn't adapt so readily; they tended to stay in their offices waiting for soldiers to show up, or they'd stick with the same approach at every base and hope soldiers would respond. I shifted my tactics each time, finding ways to connect and hoping the soldiers would come to see me as someone they could talk to—meeting them on their terms.

I knew I needed to talk differently to paratroopers than I did to the infantry; differently to engineers than to Special Forces. Each segment of the military population had their own language and interests, so I kept shifting my approach to match—as best I could—the folks I was encountering. Those who searched for IEDs were taking different trainings than those who were snipers; those who parachuted out of planes were proud of different aspects of their jobs than were those who breached walls. Again, it was like learning to change the radio dial very slightly with each group so I could pick up their signals as clearly as possible. Each branch of service had its own slang, too. A lazy, untrustworthy comrade was a "rock" in the Navy; a "bagger" in the Marines, a "Blue Falcon" in the Air Force. I layered in the slang occasionally. I didn't do it to be like them; I did it so the gap between them and me might close, even slightly.

"Good morning, Davidson," I called out to the stocky, bowlegged soldier walking in front of me as I entered the facility to which I was assigned. The cold wind was blustery and relentless that day, and we'd both hustled for the double-door entrance on the side of the building. I'd only been at this facility for a couple of weeks, but I'd made it a point to memorize the name of each person, civilian and military, who worked inside—about two hundred people. This was a particular challenge in a facility that had so many civilians because I couldn't rely on the name tags on a military uniform. Still, I couldn't imagine that they would take me seriously as a resource if I didn't take the trouble to speak to them by name. (Later, a soldier told me I was the only counselor—out of the many who had cycled through the facility—who'd made the effort to learn their names.)

As we squeezed through the doors into the warmth of the building, Davidson turned around with a wide grin and began talking about the football pool he was in for the upcoming weekend. I also knew that besides being interested in football he was going through a difficult divorce, and once we got inside, we stood in the common area as his football banter transitioned into a conversation about his sense of failure concerning his marriage.

I was always glad to catch someone while they were in between tasks—taking a break from their work or just arriving or walking between buildings. While some commanders didn't really appreciate my presence, most welcomed the support I was offering their soldiers, and they were fine with me having exchanges with the soldiers wherever that happened. It was part of my job to roam all the different areas where soldiers worked, so it wasn't unusual for me to grab a moment with someone while they were working. I never interrupted if they were in the midst of something focused or important. But if they were doing tasks they could pause, or if they could talk while working, I took advantage of the moment and it worked out just fine. The time before work and during lunch hours—or just after lunch, when things were slow—were typically good times to chat.

During the first couple of weeks, when I was still trying to memorize each person's name, I sometimes couldn't anchor the name to the person, no matter how hard I tried.

"Tell me something about yourself. Tell me a story, anything. It'll help me remember your name," I'd say when I just wasn't getting it.

"I have two blind cats," Marian, a civilian worker, told me. I easily remembered her name after that.

"My girlfriend is pregnant. I'm about to be a dad," said Micah, a nineteen-year-old who was so shy, it had taken me many days to get him to speak to me at all. After that, I not only remembered his name, I had something to inquire about whenever we crossed paths.

One day, I pulled a chair up next to PFC Deseño as she filled out equipment requests. I'd been trying to remember her name for almost two weeks. "Help me out here. Tell me something about yourself so I can remember your name."

She stopped writing and looked at the wall across from her desk. "I was in Iraq four years ago. I lost my three best friends. I still have dreams about them."

I asked her to tell me about one of those friends, and she spoke about Reynaldo, a friend she met in boot camp, who became her best buddy. They stayed in touch after they were sent to different kinds of training, but somehow ended up in Iraq at the same time and even ended up at the same base, although in different units. Every time I sat with her after that, we spent a few minutes talking about one friend or another. Deseño's desk faced away from her coworkers, so she had some privacy that allowed her to speak quietly about these things. She got a little choked up at times, but it seemed we were slowly bleeding off some of the grief she'd been carrying in her heart.

In my role on the bases, I was asking questions, talking, and listening for hours and hours, every single day. I loved supporting each and every one of the people I came to know. After a while, I knew them and their stories quite intimately. But my level of involvement was very different from what it had been in private practice. In my practice, clients had shown up, talked, and left. My appointments were spaced evenly throughout the day, with breaks in between. I had a structure to the work that helped contain it. Working on the bases, on the other hand, involved being "on" from the moment I showed up in the morning to the time I left at the end of the day. I felt like I was swimming in an ocean of clients all day, with interactions coming at me all the time.

As I juggled conversations, it wasn't unusual to turn away from one just in time to get pulled into another. One day, I was listening to a soldier talk about his struggling marriage when one of the battalion commanders tapped me on the shoulder. He and I stepped aside for a moment to get some privacy, and he said, "Would you please go talk to Sergeant Pierce? She just got some bad news." I wrapped up my conversation and went to Sergeant Pierce's office, where I found her in tears over the news of her mother's passing. When I walked back to my office,

Private (PVT) Kafley was waiting to speak to me about his decision to leave the military. If I did my outreach well and let the soldiers know I was accessible, the response could at times be pretty overwhelming. I loved it, and it sometimes wore me down.

At another base, my outreach to the soldiers unfolded in an unexpected way. During the slow hour after lunch, I was standing in the hallway talking with PVT Tellez and PVT Comber, who were teasing me about how no one wanted to come into my office for counseling.

"Why don't you put a bowl of candy on your desk? At least they'll come into your office for the candy," Tellez said. He was funny by nature, quick-witted, with a ready laugh and sharp sense of humor.

Comber was more of a follower, playing straight man to Tellez. Comber's laugh was a quiet chuckle, but when Tellez found something funny he erupted in a belly laugh that echoed up and down the hallway.

"Yeah, man . . . *candy*. That'll get them lined up," Comber said. Looking delighted with themselves, they did some sort of complicated hand-slapping sequence and went back into their offices.

I figured I had nothing to lose. Even if it didn't get more soldiers to come into my office, these two would probably get a kick out of my taking their suggestion. I got candy—not mere lollipops or hard candy, but chocolate and more chocolate, miniature candy bars of all kinds. I put it all in a shiny red bowl as big as a hubcap, and the brightly wrapped candy became a beacon to anyone walking by in the hallway. It was like putting a neon sign on my desk. Word got around, and soldiers started dropping by to see if I had their favorite kind. Pretty quickly, I knew who liked what. Sergeant Baker liked Snickers; Second Lieutenant Velasquez, Kit Kats. As I did my rounds I could say, "Hey, Jackson, you should stop by. I got more M&M's today."

A week after I'd put the candy on my desk, I left my door open while I was making rounds through another part of the building. When I got back, one lonely mini-Snickers sat in the bottom of the empty bowl. Obviously, no one wanted to be the person who took the very last candy. I smiled and refilled the bowl. A couple of days later, I came back from my rounds and found three soldiers hanging out, chairs pulled close so they could put their feet up on my desk. They were happily eating candy and talking. They looked sheepish when I walked in, but we all laughed as I leaned against the doorjamb and began chatting with them. It was exactly the kind of scene I was hoping for. Whenever my outreach paid off, I felt like I'd won the lottery.

Weeks later at this same base, Tabitha, a civilian supervisor, asked me to stop by her office when I had the time to check in with her for a moment. She happened to be on a phone call, so I slid into a chair in the corner of her overstuffed office as she held up a finger indicating she was almost finished.

While she wrapped up her phone call, I looked around at the posters she had on her wall. "Be Your Best!" said one that featured a photo of a fuzzy brown bear with a silly hat on its head. "What's to Complain About?" said another, showing a toddler completely covered in mud, a goofy, giggling grin on his face. Tabitha leaned toward flawless optimism.

"I'm glad you're here; I wanted to talk to you," she said as she hung up. Tabitha wore dresses with huge flowered prints in flashy colors, and today she had on a particularly raucous one, neon pink splashed across lime-green floating in canary yellow. Every day, Tabitha looked like she was about to board a cruise ship, and she had the happy, eager personality to match her clothes. Next to the posters hung a whiteboard that included long lists of schedules—meetings, briefings, homecomings, and trainings. She was like the air traffic controller for social services on the base. Her desk was piled high with scattered folders and paperwork that lay inches deep, but I knew that if I needed a particular form, Tabitha would reach into those piles and put her hands on the page I needed without any trouble.

"What's up?" I settled back in my chair, thinking there might be a problem with one of the soldiers or spouses.

"I've been wanting to tell you: I've seen you working with the soldiers, and you're doing something really different."

"I hope you mean that in a good way," I teased.

"No, seriously. I watch you with the soldiers, and you don't let them 'back you off.' You hang in there. You get them laughing and joking, and pretty soon they're comfortable with you, and they decide you might be all right to talk to. You have a way with them, and it works. I just wanted you to know. I've seen soldiers talking to you that I never, *ever* thought I'd see talking to a counselor."

I loved hearing Tabitha's feedback, especially after struggling so hard at the beginning to figure out how to relate to soldiers. We chatted a while longer, and then I moved on to finish my afternoon rounds. But I found myself thinking of her comment after I went to my hotel room that evening.

That night, I stood barefoot in the kitchenette area of the room, stirring leftover stew in the cheap hotel-provided pan. The coil on my little two-burner cooktop glowed bright red as it heated. The sounds of the occasional door slamming down the hallway, voices chattering as people walked by, and traffic from the nearby highway were ever present in the background.

As the stew warmed and bubbled, I wondered: *How* was *it I could hang in there when soldiers were reticent about talking to me?* I let my mind drift with that question. Part of being a skilled therapist was figuring out how to relate to a wide range of people on their terms, making contact and engaging with their stories in ways they would respond to. It had taken me a while to make substantive connections with soldiers, and I'd certainly had some missteps. But now, waiting for my dinner, I felt as if I'd been preparing for the job of hanging in there with reticent soldiers ever since I was a child.

I had grown up in a family of nine, a family that tended to be rather emotionally contained in communications, which was never my style. While there were a *lot* of conversations in our family, due to the fact that so many people had to interact with each other, those exchanges tended to focus on chores or schedules or meals or the innumerable details of running the family. Both of my parents were incredibly busy and involved, managing a family of nine and the household—and school and sports and scouts and extended family—and I imagine they defaulted to this no-nonsense conversation style out of sheer necessity.

By nature, though, I was more emotionally oriented.

If I asked a sibling or parent "How are you?" it wasn't unusual for the answer to be "Fine" and nothing more.

"How'd your day go?"

"OK."

"What are you doing?"

"Not much."

All very typical exchanges. Sure, I could chat with them about superficial things. We could talk about what time Sam had to be picked up from baseball practice or what we were having for dinner or whether or not we would go to my grandparents' that weekend, but that wasn't satisfying to my nature.

From a young age, I had felt I was wired differently. I was always interested in what I thought of as "real" emotional contact. I felt an inherent desire to know how someone was feeling, what was in their heart, how things felt to them as we walked through our days together—a desire they didn't seem to have in the least.

I remember going to see *Around the World in 80 Days* with my family when I was maybe five or six. While everyone else delighted in the adventure and the lighter moments of the film, when the movie was over I was terribly sad about one of the characters losing a friendship. My mom asked me what I was upset about, and when I told her, she was pretty baffled. That part of the story didn't even register for her or the others.

My mom joked a few times that I was "little Sarah Bernhardt" because I was so much more emotional than the others. Looking back, I don't think I was overly emotional at all; it was only by comparison with my siblings that my nature seemed amplified. Even as a child, my way of orienting felt normal to me (though, obviously, I didn't know any other way to be), but it was clearly not shared by the others in my household.

When I was an adult, my mom recalled an eighth eighth-grade friend of mine who had been sent to the hospital, my mother told me, "You absolutely insisted I take you to visit him. I never knew where you came up with these things." To me, this seems like a kindhearted gesture from a child; to my mom it was somehow odd or foreign.

When I was in college, at a university quite far from home, I took my first trip back to see my family after what seemed like a very long first semester. I was so happy to see everyone that I had tears in my eyes as I walked through the front door. My parents and a few siblings were sitting in the living room, and a couple of them rolled their eyes as one brother said, "Oh, good grief—she's crying again."

Even though they showed their love through the relentless attention and sacrifices they made in raising their children, my parents never said "I love you" to us. It was not their way. After I moved away from home, I started saying "I love you" to them every time we talked on the phone—a moment that they found quite awkward—although, eventually, they began to say it in response.

None of these thoughts were intended as criticism—they just kept highlighting for me the difference between the openly emotional world I lived in and the less emotional way my family operated. I wondered if my parents ever felt scared or uncertain, and if they had longings about things they had missed out on in life while devoting themselves to the work of raising their brood. Much, much later in life—when she was in her seventies or eighties—my mom admitted she had always wanted to travel more, and she spoke about how overwhelmed she had been as a young mother with so many children. After he retired and was much less burdened by family responsibilities, my dad opened up quite a bit and was much more available for emotional conversations, but those more intimate conversations never happened when I was young.

Through those growing-up years, I lived with being "the weird one" in the family, and it was a relief to get to adulthood where I could find like-minded people who actually enjoyed my more curious and sensitive nature. I could now see how this upbringing helped me be resilient when soldiers were hesitant to engage in conversations that might get emotional.

No doubt my choice of professions was, in part, driven by my hunger for substantial emotional exchanges. I had set myself up in a career in which I would invite people to discuss the feelings and hopes and wounds of life—all day, every day—even if they were scared and weren't sure they wanted to do so. From my childhood experiences, I had developed a finely honed ability to perceive what it might take to relate to someone; I knew how to find the thread of commonality, or the curiosity, that would provide an avenue for making that more *real* contact. Working with the soldiers not only demanded a stretching of my heart, it also called on me to use relational skills I had carried with me all along. These skills, which were born out of frustration and isolation, helped me to make deeper connections than I otherwise would have, and to find success in work that proved to be profoundly meaningful to me.

SUCCESS

Success in my work with soldiers began to happen once I better understood their sense of pride and commitment, and developed a more complex grasp of military culture. The path to success with my work was vague at first when I stumbled so frequently, saying the wrong thing or misunderstanding the point of a soldier's story. I felt relieved and proud as I got more in sync with them—that was how I defined success in my work on bases.

Success in the military takes a thousand different shapes and happens in a thousand different moments. For a soldier, success might look as simple as getting to the end of basic training and realizing you have a tribe of brothers and sisters who will fight to keep you alive. Or it might be staying physically fit in order to pass the endless PT tests sprinkled throughout a soldier's career. Success could be developing a keen sense of respect for command structure and the level of accountability each soldier is held to. Success might come from handling your duties exceptionally well or taking the initiative to consistently advance your training and education. Success may entail climbing your way steadily through the ranks or opting for the elite rigors of our nation's special operations forces (SOF).

Soldiers must handle their responsibilities with a commitment that is greater than most jobs; others could be killed if you balk or fail at your assigned task. Perhaps this is the root of the quiet pride I saw in so many soldiers. Their sense of responsibility has been battle-tested and they have hit the mark, day in and day out, for months or years on end.

When you're a soldier, success might also be the true aim of the sniper's shot that protects your buddies, the first glimpse of a unit returning to the FOB after a dangerous mission outside the wire, the silent disarming of the homemade bomb that could have taken out your unit, the plume of smoke from striking a distant target, the scorch of tires on a tilting deck, or the shuffling of dusty boots onto the plane heading home.

It might be walking into the holy embrace of your spouse's arms when you return, or seeing the unbridled joy in your child's first glimpse of you. Success could be watching football with a cold beer in your hand, feet on the coffee table, knowing you're home safe. Success might be overcoming the ravages that war left inside your body—or your psyche—and starting to feel your way into stateside life again.

Success could be putting the gun back in the drawer when temptation urges you to put it to your head. It could be calling a buddy, even when you can't find the words to ask for help. Success could arrive when you have tolerance and compassion for your overwhelming, "crazy" need to look on the roof for snipers or to sit with your back to the wall in every room you enter.

Success could be getting to know the person who came home and letting go of the person you were when you deployed, as you reckon with the changes war washed into your soul.

As I came to understand the soldiers' different ways of achieving success, I could see more clearly how much support soldiers needed to keep finding success. I could then support the individuals I encountered as they committed to and struggled with their unique path home.

Her Son

The battalion's soldiers are returning from Afghanistan this morning, and a few hundred people mill around the cavernous hangar, waiting for the buses to arrive from the nearby airport. Although it's not yet six thirty, many of these people have been waiting in the hangar for three or four hours. They feel a combination of eagerness for their loved ones' return and frustration over the constantly changing information about the troops' arrival time. In the crowd, there are wives and husbands, children, parents and grandparents, dear friends, neighbors, and soldiers who got back a few days earlier, coming to welcome their buddies home. The crowd is festive but nervous. There's happy anticipation in the air, but also a tinge of uncertainty about how everyone might have changed.

At any minute, the rumble of the buses' engines will shake the metal walls of the hangar, loud music will start, and the hangar doors will be rolled open as the soldiers march in. There'll be a cloud of artificial fog, and the weary soldiers will emerge from the haze like ghost-heroes from some spectacular battle myth.

In the midst of the expectant crowd, a middle-aged woman standing next to me asks, "Are you waiting for your son?"

I tell her I'm on base to offer support to soldiers and their families, and then I ask who she's there to welcome.

"My son. My youngest son," she says, instantly getting tears in her eyes. "He joined the day after he graduated high school. He always wanted to be a soldier, ever since he was a little boy. I haven't seen him in so long. He turned nineteen while he was over there. I sent a boy off to fight, and I'll be meeting a man this morning. I really don't know what to expect. But I can't wait a minute longer to see him."

This mom is a poignant mixture of pride and anxiety. She introduces me to the family waiting with her—the soldier's dad, young sisters, grandparents. Every few seconds, she glances over at the doors, as if she can will them open with her strong need for her son.

"But how will I find him? Do you know how they do this?" She's suddenly full of a new worry.

I explain the pattern I've witnessed during previous arrivals: the soldiers marching in, the commander saying a few words, then dismissing the soldiers to their families—and the joyous mass chaos that erupts as everyone reunites.

She nods and looks relieved, glad to have even the most general "map" of how the next moments are going to unfold. I notice she's been squeezing my arm again and again as we've been talking.

"Listen, come say hello when you find your son. I'd love to meet him."

She nods quickly, then focuses again on the hangar doors. I drift off to talk to others in the crowd.

Soon a rumble is heard from outside. Bodies turn and heads crane toward the hangar doors. The speakers start thumping with brash rock music, the fog machine cranks out thick white curls of the stuff, and the massive hangar doors begin to slide back. The crowd erupts with screams and applause as the first of the soldiers breaks through the bank of fog. They march in, tight and solemn, come to a halt in front of the commander's podium, and stand perfectly still, awaiting his speech. The atmosphere is suddenly very quiet, as if every single person is holding his or her breath. The commander welcomes the soldiers, tells them how proud he is—and releases them.

Instantly, a wild crush of people pushes toward the center of the hangar where the soldiers' formation stood rigid and clear just seconds ago. It's evaporated now. All I can see are masses of darting, hugging, squealing people grabbing on to the ones they've been waiting for. It's an explosion of sheer joy and delight.

I welcome several soldiers who seem to have no one there to greet them, and chat for a few moments with various spouses I know. I work my way out to the edges of the crowd. After several minutes, I feel a tug on my sleeve. I turn to find the mom I had been talking to. She's pulling her son over to meet me—a shy, proud young man who extends his hand like a gentleman. His family is crowded around, unwilling to get more than a few inches away from him. They look like an amoeba, endlessly shape-shifting as they jockey and jostle to stay close to their young hero. I welcome him home and tell him I'm happy he has his family there for him.

"Yes, ma'am. My family means everything to me. Especially now."

I shake his hand firmly and move on, leaving his family to enjoy his full, undivided attention.

CHAPTER 8

Soldiers are trained to stand ready to handle any order at any time, their days reflecting the randomness of the gray and brown (or green and brown, or blue and gray, depending on the branch of service) digital patterns on their uniforms.

Run ten miles for morning PT? "Roger, sir."

Move twenty-three tons of equipment from one motor pool to another? "I'm on it."

Respond to enemy fire while repairing the Humvee? "*Hoo*-ah."

They are expected to engage in the next task without hesitation or question—that's what soldiers do.

In these new environs, my days played out in a remarkably random pattern, too, particularly in the way my work came to me. Up to sixty or seventy percent of my job was outreach (chatting, explaining to soldiers why I was there, making them aware of the support I offered, etc.), and most of the counseling exchanges I had with soldiers and spouses happened outside my office.

Some of my colleagues complained about this. One of them said he felt like a therapy salesperson: "Good God. I didn't sign up to be pushing counseling on anyone. I want to do sessions. I haven't done a session in the past week. It's all roaming and chatting and trying to get soldiers to come see me. It sucks."

I knew what he was saying, but most of the time I loved reaching out to soldiers and spouses in such a wide variety of ways. I honestly believed I was part of a tremendous shift in military culture. Before the Department of Defense created the program I worked for, soldiers' access to counseling was limited to options "in the system." They either got permission from their superiors to make an appointment with on-base clinics (permission that was often refused), or they got a referral to off-base counseling through their military insurance. Either one of these options was unappealing in a culture that frowned on the "weakness" of asking for help, especially given the potentially negative impact of having the issue noted in one's medical records. I loved imagining that one day soldiers might be able to stay in touch with their emotional selves, rather than having to divorce themselves from their feelings in order to do their jobs. I wanted to be part of the healing needed by those who'd been ravaged by wartime experiences, a problem I thought was just beginning to be reckoned with by the military.

One day, I spoke to an auditorium full of just-returned soldiers about issues they might face as they adjusted to being back home. I looked out into the sloping landscape of seats, and a hundred and seventy tired faces gazed back at me while I talked about frustration, anger, feeling distant from loved ones, and the boredom that sometimes occurs after the high-octane intensity of combat.

After the briefing, I walked through an empty parking lot on the way back to my office, daydreaming about the hours I had left in my workday and the tasks I needed to address before I headed back to my hotel. A low rumble, originating behind me, vibrated through my body, shaking me out of my musings. I turned around as a grinning soldier rolled up next to me in his shiny black monster pickup truck. His left arm hung down from the window, a cigarette tucked between his fingers, as he steered with his right hand.

"Ma'am," he said, "you said something back there about us being angry? Well, I've been awful mad since I got back, and my fiancée's not too happy with me. You have any ideas?"

Since his truck was jacked up on oversized tires, I stood several inches below the window as I offered a few suggestions: Could he maybe step back from a conversation before he got too heated, or focus on any small bit of pleasure in being home, or help his fiancée understand the huge adjustment he was going through? All of those tactics would help diffuse the stress of being home, and help him to stop lashing out. He listened carefully, nodding and agreeing to give the ideas a try.

"Stop by my office in a couple of days and let me know how it goes, OK?"

"Roger, ma'am." He dropped the truck back into gear, revved the motor, and pulled away. I stood in the parking lot and shook my head in amazement, delighted that he felt comfortable enough to approach me, and tickled at this experience of "drive-thru counseling." No comfortable or steady routine in sight. It suited me. Furthermore, when this same soldier strolled into my office a few days later, he was pleased to tell me that his fiancée had already noticed a change in his manner and they were getting along just fine.

Shortly after the monster-truck encounter, while I was making my rounds, I walked through a battalion motor pool garage, ducking between huge parked trucks, neatly stored tools, and chain-draped lifts. The vast, dim garage seemed deserted at first, and I started to leave, thinking I had missed catching anyone there.

But as I neared the far end, I came upon a bespectacled private first class with a thick Texas drawl who began to tell me about his combat experiences while he worked on the engine of a Humvee. As he talked, he tinkered with the engine, shuffled tools, and wiped his hands on greasy rags. His dark buzz cut framed a tired-looking face. I chatted with him for a little while, asking what he was working on and if he liked being a mechanic. His face remained somber as he started discussing his last deployment. Focusing on the engine seemed the perfect distraction from focusing too closely on things that were difficult for him to speak about.

Keeping his eyes on his work, he shared how frightening it had been for him to see his friends wounded in a firefight that seemed to last for hours—though he admitted it had actually lasted only a few minutes. He said he felt panicked—his exact word was "undone"—as his friends screamed in pain and the bullets kept flying. The nearly empty garage offered us quiet privacy as he worked and talked, and the moment was quite touching. It was one of the innumerable instances when my ability to slow down and behave as if I had all the time in the world helped a soldier take his time opening up. It was consistently effective for me to meet soldiers on their own terms and in their own environments.

I sometimes felt I was on a kind of holy treasure hunt, seeking out these moments of heart-disclosure tucked randomly into my days. At times, I walked away from these interactions feeling as if I had just stumbled into the one predestined interaction I was meant to have that day, as if some Unseen Hand had brought me and the other person into that very moment, setting up our encounter with meticulous care and precision. I felt a pristine sense of purpose, and this sense of great purpose made the big changes in my life worthwhile. As much as I still struggled to feel at home in this new life, I couldn't deny the deepening feeling that I was doing something important and valuable. When the loneliness or the sense of missing what was familiar loomed too large, my sense of being truly useful offset all the losses.

During one sultry August afternoon, I made my way through a group of soldiers waiting to do a parachute jump for their paratrooper certifications. They'd been waiting since 5 a.m., but the jumps had been delayed again and again because a line of severe storms kept threatening to move through the area. The storms would start to move toward the airfield, then fade, then swirl close again. Rivers of sweat sheeted down my sides as I chatted with them, and my face felt hot and flushed.

They were scattered around in small groups of three or four, leaning back against their packs, sprawled on the ground in the shade, or standing in a nearby clutch to smoke. When I looked any direction into the distance, the air shimmered, foggy with damp heat. As the afternoon slowly passed, there would sometimes be a call to line up and get ready, then an order to fall out again as the storm possibility rose. Again and again, they formed up, stood for a half hour or more, then fell out into small, frustrated groups.

I asked more than one if they were upset at the delay. Most shrugged their shoulders and told me this was just part of military life: you prepared, you waited. You had no control over when things happened or what you would be asked to do.

I noticed one soldier casually ambling off to stand in the shade of a huge tree by himself, and I walked over to join him. He leaned against the wide trunk and hitched one leg backward, resting his foot up against the trunk while he fiddled with a small stick in his hands. I watched his freckled face as he shyly chatted for a few minutes about how much he loved the jump days where they got to jump "Hollywood" (that is, without all their gear and thus much lighter, making them free to take their time on the way down).

We chatted for a few more minutes before he began to talk about the fact that his parents hadn't been able to come to the base to welcome him home from Iraq because they'd been unable to get off work. He got choked up when he said he thought it wouldn't be a big deal since he knew ahead of time they weren't able to come. But when he stepped into the hangar and saw all of the other families waiting, he felt deeply hurt and disappointed. As so often was the case, these weren't things a soldier would discuss with his buddies, but under that oak tree in the stifling heat, he found himself able to admit heartbreak.

I remembered back to my early days on the base when I thought the décor of my room was going to be a problem. Now I knew that soldiers who wanted support were everywhere and that sometimes my office was the *least* likely place I would find them.

Weeks later, I walked down the wide aisle of the vast parking area of a motor pool. The aisle stretched between two long rows of armored track vehicles. Each vehicle was parked with precision, facing the empty concrete space in the middle of the rows. Since it was the one day a week the battalion spent maintaining their vehicles, small groups of soldiers clustered around the back ends of the vehicles or around engines all throughout the motor pool, checking equipment or conducting maintenance.

I noticed a blond-headed soldier with Army-issued safety goggles dangling around his neck. He was bent over a clipboard in the rear compartment of an armored track vehicle, marking off items on a long checklist. I started to walk by, but he glanced up as I passed so I stopped to say hello. He turned out to be a gregarious fellow, cheerful and easy-going. His goggles bobbed and bounced as he laughed or moved around the dark little cavern inside the vehicle. After a few minutes, as if remembering his manners, he said, "Oh hey. Come on in, ma'am. Have a seat."

I covered my surprise and clambered up into the back of the vehicle, folding myself into one of the tiny rear seats. Perching on that seat was definitely an unusual experience for me, but I could tell the setting was completely comfortable for the soldier. This was his domain: he'd spent several months in a vehicle just like this in Iraq. He knew every inch of the compartment and the function of each dial. Our chatting led to a conversation about his concerns with his upcoming marriage. He talked about whether or not he'd be a good husband and his uncertainties about meeting his fiancée's expectations. He felt unsure if he would make her happy, although his face glowed with his love and devotion for her. We talked about the importance of reaching out for support—to friends, family, ministers, and counselors, depending on the need—as they began their marriage. After we shook hands good-bye, I wished I had a photo of that moment in the back of the armored vehicle, because it was yet another peculiar place that I'd held a counseling session.

I began to relish the unstructured nature of my job. I loved the sense that at any moment I might cross paths with someone who wanted support. I had always liked thinking on my feet and working with a wide variety of people and issues, so this new role fit me very well. The immediacy of the work demanded a sense of readiness and responsiveness I enjoyed; the unpredictability suited my need to feel creative in my responses and attention. Throughout my career I had loved the real *art* of therapy: the honed, intuitive ability to respond instantly in a creative and compassionate way to issues that suddenly arose. The unstructured nature of this work ensured that I kept getting pulled into the soldiers' world in a very pure way.

Learning to look past all the machismo and the tough-soldier presentation to see the very real human being that was just behind the military persona was immensely rewarding for me, and as I let go of the confines of a counseling office, whole new worlds of vulnerability and connection opened up—inside me and within the soldiers.

LETTING GO

I'd had to let go of my preconceived notions of soldiers in order for them to show me who they *really* were in all their different personalities and identities. I'd had to let go of working in familiar ways and thinking the best counseling happened in an office setting. With each assumption I shed, I could meet soldiers and spouses on their own terms—and in their familiar environments—laying aside what I *thought* they needed and listening carefully to their stories in order to understand what they *really* needed, truths I found in layers that were previously hidden from me.

On the other side, soldiers who reached out to me had to let go of their biases about seeking counseling or needing help. They had to face a belief held by many in the military that soldiers were weak if their combat experiences were troubling them. If they were to admit to struggling with the internal fallout of combat, they had to see this as a brave thing; they had to see that getting help for a crumbling marriage was an act of courage, not a sign of failure.

For both the soldiers and me, the act of letting go created better understanding—a bridge between two worlds. This same bridge of letting go is needed from civilians, too.

Innumerable soldiers have told me they don't want to be thanked for their service and they don't want to be seen as heroes (or, for that matter, villains). They want to be respected for the job they did and the pride they took in doing it well. They want to be able to say they're proud of their service without feeling like they're facing judgments from those who might not understand the commitment and sacrifice they made. They want to ask for support without being blamed for having been in such horrendous situations.

In an NPR interview, General Martin Dempsey, former Chairman of the Joint Chiefs of Staff, stated that the military "face[s] a deficit larger than our budget. And that is a deficit of understanding between those of us who serve in uniform and our fellow citizens."[8] Referencing this same dialogue between civilians and military to further a real sense of understanding, Phil Klay, winner of the 2014 National Book Award for *Redeployment*, his book of fictional stories, commented: "I can't think of a more important conversation to be having."[9]

In my years of working with the military, I noticed the misunderstanding soldiers sometimes faced from the civilian community. Rather than being seen as protectors—as warriors have been viewed in past cultures—our current culture struggles with how to view combat veterans.

The cultural dissonance about recent wars spills over into our feelings about soldiers, creating another layer of difficult struggle for soldiers who fought and served.

As I worked with the combat veterans, I began to understand: soldiers can't really arrive back home until we are able to *receive* them—not with parades and reintegration programs, but with a deep and profound willingness to honor their individual journeys into combat and back again. We need to reach out, listen, and understand the burdens they carried—to grasp the enormity of the task they undertake in the name of service to our country.

After War Comes the Battle

I look up from my paperwork and see a grinning, slightly disheveled soldier striding into my office, offering his hand as he makes a rather startling beeline for the front edge of my desk.

"Sergeant Richards, ma'am," he booms. He speaks a little too loudly and a little too quickly. His manner is stiff and unsure, like he's trying to imitate how one offers a greeting, but not grasping the finer points of how to start up a conversation.

Although I've worked with this battalion for a couple of months, I've never seen this soldier before. He's a tall, russet-haired guy in his late twenties, with deep-green eyes and a barrel chest that leaves one with the impression he's been spending time in the gym.

I extend my hand, introduce myself, and watch as he stands awkwardly in front of me, unsure how to proceed. He shuffles his feet and sways slightly in various directions, his body in constant motion. His eyes dart all around the office, like he's tracking dots on a computer screen set to a random pattern. He looks at the posters on the wall, the shelves of books, and then the clock. His eyes skip to the view outside the window, the carpet, the plant on the table.

"I haven't seen you around here before, Sergeant. Did you just get back?" I ask, wondering if he's just returned from combat in Afghanistan.

"Yes, ma'am. Two days ago." His voice still too loud, too strident.

"Two days ago? You must be happy to be home."

"Oh yes, ma'am."

As we talk, his eyes keep moving around. He's jittery.

"How is it, being back?" I venture.

"It's good. It's really good." But his face looks flat and uncertain. We make small talk about the base and the various offices along the hallway. I keep watching his body with its stiff, jerky movements, his roving eyes, his out-of-sync affect. When he speaks of the long plane trip home, he goes into great detail and has a big smile on his face. When he speaks of his wife and kids, his eyes are fairly empty and the smile is replaced with a tight, straight mouth.

I keep him talking, using small talk to reach through his frenetic scanning. We discuss the weather and his buddies still overseas. I ask him if he's enjoying home-cooked meals after endless months of Army food. I'm hoping the conversation will help him to anchor. He stays and chats for a good twenty minutes.

All of a sudden, he gives me a too-wide smile and an incredibly eager handshake. "Well, ma'am, I'd better be going. I'll see you around." He steps back out into the hallway and disappears.

Welcome home, *soldier.*

CHAPTER 9

One afternoon as I neared the end of an assignment, I stood outside a DFAC with my colleagues Sam and Carol, waiting for the doors to open for lunch. We talked about the things we had to do to wrap up our work on the base, and just as we started to discuss our future plans, the doors were pushed back by a white-clad kitchen worker and the line began to stream inside. It was a typical cafeteria-style facility, and we split up as soon as we entered, making our way through different food lines: salad bar, hot meals, sandwich lines, beverages. We met up again on the other side of the lines to find a table together. The ever-present DFAC televisions droned in the background, a hundred loud conversations jammed the air, and the scraping of chairs and trays added to the din. Carol, Sam, and I had a habit of going to different DFACs together on different days (there were several on the sprawling base), in order to have some variety in our lunchtime surroundings. But wherever we went, the din was always the same.

"What are you going to do next?" Sam turned his tray so his meat-loaf was right in front of him. "Are you heading to another assignment?"

"Not right away. I'd like to find a quiet place to catch my breath before I do another stint, but I don't have anywhere to go. No home base to go back to, remember?"

He nodded, talked about his own plans to go home to rest up for a while, and then graciously offered me the use of his family's mountain cabin for as long as I might want to stay. I accepted his offer. I was finding it a challenge to live like a nomad, going from one temporary location to another. It was a relief to know where I was heading next.

As the assignment ended, I started closing up shop—a blur of activity similar to my arrival but in reverse, like a film rolled backward through a projector. Instead of greetings and unpacking, my days were filled with saying good-byes and packing up. I walked into offices along the long hallway and shook hands with all the soldiers I'd come to know. The handshakes I offered each of them were firm and full of appreciation.

"You leaving already?" they teased. "You just got here."

In some ways, it did seem like I'd just arrived. But when viewed through the lens of the confounding and deeply connecting moments, it seemed a much, much longer time than the three months I'd spent on this base. I had grown fond of the soldiers during the time I was there, individually and as a community. I would miss knowing what happened to SGT Sullivan's plans for college and whether 1LT McElroy's baby was a girl or a boy. I would wonder what happened to a few soldiers I'd worked with who were heading downrange. Would they fare well in combat and return to their loved ones and families? And how would they and their spouses handle the long months apart?

I'd never know. I wasn't allowed to stay in touch with soldiers after I moved on from an assignment. Their stories would remain unfinished in my heart.

As always, packing up meant that boxes and clothes and shoes went back into my car. The hotel room walls were stripped of all photos, poems, and quotes. The blue cup and plate, the pillow, the deep-red quilt went into my car trunk. Looking around my empty hotel room as I got ready to depart, I shook my head in amazement: I never would have imagined my life would have me living in a hotel room in a small military town, surrounded by parking lots and fast-food joints. This was a thousand miles—literally and figuratively—from the simple cottage and settled life of my past.

On my last afternoon, as I drove off the base, I felt a weight lift off my shoulders. Those unconscious assumptions I'd brought with me when I first started out had been lightened more and more with every base I worked on. While I still didn't grasp every aspect of military life, I now felt a familiarity with it. I knew rank insignias, and I knew the heartache that deployed soldiers sometimes faced. I was beginning to understand the relationship these men and women had to their years of service. I had a growing understanding of the protocol and integrity that guided their days. I felt a basic knowing of their families' sacrifices, too.

I also felt a sense of loss as I left the safety and security of the ordered calm that had started to feel familiar. The civilian world felt different to me now. I noticed unruly crowds more. The vying for space that happened in traffic and in stores, the kind of rushing, darting, pushing tone to things that was normal in the civilian world, was almost completely absent on the base. I had come to appreciate the difference. Twenty-five miles per hour now seemed like a good speed for local driving. The respect and consideration that were norms on the base were often missing in civilian life. I'd gotten used to "Good morning, ma'am" and the basic sense of graciousness in which the soldiers were schooled. Compared to the structure of the base community, it felt like there weren't any rules in civilian life. Certainly, things felt freer and looser off the base, but they felt less clear and less simple, too.

I drove to my friend's cabin and for the next two months "shut my engines down." Mostly, I relished the fact that I didn't need to listen to anyone. I felt relieved that I didn't have to attend to conversations with the intense focus and careful scanning required to help me know when soldiers were trying to hint at something serious and important in our casual exchanges. I had time to feel the changes that were occurring in my own heart.

Most mornings, I sat with my computer at the cabin's kitchen table, warming myself in the sunlight shining through the windows and checking my emails. When I perused the news online, I found myself clicking on articles about the military—articles about policy, combat deaths, military family issues. If I watched the evening news on television, I got teary when I saw footage of returning soldiers or wounded warriors. I had a relationship to that world now, and I felt pulled to stay in touch with it. I understood all the reports and stories at a different level and was able to interpret the information through the filter of ranks, battalions, commanders, and missions.

In the meantime, I soaked in luxurious solitude. Like a pendulum that had swung very far in the direction of constant interactions, my life now swung just as far in the opposite direction, toward silence. I slept deeply and went for long hikes on the nearby trails, ate simple food, and watched as the wind danced in the trees.

In between assignments, I was always processing not only my adjustment to working in the military, but also the leaving behind of my pre-military life. As I hiked for miles, I let my mind wander. I thought about how much I had lost: friends, home, career, familiar places—my favorite Mexican café, the coffee shop, the neighborhood park where I had walked my dog every day during the last year of her life. All were far, far back down that first highway.

Even the hiking trails were different in this new chapter of my life. During this particular break, the vast skies and the wide open vistas from Tucson were gone; I hiked in thick mountain forests, the trails like narrow hallways cutting through the woods.

I pondered what I had gained, too, sifting through my memories of thousands of powerful moments I'd experienced on base: meeting a wounded warrior for the first time and understanding the difficult future she faced; listening quietly and intently as a soldier began to speak of his inner wounds; watching a shy private from a small town start to talk to me, knowing he was doing his best to ask for help. I found it absorbing and necessary to have the time to reflect on my new working life. Like a soldier just returned from deployment, I went through a period of "debriefing" after each assignment: reviewing everyone I had met, the conversations I'd had, the moments that had been overwhelming or painful or deeply touching. I filled my days with silent reflections.

IN-PROCESSING

When soldiers return from combat, they go through a regimented process called "in-processing." They move through a tightly defined system that involves filling out forms, checking in about medical concerns, turning in their weapons, and finding their way through the maze of tables and check-in points until they are considered officially "returned."

But none of the in-processing addresses the layers of subtle but profound inner adjustment required to *truly* come home. Although there are briefings, workshops, retreats, and reintegration fairs offering support services, dedicated attention is not given to each individual's process of returning home and—more precisely—each individual's process of integrating their combat experience emotionally, psychologically, and spiritually, so he or she can fully return and rest. Although homecoming rituals are woven into the military process—bands, honor guards, blissful hugs with loved ones, and the relief of a mission completed—the inner work of coming home takes much longer, and most soldiers aren't prepared for it.

One soldier said to me, "They trained me for months on end to adjust to combat. They wanted me fully prepared for what it means to fight on the battlefield. But they never gave me any training on how to leave all that behind."

Some soldiers told me that when someone asks, "When were you in combat?" they feel the most honest response would be, "I'm still there."

As the joy and relief of making it back home sets in, so does the subtle, intricate process of suppressing memories, smells, sights, and traumas carried home along with the rucksack, gun, and uniform. The suppression is necessary, and it can be all-consuming for a while. Spouses talk about veterans who return that are shockingly quiet, distracted, or "absent" for months or longer.

Keeping memories and feelings well suppressed can require an avoidance of intimacy—if you let someone close to you, you might relax and those hidden emotions might emerge. Many veterans shun things as seemingly simple as Fourth of July celebrations because of the triggering sounds. Family time might be awkward because their position in the constellation of family dynamics has become uncertain. A lot of veterans avoid crowds and noisy places that would overstimulate a nervous system already busy managing and coping.

Someone asked me why so many soldiers avoid speaking about combat experiences. I responded, "I think they're working so hard to be home, to protect themselves from their experiences downrange, that they can't possibly hope to dip into those experiences 'on demand' and still keep themselves on steady ground emotionally."

On the other hand, remembering combat experiences with other veterans often provides an avenue for real emotional contact. "We were both in Fallujah," one soldier told me by way of explaining the bond he felt with a new veteran friend. They didn't need to be there at the same time or have the same battle experiences. Just the fact that they both had walked through similar hells was enough to give them mutual respect, right off the bat.

In-processing needs to include the inner return as well as the outer return. Until that gets addressed adequately, soldiers are left trying to bridge the vast divide between war and home without the advantage of having a cushion of time devoted to letting their nervous systems and their psyches integrate all they've carried home.

Morning Formation

I'm watching soldiers gather in front of the battalion building, less than thirty hours after they've returned from combat. This morning's formation is their first formation back on home soil, back in front of their familiar building. Just this once, they're allowed to wear civilian clothes, so it's an unusual sight: tight lines of straight-up bodies in wildly baggy shorts and oversized sports jerseys, flip-flops or sneakers. The soldiers are still lost in jet lag, barely even registering that they're back home, so there's a hazy quality to their interactions. After roll call, their commander, an officer named Dickerson, talks about the briefings that are required in the coming days and speaks forcefully about keeping themselves safe while they're adjusting to being back. He asks them to watch out for each other during the transition. Dickerson releases the formation early, and most of them mill around and chat, enjoying the morning's lack of schedule.

Watching the scene from a distance, I see the soldiers' faces and can hear their laughter as they're dismissed. The whole formation seems casual and easy, so I'm surprised when Dickerson turns around to walk back to the battalion building—his face is dark and tense with concern. He starts toward the building, but as soon as he notices me, he changes course and comes over to talk.

"I'm worried about this unit," he says, after shaking my hand and offering a greeting.

"Tell me what you're worried about."

"These soldiers are tightly bonded; we're going to have some adjustment problems. Here's what I can tell you: This unit was engaged in active combat over there. They took fire every single day, the entire year we were over there. They had one another's backs; they were each other's lifelines. These soldiers came home because of each other. So it worries me. They know what they've been through and know what they had to do to get back here. They understand each other without question.

They are as tight as a group of people can possibly be. I'm afraid they're not going to let their spouses and families in. You see what I'm saying?"

"Yes, sir. I appreciate your concerns."

Actually, I admired this officer's perceptions and his sharp attentiveness. Sometimes returning troops were simply expected to figure out how to make the adjustment to being back home. While there was always support available, soldiers often tried to adjust without any help at all. I'd never worked with a commander who was so frankly articulate about this kind of concern.

"So, what do you think might happen, sir?"

"I'm concerned they'll want to spend all their time with one another. That's what is familiar and comfortable, but it might make things rough at home. I'm worried about divorce or domestic violence. I'm worried about suicide—or getting out of control because they don't know how to adapt. I'm not really sure. I just know how tight they've grown. I know the level of structure and pressure they got used to. Trying to relate to people outside of the unit is going to be a tough, tough shift for them."

We spend a good hour or so talking about ways to address his concerns, and I know he'll be in close touch in the coming days. His soldiers are fortunate he's watching out for them so carefully. I hope his attentiveness will give them a better-than-usual shot at making their way through the upheavals of returning home from that other world.

Moti

I've spent the morning in an auditorium, giving briefings to three hundred soldiers who've just returned from their year in Afghanistan. I've conducted the briefing so many times now that I'm able to relax and joke around with them while I make sure they get the information about the counseling program. I tell them the counseling is strictly confidential, and then I say, "I know, I know. You don't believe me. But here's the thing: Even if your commander comes to me and says, 'Did Morris come and see you?' I will *lose my job* if I answer that question."

I let that sink in for a minute and then I tell them, "I *really* like my job. I want to keep it. Telling anyone you came to see me is not going to happen." I watch a few of them sit forward at that part, and I hope they're starting to believe they might be able to ask for help without suffering repercussions.

I'm glad things go well while I'm on stage, but I feel I make the most impact during the breaks when I hang out in the courtyard of the community building with soldiers, chatting and making contact one-on-one.

The breeze in the courtyard is brisk, but the air has the freshness of an early-spring morning, so no one seems to mind the chill. During the break, soldiers gather there in twos and threes, smoking cigarettes and chugging energy drinks. I tease one private by telling him I'm tracking the number of energy drinks he guzzles during the day's briefings. He laughs and says, "I'm on number three already."

While I'm chatting, I notice a young soldier standing off to the edge of the group. She's not talking to anyone and looks awkward—like someone who seems to always get left on the sidelines. I'm concerned she might be having a hard time, so I make my way over to her. I glance at her name tag and see that I'm talking to SPC Katel.

"Hey, good morning." I lean against the wall next to her, looking out at all the soldiers in the courtyard.

"Good morning, ma'am."

Katel doesn't make eye contact, and her voice is so quiet I can hardly hear her response. I have a hunch that she's just very shy, so I lower the intensity of my voice and ask her where she's from.

"Wisconsin, ma'am."

"You headed there for block leave?"

"Yes, ma'am."

I'm wondering what topics might help her relax a little, so I keep probing.

"You have family there?

Katel nods.

"What's your favorite part about going back?"

With this question, she turns to face me. A grin starts to spread across her face and her eyes start to sparkle with pleasure. The change in her demeanor is so sudden, it takes me by surprise.

"I'll get to see my dog, Moti." The grin gets bigger. "I missed him like crazy. I've had him since he was two months old, and now he's five, and my folks kept him while I was deployed, so I can't wait to go get him. I'll bring him back here with me."

"I'm happy for you," I say, and we spend the next ten or fifteen minutes talking about what kind of dog Moti is ("Pure mutt," Katel says), where he got his name (a suggestion from a family friend who lives in India), and the kinds of tricks she's taught him. Katel is animated, engaged, and eager while she talks about Moti. It's as if the months of stress and loneliness have disappeared. Our conversation makes me thoughtful about all the different ways soldiers find rest and recovery between assignments.

Often, when soldiers return from combat, they are given an extended leave, then get assigned to new bases or new duties. In that sequence, leave becomes a critical time for recovery from the pressure and exhaustion of deployment.

For Katel, time with her dog would be the soothing tonic of recovery, and I would imagine time with pets is key for many soldiers during leave. For others, leave entails time with family: beach vacations with the children and spouse, Mom's home cooking, fishing trips with cousins. It strikes me that connection is very often the path to recovery and regrounding in daily life once soldiers are back home. Sometimes that's Mom or Dad, or a sweetheart or spouse, or a child.

Sometimes, it's a Moti.

CHAPTER 10

Each time I took a break between assignments and spent time alone, I felt my sense of resiliency restored, so I submitted my name to the system for another assignment and headed to a new base. My work life fell into this rhythm: several months on a base supporting soldiers and spouses, then a month or so off to recover from the intensity of my work. I soon knew that the first days on every base were guaranteed to be an overwhelming influx of information and orientation.

On the first morning of one assignment, I walked into the lobby of my hotel and met Laura, the counselor I would be replacing. With her dark curly hair, ready laugh, and warm friendliness, Laura put me at ease right away. Her arms were full of the handbooks and paperwork I would need, and as we got into my car for the twenty-minute drive to the base, she reassured me, "Don't worry. This base is really friendly, so you'll get to know everyone pretty quickly. I'll introduce you to some folks, and then we'll go to the community services staff meeting. You'll be expected to attend that every week. And then we'll . . ." and we were off and running.

During the drive, she filled me in on protocols and expectations for the assignment. My back didn't stiffen and straighten as we passed through the guardhouse. The passage from the civilian world to the military world now felt as familiar to me as opening my office door in the morning. I still felt the dramatic change in environment when moving from one to the other, but I no longer felt intimidated by the process of entering the military world. Laura and I began our rounds. "This is the headquarters building," she told me. "Here's the commanding general, and here's the CSM. OK, now here are the battalion offices, and here's the Rear D commander. Here are the company commanders. Now, let's meet the community services staff—you'll be working closely with them. And now it's time to make an appearance at formation to introduce you to the soldiers. After that, let's get you over to the community center to meet some spouses. Oh, and I need to hand you the schedule for next month's briefings. And be sure to remember the offices in that two-story building over there. You're supposed to cover those, too."

And that was just the first two hours.

The jumbled whirlwind of information wasn't Laura's fault. She was doing a spectacular job of trying to offer me as much information as possible during the two days our assignments overlapped. I took copious notes as our agenda shifted from buildings to meetings to scheduling, to maps of the base and specific, important buildings, to a lunch spent covering still more details. We were in and out of the car more times than I could count, entering a building, doing a quick pass-through to make various introductions and explanations, then walking out again, and on to the next one. I plastered a smile on my face and tried to grasp threads of information as they flooded my consciousness.

That night in my hotel room, I opened the windows wide and let in some cool fresh air. I took my time changing out of my work clothes. I stood near the closet and took off my name tag; taking my name tag off had become the demarcation point between being on duty and leaving my day behind. I kicked my shoes into the closet and hung up my dress slacks and tailored shirt. I washed my face, thinking, *Here I go again.*

Here comes the deluge. I took deep breaths and tried to calm my system down for the evening before I had to go back into the fray the next day.

My evening routine comforted me—cooking my dinner, doing some paperwork, breathing through the edges of panic that kept rising up and filling my mind. My thoughts would start circling around all the tasks I needed to remember, or my heart would start jacking up its rhythm as I tried to remember the name of a commander I'd met, or I'd begin to feel overwhelmed and I'd have to stem it quickly so as not to drown in dread of all the new responsibilities I was now carrying. If I wasn't careful, I would lapse into feeling that I would never be able to keep up with the schedule of returning soldiers, or I wouldn't remember to go to the family support meetings I was supposed to attend. Listening to a thousand different "important" details all day long always set me up to experience some real nerves the first night or two. At times I didn't fall asleep until early in the morning hours, unable to quiet my mind.

I kept the room lights off except for one next to the bed so the room was lit softly and my system could calm down.

No matter how many bases I worked at, the first two weeks always manifested this same incredibly intense learning curve. According to the structure of the job contracts, I only stayed at each base for a few months, so I regularly began again as a matter of routine. It was like starting an entirely new job each time—new commanders, new expectations, new schedules, new needs, new protocols, new people and personalities, new geography, new buildings and offices—and sometimes even dramatically different weather.

Still, I came to understand how soldiers got used to the repeated moves their jobs required of them. I developed a rhythm of unpacking, working, making connections . . . then saying good-bye, packing, and heading into the next swirl of transition. Like them, I got acclimated to the rhythm and learned to lean on my mission—in my case, supporting the soldiers and spouses—to sustain myself through the constant changes.

I got used to long hallways with countless doors and the commanders' offices always at one end or the other. I got used to noisy dining facilities and huge motor pools and the fifteen-minutes-early rule. I got used to being called "ma'am" and the polite, uncertain reception I would receive whenever I first arrived. I got used to reaching out, all day, every day, to every soldier or spouse I came in contact with. One soldier fresh out of boot camp told me he wanted to set up an appointment "because you've smiled and said hello every time I've seen you." That was how it worked.

That first night of this particular assignment, after I'd changed clothes, eaten my dinner, and reflected on different moments of Laura's introductions, I reached for the phone in my room to call my friend Julia and tell her about my day.

"I don't know how you do it. I couldn't keep starting from scratch again and again," Julia said.

"Well, if you knew that you'd have a couple of weeks of being overwhelmed, then months where you'd feel a sense of destiny like you'd never felt before, wouldn't that seem like a decent trade-off to you?"

It was true. Helping others had *always* given me a strong sense of fulfillment, yet the powerful fulfillment I found in working with soldiers was remarkable.

CALLED

Being sent downrange again was a complicated prospect for most soldiers. I don't think I came across too many soldiers who were excited to deploy again. To some soldiers, being in combat was their job, nothing more. From the time they enlisted, preparing for and facing combat was their occupation. They put in their time, did what was asked of them, and met the standards they were expected to meet. When they got their notice to deploy again, they shrugged into their rucksacks, lined up, and left. They might grumble about what they knew was waiting downrange—blasting heat, sandstorms, bombs, and boredom—but it was the job they'd signed up to do.

Others—particularly those who considered the military their *profession*—conducted themselves with a conscientious, professional dedication. For them, going back into combat was a serious responsibility. They knew what awaited younger troops when they hit the battlefield. These soldiers had tested skills, significant insight, and more maturity, all of which were invaluable to less experienced troops. Many of these more experienced soldiers spoke to me of watching out for younger soldiers while deployed.

And then there were soldiers who felt the military was their *calling*. They might have been deployed six or seven times, but they approached each assignment with somber willingness and fortitude. Any complicated feelings about deploying again got filtered through the sense that they had been called to military service.

In reading different definitions, I came to understand that a calling involves a number of key elements: work that's done in the service of a higher goal, self-sacrifice, and a dedication to one's role that transcends self-interest. Soldiers who felt the military was their calling anchored their deployments in the values of "duty, honor, country," expressed in the oaths they'd taken to serve and the military creeds they professed. Those values served them well as they deployed again and again. Their personal feelings or preferences stayed in the background.

First and foremost, they were called to serve.

The Notice

It's the end of my day, and I'm ready to head back to my hotel and collapse with weariness. As I pull my office door closed and turn the key in the lock, I hear a shaky voice behind me, "Please, ma'am, can I talk to you?"

I turn the key back the other way, and as I push the door open again, I look over my shoulder to see SGT Hayes standing behind me, his face a storm of changing emotions I can't read. He's usually a light-hearted man, but the face I'm gazing at now is full of struggle. I flip the lights on and motion toward a chair.

"What's happening, Sergeant?" I take a seat across from him.

Hayes is a soldier I've gotten to know quite well during the time I've worked on this base. He's a devoted husband and father, a dedicated soldier with a sharp mind and quick wit. His soldiers adore him for his fairness, his willingness to work right alongside them, and his ability to make menial tasks seem important and challenging. I often see him moving from one soldier to another, keeping his unit smiling and morale high. He's young—maybe early thirties—but he carries himself with the demeanor of a much older man. At one point, he talked with me about the challenges of raising his autistic son, and he has spoken frankly about powerful moments he experienced in combat. Perhaps these factors shaped the easygoing maturity I'd seen in him. As he sits across from me now, his typically sunny manner has vanished.

Hayes holds a piece of paper in front of him with trembling hands. "I just found out. I mean, I just got this."

He glances at me, then down at the piece of paper, then back at me. He gulps down a couple of breaths, starts to speak, then gulps more air. "I'm on the list to be deployed again."

We stare at each other for a moment. He keeps quiet, looks out the window and then down at the paper in his hand. He smiles a brave smile; instantly, it fades.

I keep waiting, watching.

He holds the printed list out toward me, pointing at his name. I take it from him and glance down. He could be gone in a matter of weeks. His words begin to take shape, like a melting ice floe starting to move.

"I kind of knew this was coming. I mean, for a few months I kept feeling like it was going to happen. I don't know why. I get a feeling about things sometimes. And now it happened." His voice gets quieter with each sentence, and then it trails off into silence. I realize that much of what I see in his face is shock.

"So tell me, honestly, how does this land, Sergeant? How are you feeling?"

"I really don't know, ma'am. I mean, I've felt a need to go back. It doesn't feel right that I've only gone once, while others are going five and six times. But this seems so sudden. It's hard to know what to feel."

He turns to gaze out the window again. He shuffles his feet on the carpet in front of his chair, rubbing them back and forth in a pattern of two straight lines, as if he needs to feel assured of something solid beneath him. He's folding and unfolding the notice in his hands, not even realizing he's creasing it in half, then opening it, then creasing it in half again.

He takes another deep breath, looks over at me, and says with certainty and a slight nod of his head, as if he's finally gotten a hold on his feelings: "It's mixed, ma'am. I'm proud to go back. I want to do my part, and it's my turn. And I can take better care of my family—you know, provide for them better with the combat pay. But to be away from my kids and my wife for a year . . ."

His voice shuts off again; his eyes blink rapidly.

He whispers, "I don't know how to miss them so much."

Suddenly, his cell phone beeps. He looks at it. "It's my wife. I sent her a text, telling her we needed to talk when I got home, but I didn't tell her why."

He flips the phone open. "Hello?"

I hear his wife's voice coming through the phone. I can't hear her words, but her tone is rapid, pressured. She wants to know what has happened, what's wrong, what they need to talk about. He interrupts to tell her about being on the deployment list, and suddenly it's dead quiet on the other end. The silence stretches on and on. He waits. She says nothing, her world tilting at an alarming new angle.

Eventually, he says, "Hello? Are you there?"

No response.

"Are you there?"

Nothing. He unconsciously moves his hand to the center of his chest, just over his heart, and starts tapping his fingers there while he waits for her voice.

"Talk to me, baby."

She finally speaks, and now I can hear her voice telling him, "Come home right after work. Don't do anything, just get home."

Hayes agrees, hangs up, and shakes his head, trying to clear it of all the thoughts pouring through, as if the shaking could slow down the race of time he's now swept up in.

I ask him how he thinks his wife will respond to the deployment, and his voice becomes steadier for the first time. "She'll do OK. I've told her I thought this was coming, so we've been talking about it. We'll do fine. We'll be OK."

I watch him orient himself in a new direction, like a compass suddenly turned, the needle skittering before finding true north again. He looks at me steadily, gives a quick nod.

"Well, I don't really need to say anything else right now. I just wanted someone to know."

As he stands to leave, I ask him to be sure to keep me posted if he hears anything more. We shake hands solemnly, as if we're already saying that other good-bye.

The Wait

On this cool, overcast Saturday afternoon, a long line of tan buses hunkers nose-to-tail at the edge of the battalion's parking lot. They're empty, waiting to be filled with two hundred and eighty-five soldiers deploying to Afghanistan for a year. The buses with their idling engines are a concrete reminder in everyone's field of vision: *Soon. We're leaving soon.*

My name tag identifies me as one of the base counselors as I move through the crowd, looking for anyone who could use some support, a brief conversation, a little reassurance. A tall, muscled soldier off to my left holds his tiny baby up close to his face and smells her wispy brown hair. He closes his eyes as he draws in her sweet baby scent. His huge hands, tanned from weeks of training in the hot Texas sun and scarred with the rough work of soldiering, cradle the baby like he's holding a fragile teacup. His wife leans into his side, trying her best to look strong and capable of making it through the next year without him. When she nudges her face into his shoulder, a cascade of long dark hair falls across her face. She doesn't push it back; maybe she's relieved to have a curtain to hide the anguish she's feeling.

I look to my right and watch a mother struggling to chat with her soldier-son, her eyes blinking rapidly as she wills her tears to hold off until he boards the bus. She keeps the stilted conversation going by tossing out inane observations about the weather or the buses, even as her voice cracks with emotion and ripples of fear move across her face. Her son is barely listening. He's glancing around, jumpy and distracted, wanting to get this part over with and get on his way. His right hand is spread open on the side of his thigh, tapping out an agitated rhythm against the leg of his uniform.

All around, young couples stand in silent embraces, holding each other for long stretches of time before pulling back to look at each other's faces, then pulling each other close again.

To start conversations, I sometimes put my hand on someone's shoulder and ask them whom they're looking for. Different companies within the battalion have gathered in different areas, so I point out where to look for the relative or friend they've not yet found. I don't ask them how they're doing; for all the ones teetering on the edge of falling apart that question would be too direct. It's a delicate challenge not to intrude on moments so full of tender grief for these warriors and families. I know their hearts are shivering with the looming loss of companionship and comfort, so I begin to ask, "Who are you saying good-bye to today?" This seems to be the perfect invitation.

"My son."

"My granddaughter."

"My husband."

Sometimes these responses expand:

"My son—he's been deployed before, and I really wish he didn't have to go back."

"My granddaughter. I have a grandson over there, too. I know she'll be OK. I just want her to come back safe."

"My husband. We've only been married two months."

The atmosphere is surprisingly subdued. This is not the time for hysterics or drama. Soldiers are tense but keep up their professional demeanor. Loved ones look teary but maintain their composure so as not to inflame these last moments with more angst.

I walk up to a couple who look like they're well into their sixties. While they balance on the edge of the curb to get a better view across the vast area, I ask, "Who are you saying good-bye to today?"

"Our nephew," they reply at the same time. Their Kentucky accents are so thick it takes me a moment to process their words. They're large, rounded people with graying hair and bright eyes. Trading off back and forth, they tell me their story.

"We drove fourteen hours to be here with him," the uncle says.

"We didn't even stay at a motel," his wife adds.

"We just came straight here to find him. Is this everyone? We don't see him," he says, worried.

"He's got to be here," says the wife.

I point out a few other areas where they might find their nephew. As I wander, I bump into them a few more times. They're still searching, and each time I see them, worry has etched deeper into their faces.

I nod to a young woman who's standing by herself, clutching a scuffed black handbag up against her chest, her arms curled into her body with distress. The gray sweater she's wearing over her dark blue dress is fluffy and looks brand new. Clearly, she wants to look her best on this unhappy day, but her new clothes don't hide the fragility in her eyes and posture. She tells me she's trying to find her husband, that they've been married for less than a year, and that she's scared to be without him. Seeing my name tag and assuming I know all the answers, she turns her watery eyes on me and asks rapid-fire questions: How will she know he's OK? How often will they be able to speak to each other? How can she get news of him? Will he come back *different*? When her questions ebb, I tell her about the family support groups that will help with all of those concerns. She writes down a few contact numbers and then heads off into the crowd to find her guy.

After the young wife walks away, I turn toward a tribe of eight relatives who've come to say farewell to their daughter/cousin/niece. As they stand in a circle around her, they tell me how proud they are of her, but behind the pride I detect fear and sad nervousness. The corporal smiles shyly at all the attention and holds her duty cap rolled tightly in her hand as she waits for departure. "She'll be OK," the aunt keeps saying, as if repeating the words again and again will keep her niece safe.

A petite, pretty woman sobs into her soldier's chest. He's not speaking, just holding her tightly and placing soft kisses on the top of her head. There are no words that will make his leaving any easier—a year seems like an eternity. The pungent smell of diesel fumes wafts through the air at that very moment, another subtle cue that departure looms.

Overall, the troops are doing better with these farewell moments than are the loved ones and friends. They're used to waiting, used to standing by until the moment of being called into action. They understand the anticipation of being told what to do next. It is the air they breathe, day in and day out.

A soldier walks by me wearing a backpack that seems twice as big as he is. He's bent almost double in his effort to lug the pack over toward the buses. His buzz cut is so new: the sides of his head are nearly bald and his bright-white scalp shows through the fuzz. This fresh-faced private has a huge grin on his face, and when I wave to him, he waves back with eagerness, ready to go. Perhaps his good-byes have already happened. Now he's anxious to move out and get busy with the adventures he's conjured up in the daydreams of an inexperienced warrior.

A honk from one of the buses blasts through the air and for a split second the entire crowd freezes: *time has run out.*

"I'll see you soon, bud," says a father. He shakes his son's hand—but then he suddenly pulls his son into a tight embrace and buries his face against the young man's shoulder. The soldier awkwardly pats his dad on the back, his eyes brimming with tears as he says, "OK, Dad. OK."

"Oh," says the worried mother who's been trying to keep her conversation upbeat. "Oh," she repeats, having no way to fill the emptiness that's starting to rise up. Her son's already walking toward the buses with his squad.

"You take care, honey," the aunt says to her niece. "Now, we'll see you soon, OK? I mean it. We're going to be right here when you get back."

Most of the couples don't speak. They just hold on to each other, and savor the last hug, the last physical imprint of the one person they never want to be without. Many of the soldiers don't look back as they walk away, avoiding the searing pain of that last glance.

The crowd disperses—those in uniform move toward the buses, family members watching in silence. The buses will carry the troops to a nearby airfield where their long flight will begin. The loved ones will be left standing in an empty parking lot, counting the first of the hundreds of thousands of minutes that must pass before the buses bring the soldiers back home again. And the praying begins, too—prayers that the wait will last only this one year and that their loved one will return to them safe and whole.

CHAPTER 11

As I began my second year of working with soldiers, one unique experience amplified the sense of destiny I had begun to feel in my work. It was 3 a.m. on a shockingly cold February morning. I found myself standing out on the tarmac at an empty airfield, scanning the distant skies. The night was bright and clear, as winter nights can sometimes be. The stars sparkled and blinked against the deep velvet sky. A fierce wind kept whipping my coat open, and when that happened it felt as if the cold swirled right through my body. I shuddered with cold, but I wouldn't have traded my circumstances for anything.

Four commanders stood slightly off to my left, and a noncommissioned officer (NCO) stood just behind us.

"There, sir." The NCO pointed to the north.

We all strained to follow the path of his finger, and finally found the one steadily growing bright white light among all those stars, the headlight of a plane carrying one hundred and seventy soldiers back from their year in Afghanistan.

"Four minutes ETA, sir," I heard the NCO murmur.

Watching the blue-white light grow ever-so-slowly bigger as the plane neared, a part of me stepped back and marveled: How had I come to this exact moment, to the tarmac of this airfield, waiting to greet these returning warriors? I was full of wonderment. How had a kid who grew up in Oklahoma and Texas become someone commanders would invite to be a part of the welcoming contingent for these warriors? How had all my hours of struggle and confusion within the military world added up to my being included in this small group? I honestly couldn't grasp the enormity of the forces that had aligned to bring me to this specific moment. I was deeply, deeply humbled. In that instant, it seemed the events of my entire life had somehow led me into this very moment. I watched that light grow brighter in the sky and savored the experience.

The plane landed far out on the runway and began taxiing toward us. It crawled along the tarmac, turning slow angles and making its way toward the hangar, while a tiny band scurried into place next to where the plane would eventually come to a stop. Flag bearers took up their places next to the band. At this base, the soldiers in the band and in the color guard met every single plane that brought troops home, no matter what time of the day or night, no matter how many planes came in each day.

The commanders grew silent and automatically ordered themselves into a receiving line according to rank. I stood at the far end of the line. There were no family members present. The airstrip was an hour's drive from the base and soldiers would be bused there after they processed through several registration lines in the hangars behind me.

As the plane taxied to a stop, a set of stairs was rolled up to the door and the band started playing "The Star-Spangled Banner." The air was tense with anticipation as all eyes stared at the plane's door. For several minutes, nothing happened. The door didn't budge. I looked at the officer next to me and asked, "What's happening?"

"They're getting a quick debriefing, being told to check around their seats, and given a rundown on what they need to do to in-process in the hangar. It'll be a minute."

As he finished speaking, the door slammed back against the side of the fuselage, and a river of soldiers began clattering down the metal steps. I shook every soldier's hand and offered a greeting.

"Welcome home."

"Good to see you."

"Glad you're back."

"Well done, soldier."

"Proud of you, thank you."

"You made it. You're home now."

Their faces told the complicated story of homecoming—some were elated, infused with joy; others were serious, heavy with the uncertainty of what it would take to truly come home; still others were bleary-eyed, sleepy, just following directions, doing the next thing in front of them. A few nodded sheepishly, shy in the face of this effusive welcome. Some averted their eyes, wouldn't speak, their faces tight with tension.

After the last soldier had disembarked, I followed the troops into the hangar and stood chatting with them as they waited in various lines. One of the female soldiers had a small purple teddy bear tied to her rucksack.

"You're bringing home a teddy bear?" I asked.

"It's for my son. He's two. I've missed him so much." Her voice was nearly a whisper and her eyes grew misty with tears.

"Well, you're almost there. He'll be glad to see you."

We both smiled as she shuffled forward toward the next check-in table.

"Hey, how are you?" I asked a private who was grinning broadly and seemed practically giddy. He looked so young and fresh, as if he might have been sixteen, his string-bean body all angles and gawkiness in his uniform.

"I couldn't be better. I'm fantastic. I'm great. I'm just awesome, ma'am!"

"So . . . you're glad to be home?" I teased, as if I was trying really hard to figure out the most obvious thing in the world.

"Glad to be home, ma'am. Glad to be back in the USA. I love this country. Man, I've dreamed of this day for a whole year. I made it."

He, too, shuffled forward in line.

"How are you doing?" I asked a specialist who seemed nervous and wired.

"Ma'am, I don't mean to be rude, but I just want a cigarette."

We both laughed and I pointed him to the area where he could smoke once he'd finished moving through all the in-processing lines.

This wasn't the time for long conversations about their experiences. It was a time to scan for troubled faces, to make sure as many soldiers as possible saw my name tag and knew I was available to them. It was a time to join them in whatever kind of homecoming moment they were in the midst of: happy or downcast, tense or full of relief. I would learn their stories over the coming weeks; for now, I savored the bright moments of welcoming them home.

After they finished in-processing, the troops boarded buses and headed to the base, where their families waited. I traveled back to the base with some other staff members and watched all the ecstatic reunions, feeling vicarious joy as folks hugged, cheered, screamed, and burst into tears. I watched a soldier hold his two-week-old daughter for the first time. I asked him how that felt, and he stared into his baby's eyes. "No words, ma'am." I backed away and blended back into the crowd, leaving him and his wife to savor the miracle of that moment.

I worked through the night and drove back to my hotel as the dawn started lighting up the eastern sky. I was utterly exhausted, and I was elated. I felt like my heart was a million miles wide, and I felt like embracing every single one of those soldiers—and their families—with sincere gratitude, pride, and welcome. I felt deeply humbled as I thought about all they encountered in the course of doing their jobs. They faced experiences many of us would never agree to face; they carried burdens that would break even the strongest among us. The moments I'd just walked through, the homecoming I'd just witnessed, left my heart so overfilled with emotion I couldn't fall asleep.

I paced back and forth across my hotel room, recalling the exchanges I'd had in that hangar and letting myself feel every layer of the emotional impact. Unable to stay cooped up in my room when my heart felt so open, I changed out of my work clothes and sat in the sun on the silly little patio at the bottom of the hotel stairway, which was the size of a child's plastic pool.

I watched traffic whiz by on the road below the parking lot, the morning rush hour beginning as my work day was just ending. I leaned against the brick of the hotel in my comfortable sweatshirt as everything in me relaxed and savored the experience. My mind drifted back through the night before, and I tried to remember as much as I could about every soldier I'd met. The woman with the teddy bear, the guy who just wanted a cigarette, others I hadn't spoken to but whose weary faces I could recall. The crush and shuffle as soldiers worked their way through the in-processing lines, that blue-white light growing brighter in the dark winter sky. All of it.

Welcoming the soldiers home was a defining event in life for me. Whatever destiny had carried me there and deposited me in that receiving line, I bowed to it.

Altogether, this base welcomed back seven hundred and fifty soldiers in the space of a couple of weeks. After the early groups began to arrive, I felt a great fear rise up in me as I imagined the level of need rolling toward me. I was the only counselor on this base. Knowing that I was responsible for serving the seven hundred and fifty soldiers arriving, plus their spouses, plus other family members, all of whom were certain to be experiencing emotional reactions to the challenges of return . . . I was overwhelmed. I couldn't imagine being able to respond sufficiently to their concerns.

I called a colleague who was working on a distant base. "Hey, Becky. I'm getting scared. With the ones who have already gotten here, I see so much need—and there's so many more coming in the next couple of weeks. I don't know what to do." My voice cracked and tears began rolling down my face. It's hard for therapists to contend with a need so great; there's such tension between our longing to truly help and the limitations of what we can realistically give.

"I've been there," said Becky, "I know. It's overwhelming, isn't it? With just about every assignment there's a moment when I freak out about how to address so much need."

Becky and I talked for another half hour about my fears: What if I missed someone who was really struggling? What if I got too worn out? What if I wasn't capable enough? What if I didn't know what to do? All of these fears were churning in me, and talking with Becky—and a couple of other colleagues I reached out to—helped to soothe my frayed nerves and fears.

"You can't meet every need," Becky reminded me. "But you'll be sufficient for the ones that come your way. Don't try to do *everything*; settle down into doing the pieces that show up at your door or in front of you."

That made so much sense. I slowed down. Once I did that, I was able to move back into trusting my sense of destiny, the sense that I could make a difference in the right places and with the right people. I walked into the ferocious swirl of returning soldiers and anxious spouses, and I began to meet each moment with as much of me and my heart as I could muster.

As more planes landed, I found a pace I could sustain. I bounced from hangars filled with family reunions, to reintegration briefings for large groups of soldiers, to planning meetings for reunion events—such as picnics and family fun days—to sessions with couples straining to reconnect, to spontaneous interactions with soldiers who were faltering. In another month, more counselors would arrive to help soldiers get integrated back into their home base and their families, but by then I would have handed over my position to my replacement. In the meantime, I steadily worked my way through the schedule of each day's need and response.

It was overwhelming and beautiful and exhausting and meaningful. By the time the last plane arrived with the last of the returning soldiers, I wouldn't have traded the experience of those very intense weeks for anything in the world. Through the experiences I had during those hectic days, I'd come to comprehend even more about military life and the sacrifices, honor, and giving that soldiers represented. It was terrifically humbling. I was very proud of the work I had done and the hearts I had touched.

It's a Party

There's loud music playing, and the vast, hulking hangar is full of people waiting for the soldiers to arrive. The expectant crowd is huddled in twos or threes, closely melded together in their exquisite waiting: soon, over two hundred battle-weary troops will march into the hangar and reunite with families and loved ones they haven't seen for a year. It's close to midnight, but once you've walked into the hangar—the assault of music, the people, and the bright lights—it feels as if you've just arrived at a raucous block party in the middle of a summer day.

I walk through the crowd and notice a soldier's wife I've talked with in recent weeks. Her husband is one of the soldiers scheduled to arrive tonight. I walk over and meet her three young daughters. The girls are eight, five, and one and a half, and they're all dressed up in matching pink dresses. I lean down close to them and ask, "Are you excited about the soldiers coming home?"

Before any of them can answer, I notice their mom frantically trying to get my attention from where she's standing just behind the girls. She whispers, "They don't know their dad's coming." This is common for military families with small children. The return schedules change so often, it's kinder to leave younger children in the dark, so they don't get disappointed over and over again when planes are delayed.

I direct the girls' attention to other topics and they don't seem to notice. We talk about how pretty their dresses are, and I admire all the frills. I notice the delicate edges of lace on their little white socks, and they giggle with pleasure. I tease them about being up so late, asking them if I can just lie down on the concrete floor next to them and take a nap. They think I'm silly.

We keep chatting for a minute, then I ask them what's going on with all these people in the hangar. The five-year-old—the most precocious of the three—dances on her toes and squeals, "It's a *party!*"

"It *is?* Well, why are we having a *party?*" I ask her in highly conspiratorial tones.

Her whole body wiggles as she shouts, "Some soldiers are coming HOME!"

She's yelling with excitement. Her sisters watch her wiggling, and the older one rolls her eyes, embarrassed by her sister's effusiveness.

"Oh good!" I say, "I love that kind of party. I like it when soldiers come home."

The eight-year-old nods. "My friend Caitlin? Her dad's coming home."

Their mom joins in, smiling. "We're happy for everyone, aren't we, girls?"

"YES!" the girls chorus, caught up in the joy of homecoming, no matter who's arriving. Even the one-and-a-half-year-old is nodding and giggling now, and she's doing her own wiggly dance of excitement.

I stay a while longer, then move off to talk to other people I know in the crowd. A half hour goes by before the hangar doors start to slide open. The music suddenly changes to the pounding theme from *Chariots of Fire*, and a cadre of battle-worn soldiers marches in.

Standing off to the side, I watch the girls shuffle and bounce with excitement as the level of anticipation skyrockets. The girls wave to neighbors and friends. They stomp their feet to the music and hang on to their mom while they watch the soldiers file in and come to a tight formation in the center of the hangar. After a few words from the commander, the soldiers are dismissed and the formation begins to crumble and dissolve, like a sand castle washed apart by the ocean. Soldiers rush in every direction looking for loved ones, and the hangar is filled with happy chaos.

The little girls don't see their dad until he's just a couple of feet in front of them. The eight-year-old opens her mouth, then forgets to shut it. She's staring at her dad like he's a ghost, a phantom soldier, her whole body frozen in shock. The five-year-old screams, "DADDY!" and runs into his arms at the exact same moment the littlest one starts to cry and break into a wobbly little toddler's run. She propels her tiny body straight into her daddy's legs and sticks there like she's plastered to him forever.

Their mom hangs back just long enough for the girls to have their moment of ecstatic surprise. Then she runs forward, too, and she's crying right along with them. In about two seconds, they're all clinging to each other, crying and hugging and swaying in each other's arms. Her husband's embrace pulls the whole family in. He's got his head buried in his wife's shoulder, but his hands are constantly making sure his girls are right there, too—his love a force field around his beautiful family.

CHAPTER 12

The longer I worked with soldiers, the more emotional turmoil I had to tolerate within myself; as I understood the depth and the more subtle or more complex aspects of their struggles, I had to bear witness to—or "hold the space" for—deeper and more acute suffering. Naturally, their suffering prompted emotional responses in me: grief, sadness, compassion. The intensity of their stories and their struggles could be overwhelming, and yet the last thing they needed was a reaction of pity or an attempt to "rescue" them. Those are common responses when we try to feel another's pain, but they weren't useful in the work I was doing with soldiers.

They needed for me to stand steady, right across from them, able to absorb what they needed to share without flinching or ducking. So often, I sat across from soldiers who'd look me in the eye as they described their experiences, watching for me—the civilian—to judge or flinch or push away. There was simply so much they had seen or lived through; nothing I could say would soothe them. So I held still in myself and listened. And sometimes I felt tremendous helplessness.

In private practice, I'd sat with people who faced devastating difficulties, but those clients were not struggling with having seen a dear friend—or several—get blown up. My previous clients hadn't been away from their families for a year, several times in succession. Those clients were not trying to carry on bravely in the face of the tremendous fears and unknowns of the battlefield, or tolerating the relentless tension in training rooms, knowing their days in combat were fast approaching. They weren't struggling with the ravages war had wreaked in their emotional field, damage that could feel hopelessly immense.

I couldn't say any one person's struggles were more or less important, or harder, than another's; there was no way to make that comparison. Yet I was stunned at the levels of helplessness I reached while listening to soldiers' struggles. In my private practice, the instances of feeling like that were far fewer in number, and certainly less in potency. Usually those moments arose with clients whose history included severe trauma. With the military work, I faced astounding powerlessness and vulnerability almost daily as I listened to the terrible knowledge the soldiers now had to carry with them, the knowledge that life could become wildly tragic and immensely frightening in a microsecond. That truth could leave them feeling isolated and misunderstood, on top of the trauma they might also be struggling with.

My ability to contain or manage my emotional responses—whether heartbreak, sadness, helplessness—in the face of their awful knowing was key to a soldier's willingness to talk about those searing moments; the only way they could face feelings that seemed otherwise impossible for them to admit. I sat with them in swamps of grief, shock, terror, bitterness, and loss. I stood by them as they recalled crushing blows to their hearts and psyches. I wanted to help them get to the other side of the ocean of struggle in which they were drowning, the place where their feet might find solid ground again.

On a sunny spring day halfway through one of my assignments, Staff Sergeant (SSG) McComber and I bumped into each other in the reception area of the education building and chatted for a while. The wide skylight-lit hallway felt warm and relaxing. McComber leaned against one of the pillars that held up the lofty roof of the building, his books under his arm and his cap scrunched up in his right hand. We talked about the fine weather and laughed when he bemoaned the upcoming exercises that would keep him out in the field for at least two weeks, maybe four.

Suddenly his face got serious as he swallowed hard and blurted out, "It's hard for me to talk to my wife these days. I kind of freeze up and I really just don't know what to say. It's not working out very well."

I had started to suggest basic ways to communicate better when McComber said, "You know, I didn't grow up in a good way. I didn't really get to learn about other people much." He began to describe a horrifically difficult childhood full of abuse, neglect, and shame.

As he opened up about his concerns, I felt myself in a bind. By contract I was supposed to work only with short-term issues such as adjustment concerns, relationship issues, grief and loss, communication skills, parenting, daily living skills, etc. Specifically, I wasn't to address PTSD issues, issues that called for long-term counseling, medications, psychiatric review, or any kind of diagnoses. The program I was working for was designed to be a basic support resource, rather than an option for more intensive concerns. "Brief, solution-focused counseling, not long-term support" was the phrase used; we were to limit our contact with an individual to a maximum of six sessions as part of the program's parameters. This, of course, was a difficult line to walk, and I felt it wasn't realistic to deftly avoid soldiers who were suffering with deeper concerns—especially when I saw so many struggling with serious issues.

Soldiers with PTSD were referred to military behavioral health or medical venues on the base. As I was talking to McComber, he had unexpectedly moved the conversation toward deeper issues that were more serious than simple communication problems. I had the skills to diplomatically communicate the limits of my work. But the act of speaking up and admitting he needed help was monumental for someone like McComber. In such moments, it was tricky to turn around and refer them to other resources. I talked with McComber for another half hour, and then referred him to the on-base military health clinic. He said he knew where it was and we said good-bye. I had the feeling he wasn't going to seek help there.

Months later, on a different base, 1LT Franklin said to me, "Don't let anyone tell you this isn't a good ol' boys network. I've been passed over for promotion so many times I might as well pack it in."

I started to sympathize with her, but she interrupted me to tell me how badly the situation was affecting her marriage and her outlook in general. As she talked, I realized she was describing a fairly serious depressive episode, and once again I was outside the bounds of what I was allowed to discuss.

Serious, complicated issues arose without warning or intentional probing. I often found myself following a soldier's story into emotional territory that my restricted counseling directive excluded. PTSD issues often emerged while in the midst of more casual exchanges. When soldiers felt someone was truly listening and ready to hear, their heart's concerns came forward in our conversations.

Offering them solace at the same time I was trying to maintain the dictates of my job description was stressful. I didn't want the soldier to feel handed off at such a vulnerable and tender moment. At times, my natural capacity for listening intently and my compassion for how much a soldier or spouse was struggling won out over the directive to limit the process, as in the case with PFC Petri.

Petri had been greatly damaged by his time in Afghanistan the previous year. He hesitantly showed up in my office one afternoon, reaching out for the first time. His eyes brimmed with tears and he was almost nonverbal as he tried to tell me he was hurting. I could tell he was most likely in the grips of a PTSD reaction, and I knew I had to refer him to the military mental health clinic on base, but I also knew he needed to feel like someone was responding to him "right now," so that he would keep asking for help.

We spoke for a very long time, and at the end of our time, he asked if he could come talk to me the next day. I agreed. I also mentioned the referral to medical services. When we spoke the next day, he asked to come back again the next day. It was painful for me to keep nudging him elsewhere when it was clear that he desperately wanted me to hear the terrors in which he was tangled. I met with him again and kept nudging him toward the medical system.

Eventually, he followed the recommendation. But to this day, I remember the inner pressure I felt in knowing I'd violated the rules by listening to him after that initial meeting. In these moments, I felt the military was not yet in sync with the depth of service members' psychological needs and the ways they preferred to reach out. Soldiers didn't want information about their struggles going into their files, because they feared it would impact their career. They usually faced long wait times at the base's health services, and they often didn't feel understood or truly helped even after they were finally seen by someone.

"So, I went to behavioral health," SSG Dallas told me. After a conversation with him a couple of weeks earlier in his company's training room, I had suggested he go to behavioral health services for his anxiety and trouble sleeping.

"How'd it go?" I asked.

"They gave me a prescription and told me to come back in three months." Disgust saturated his voice, and he rolled his eyes as he said this, frustrated at being left on his own when he was clearly struggling so much. He didn't think meds were the answer, and the medical clinic's response let him down. Soldiers were often disappointed when offered medication. What they wanted was an authentic, empathic response from someone who truly understood what they were coping with. Typically, when I checked back with soldiers I had referred, I learned that they had never pursued getting help on the base.

Whether hints buried in things said or telling facial expressions or a reticence that I sensed would soon melt, there were innumerable subtle indicators present when a soldier wanted help: a flicker of pain across the eyes, a stumbling sentence when the topic moved to combat, a voice that suddenly went silent, or a quick change of subject when we began to speak about buddies lost forever.

Working less intensively would have protected me from feeling the level of trauma and pain the soldiers brought forward. Many of my colleagues chose to interact with soldiers in a more sociable, supportive manner. They spent their days chatting with soldiers and spouses, and offered friendly support—without giving any indication they saw or noticed any struggles on the soldiers' part. One colleague told me our job was to be "available" to support service members, so in her mind as long as she was around the soldiers, she had met the job requirements. For her, there was no need at all to be more active in responding to their concerns; chatting and hanging out was enough.

I could have ignored the pain I sometimes saw in a soldier's eyes, limiting our conversation to more mundane concerns or indicating to them I wasn't available to hear the depths of their woundedness, but it wasn't in my makeup to do that. Besides, most soldiers were *very* perceptive about this kind of avoidant response. Instead of limiting the interactions I was having, I threw myself into them, and with each assignment my heart was getting more and more saturated by the traumas that were disclosed to me. Soldiers who were fragmented by their combat experience were especially noticeable to me, and I felt special care and concern about their burdens.

In discussing all this with one of my colleagues who was a retired Navy corpsman, she observed, "Soldiers hate bullshit. I think they instinctively know you're someone who can handle what they have to say. You don't flinch. That's what they need." I felt the truth of her observation, and saw it in practice daily.

Another friend who was doing the same kind of work with the military emailed me and said, "You're a counselor whose instinct, training, and skills take you to deep places, *quickly*. You intuitively sense those places and kind of instantly identify the work that needs to be done by an individual or a couple. And you go there. Soldiers sense that in you."

Commanders noticed my work with their troops was more direct, and they often asked that my contract be extended. This was a nice acknowledgment, but it was less about me and more an indication they knew their troops needed more help, and the commanders wanted them to receive it. Over the course of my assignments, I felt more and more capable of understanding what kind of support soldiers truly needed, given their particular wounds and bravery. At the same time, my new job befuddled some of my friends and colleagues from my past life.

One evening, I was sitting in my hotel room, sipping tea and watching the sun go down. I was always delighted to get a room that faced the sunrise or sunset, and this room had a west-facing view out across a big open field instead of the usual parking lots. I had just called my friend David, who was a counselor back in Tucson.

"Seems working with all those soldiers has to make you feel more and more antiwar, doesn't it? Antimilitary?" he said sincerely.

"I know it sounds strange, David, but it has the opposite effect. It doesn't make me hold any appreciation for war, but it makes me feel utterly detached from a stance one way or the other."

The sky was darkening by the minute, the field disappearing in the darkness.

Elizabeth Heaney

David pushed further. "But surely you see soldiers who are sacrificing themselves for no reason, off in other countries in crazy wars. That's how it seems to me. Sometimes, I don't see how anybody could work for the military like you do."

I no longer knew how to respond to comments like David's. I believed in the work I was doing. I felt drawn to reaching out to soldiers and helping them with the stresses and traumas they carried—traumas that were understood by so few. It had nothing to do with believing in the wars they were fighting. As I saw how much soldiers were suffering, all I was focused on was fellow human beings in need.

Sometimes I felt angry with people who felt a comfortable certainty about their opinions concerning the military—or about service members, specifically. In my anger, I felt like pushing back hard at their assured opinions by asking: "How many soldiers have you talked to? How many soldiers have you actually sat with and asked about their lives; why they do what they do; what it means to them? How many have you really, *really* listened to—not to convince them of your viewpoint, but to help yourself understand theirs?" But I mostly kept quiet. Challenging them seemed useless because they truly had no clue about the things I had seen in my work.

During one of my breaks in between assignments, I visited a good friend, joining her and some of her friends one morning for coffee. When one of the women heard about the work I did, she said, "I can't understand why anyone would sign up to get killed."

She screwed her face up into a look of disgust and her body straightened in certainty.

"Well," I said, "in the time I've been working with soldiers, I've found they have a variety of reasons for signing up. Have you ever asked a soldier why they do it?"

"Oh, I'm not interested in talking to them," she said disdainfully.

I suddenly understood more fully how frustrated soldiers might feel not only when they are misunderstood and judged, but also when they

166

encounter this kind of adamant refusal to even *want* to understand. For myself, I found I could no longer hold opinions that didn't honor the astounding heart and integrity I saw represented in their dedication to their work.

TERRIBLE KNOWLEDGE

In 1991, some twenty years before I began working with soldiers, I read an exceptional article titled, "Terrible Knowledge," in a psychotherapy journal.[10] The article described the deeply distressing fallout one experiences after a traumatic event; life no longer feels safe or predictable or assuredly reasonable. And the one who experienced the trauma now carries the terrible knowledge that life can suddenly veer off the rails and into dark, enormously surreal and horrifying territory.

In combat, life suddenly becomes wild, chaotic, far outside the boundaries of normal. After being in combat, most soldiers can't hold on to the safe, secure assumption that life will unfold in a fairly sensible way. They can go back into "normal" life, they can walk their neighborhood streets, applaud their kids at football games and recitals, sling an arm across their loved one next to them in bed—but they can never forget that *at any second* normal reality can come crashing down and morph into surreal insanity. Even if this collapse of reality never happens again, they have the knowing that it *can*, and this knowing makes them different from those of us who have never experienced the shattering of the fragile glass structure we call normalcy.

I cannot count the number of soldiers who began to stutter or got a very distant look in their eyes or struggled to speak coherently when telling me about the moment the shattering happened. It was nearly impossible for them to find the words to wrap around a kind of chaos that most people never experience. The experience of combat has often stolen their sense of meaning in life, too. If you know life can get that crazy in a heartbeat, how can you ever relax again?

"Surreal" is the word most settle on.

"Seeing my buddy shoot himself was . . . I don't know . . . surreal."

"I lost count of the buddies I lost. What do I do with that? What do I do with the fact that I can't remember how many? It's so goddamn surreal, you know?"

"When I realized the whole bottom half of his body was gone, it was . . . uh . . . it was . . . surreal."

Again and again, they echo the word that indicates something that will not be kept within the bounds of "real" life—disorienting, almost hallucinatory in its fantastical horror.

They are left to live alone in their memory of things their hearts can't bear, isolated in their terrible knowledge and hanging on day to day, trying to cross back across some invisible line that would let them be just one of us "normal" people again.

I found myself wishing that all of these veterans in possession of such terrible knowledge would be surrounded by people who would continue to reach for them, in a hundred different ways: sitting next to them, honoring their knowledge, understanding their isolation, making room for their shattered sense of safety. I began hoping that we—civilian and military alike—would come to respect how very far war has pushed them from the home base of "normal," and that we would exhibit enormous patience and extend tremendous grace for the time it takes them to find their way home. I came to see that we need to grapple with our own knowing that they can't ever get back across that line, rather than expecting them to easily rejoin the ranks of "normal."

Now, and for the rest of their days, they live with terrible knowledge.

Razor's Edge

While walking from the motor pool to the battalion offices, I bump into PFC Hernandez, who returned from Afghanistan less than a week ago. We sit at a picnic table outside the battalion building and chat while he smokes a cigarette and gazes at the sparse landscape surrounding the base.

"Gosh," he says, "this landscape is so damn flat. Bunch of brown, with mountains on the edges, huh?"

I nod, then wait.

"Reminds me of Afghanistan. Looked a lot like this."

"Really? Similar to this?"

Then I keep quiet. I don't press, I just stay right alongside him. Sometimes soldiers aren't even aware of what they're trying to bring up when they start chatting, but the subtleties tell me everything. I watch his face change to a kind of distant wistfulness, and his voice is thinner and tighter when he speaks.

"Yeah. It was like this. Seems like I never got used to it. I still feel a kick in my gut when I think about it. You just never get used to it."

"Never get used to what?"

"The damn tension. Never knowing what's going to happen. You live with it. It sits inside you. But it's wild. Any second of any day, you could be gone. That's intense. The adrenaline gets you through, makes you feel invincible. Sometimes I felt like I had X-ray vision. It felt like every second was ten minutes long."

Hernandez pauses, squints a little as he blows the smoke out of his mouth and shakes his head. "It's always there in your gut—that feeling that you're on some razor's edge, and in the next second you could be finished. It's weird to live like that, you know? Every damn day. And it doesn't leave you just because you come home. I still feel it. I still feel like I'm on that edge. You get used to it, and you can't really just let it go."

"So how do you deal with it, now that you're back?"

Hernandez laughs, gives a slight shrug with his shoulders. He's said enough for now, and he's ready to make it "no big deal."

"I go to the gym a lot. Keep busy. Don't let my mind relax too much. It'll wear off. I just have to get through this part where everything feels so . . . I don't know . . . 'off.' The bad part is, they don't really have anything for us to do right now—they want us to rest and relax. What a joke. You can't relax—it's not possible. So I find things to keep myself occupied. I think I'll rebuild the engine in my car. That'll take me a while."

Soldiers often have a good deal of free time when they return from combat, and while many go home to visit loved ones, others don't have anywhere to go, so they hang around and try to keep themselves busy. If they're working, their work schedules are more relaxed, as in Hernandez's case. We talk a bit longer before he has to go back to work, and I offer to meet with him again soon. He nods and thanks me, says he'll see how it goes.

After walking about twenty feet toward the battalion building, Hernandez turns around and comes back. "Yeah. I think I'll set something up with you. I think that'd be a good idea."

Music Man

At the third base I'm assigned to, my office is down a side hallway, off the beaten path of most of the battalion hustle and bustle. There are only two other offices on that same small hallway, and a few days ago SSG Hicks was assigned to the office next to mine. He's new to the battalion—a thin, pointy-faced soldier from Wisconsin, with a nasally upper-Midwest accent and a nerdy pair of glasses that look more like goggles. He tells me he got the glasses issued downrange because they were cheaper there, and "the best thing about them is they're safety glasses." When we introduce ourselves and chat for a while, I notice he has a habit of repeatedly tugging his unruly black hair into place while he's talking.

Hicks is the new reenlistment person for the battalion. He's awkward and stressed about his new position, nervous that he's expected to produce certain numbers in order to show he's being effective in his job. He tells me about all the "goodies" he can give to folks when they reenlist—duffel bags and backpacks with military emblems on them and other items, all similarly emblazoned. I joke with him that I'm going to sign up just to get some of the goodies.

Hicks strikes me as someone who could use some support and encouragement. He seems a little tightly wound by nature, making him feel his stress even more intensely. I notice that humor is a good way to connect with him, so as we spend our workdays focused on our various responsibilities, I keep my eyes open for ways to joke around with him so he'll feel more comfortable with me.

One morning while I'm sitting in my office, I hear rap music from somewhere nearby. I'm surprised. I've never heard any music being played in the offices. I walk into the hallway and follow the sound and arrive at Hicks's door. He's busy at his desk, his back to the door, and the music is coming from his computer. I figure this is my chance to tease him a bit and, I hope, to weave a little more connection between Hicks and me.

I stand at the doorway and try to look officious as I declare, "Oh no, Sergeant. No, no, no. This is *my* hallway, and in *my* hallway, *we don't play music. We work.*"

Hicks swivels his chair around to face me, looking worried and a little shaken. I continue.

"We're here to work, on my hallway! There's no time for *music* when we're *working*! No sir, not on my watch! We stay focused and busy. I'm telling you, this is *not* going to happen on my hallway. Now get that music turned off."

Hicks is new enough to the battalion that he's slightly unsure of my position. He knows I'm a civilian, but he's not sure what the counselor role entails here. Maybe I really do control this end of the hallway. Maybe there is some rule about playing music. Maybe I could report him to someone up the chain of command.

He reaches across his desk and turns the music off.

Still keeping my demeanor as serious as I can, I ask, "Now, who was that you were playing?"

"Eminem, ma'am." He's scooting back in his chair, and I can tell he's trying to read my face and get a feel for what's going to happen next.

"Eminem? Can you honestly tell me you think Eminem's going to help you get soldiers to reenlist?"

He looks at me for a moment, thinking he needs to answer the question, but then it dawns on him that my last question was a purely ridiculous thing for me to ask—he starts to smile, just a tiny bit at first, testing the waters, waiting to see if I'm going to smile, too.

I start laughing. "No, I'm just teasing. I'm fine with the music. I just wanted to start your day off with a little adrenaline rush." I wink at him for good measure, and his body suddenly relaxes in his chair.

"Good one, ma'am! Good one."

This small and silly exchange establishes a very solid bond between Hicks and me. In fact, over the weeks we share the hallway, he sometimes pulls harmless pranks on me when he gets the chance. One day, he closes my office door while I'm gone, locking me out—I didn't take my key since I'd left the door open—and then laughs at my predicament for a while before he produces the key to open the door. Another day, he takes my lunch; I accidently left it on my desk and then can't find it when I'm ready to eat. After fifteen or twenty minutes, right when I resign myself to buying my lunch at the DFAC, Hicks surreptitiously sets my "lost" lunch bag right in the middle of my open doorway, so I will see it the next time I look up from my desk.

He also starts stopping by my office when his numbers are down, when he's feeling unsure of his work, or when he feels homesick for Wisconsin and his large family back home.

I'm at the base for another few months, and Hicks is truly sorry to see me go when my assignment there draws to a close. I'm sorry to say good-bye to him, too. I ask him to play Eminem one more time for me on my last morning, and we both have a good laugh about the morning months ago when we were still getting to know each other. As I walk down the hallway for the last time, Eminem's "When I'm Gone" is playing nice and loud.

Marathon

Ms. Linnon introduces herself with an intensity that's a little shocking, leaning forward as she shakes my hand and making harshly direct eye contact. As she leads the way to the patio of the empty café where we've decided to meet, she says, "Let's sit over here."

She directs me to a specific chair at a particular table. I wonder about her need to be in charge, but then as we sit down her eyes quickly fill with tears, and the first words out of her mouth are, "Ma'am, I'm *desperate*. I need your help."

Settling her stocky frame into the chair, she flips her long auburn hair behind her shoulder on each side. She leans halfway across the table and begins to tell me about her soldier-husband who came back from deployment a changed man. Her formerly funny, warm, easygoing guy came back sullen and dark. He didn't talk, he scowled at her most of the time he was home, and he began to stay at work longer and longer as the weeks went by. She figured they'd get through it, but without warning he divorced her, and then spent three years taking the house, the money, and—eventually—their child. She told me she'd been shredded in one court proceeding after another by this man who seemed intent on destroying her in every way.

"I kept thinking he'd wake up and see what he was doing. I kept trying to talk to him, asking him to get help. I can't tell you how many times I tried to find some part of him that would remember how we used to be. But it was like talking to a stranger, someone so distant and 'gone' I could never reach him." Ms. Linnon seems like she's not breathing. She never looks away and never sits back in her chair.

Manipulating the legal system, he'd prevented her from seeing their young daughter for over a year by convincing the courts she was an unfit mother. Eventually, she got partial custody, but by then the damage was done. Her voice breaks as she tells me this. She's deeply anguished by the loss of that time with her little girl.

One day a few months ago, she tells me, after years of this brutal emotional and legal assault, her ex broke down sobbing and said he regretted everything he had done. He didn't want her back; he was living with a new girlfriend. He'd just had a moment of awareness. The next day, he was harsh and hostile once again. He's been diagnosed with severe PTSD and depression, but she sees no hope of his getting any real or ongoing help as his frantic need to be "fine" drives all his choices and erratic communications.

Ms. Linnon heaves a huge sigh and flips her hair back again. "It's three years down the road now. I'm working so hard to rebuild my life. I had to find a new job and rent a new place to live. I had to change all my banking and credit cards. Had to find myself a used car I could afford. It's been difficult. But I'm getting there. I still feel like I'm trying to get on solid ground. I still don't feel sure he's not going to surprise me with some sort of attack. But I'm doing better. Then last week, the worst thing happened."

Here, Ms. Linnon looks down at her lap for a long time, then clears her throat several times. She looks up, holds my gaze. "My daughter has tried to commit suicide a couple of times. She's a teenager now, and I'm scared to death. I didn't hear this from my ex. Friends of mine called me to make sure I knew Daniella was having trouble like that."

Ms. Linnon's eyes are wild with grief and fear. She's terrified that the lack of communication with her ex-husband means she won't know how badly her daughter is suffering until it's too late.

Throughout the forty minutes we've been sitting together, she's talked nonstop, and the words have come out in a torrent. Other than the one time she looked down at her lap, she's held my gaze the entire time to make sure I'm closely following every detail and every twist in her story. I meet her gaze and meticulously listen to each layer of agony. I offer her nothing, except words of validation: "I'm so sorry" or "That sounds terrible."

Clearly, she needs someone to understand the enormity of what she's gone through, but she also needs some specific ideas about how to help her daughter. We talk about getting a release so she can talk to Daniella's psychiatrist directly. Since Daniella prefers text messaging to talking, Ms. Linnon agrees to upgrade her own phone so she has one that can send and receive texts. We discuss ways for her to engage her daughter's father neutrally so he might be willing to share more information with her.

While she's clear and definite about all of the trauma she's endured, she's not bitter or vindictive. She's trying to move forward. She's trying her level best to understand that her ex-husband was severely changed by what happened to him downrange.

She's not completely forgiving yet, but she's well on her way.

By the end of our time together, her eyes are clearer, her resolve once again in place. She speaks with a steady voice when we part. "There'll be an end to this. I know there will. I just have to keep going until I reach the other side of it, right?"

I nod, and her tight hug tells me that her hopeful certainty carries her forward in this marathon of anguish and strife.

CHAPTER 13

"What are you going to do when you finish here?" asked Melissa, a civilian employee. She knew my time at the base was winding down.

"I'm going to a retreat center for a few weeks. I'm going to stay in a little cabin in the woods all by myself."

"Oh, you're going to *hate* that!" she said with absolute certainty.

Her reaction brought home to me just how successfully I'd done my job. Since she had seen me doing so much outreach and being so sociable, she truly believed I wouldn't like being alone and quiet, but I was starving for it. My passion and ease in relating to others were counterbalanced by a deep, introverted side to my nature.

At each base, I relied on predawn walks through silent neighborhoods to settle myself before I headed into the fray of daily communications. I was flooded with endless and immediate connections during my work hours, so whenever I arrived at a new assignment I sought out a neighborhood where I could walk each morning. Usually, I could walk right out the door of the hotel and wander up and down hushed streets. During one assignment where the hotel was in the midst of a commercial area, I drove three miles to a quieter neighborhood with tree-lined streets, a rippling lake, and rolling hills.

"You're *crazy*, getting up that early!" said my coworker, Magdalena, as we worked an information fair in the base gym during another assignment. Magdalena was one of my favorite colleagues. She was bright and funny, and she had a fierce dedication to soldiers and to the work we were doing. We were talking about our services and handing out brochures to streams of soldiers and spouses who passed by our table. Even though the fair meant extra work for us, we both enjoyed the switch from gray motor pools and battalion offices to the loud, colorful setting of the base gymnasium. Information tables were set up throughout the cavernous space, and the atmosphere was festive with free giveaways and flashy posters hanging behind colorful displays. In brief lulls in the flow of people, Magdalena and I chatted about our schedules.

"You can't imagine, Magdalena. Getting up at 5 or 6 a.m. is so worth it to me. I get some fresh air and peace and quiet before I talk to people all day long. Think of it as my sanity-saving device."

We both laughed, but I was serious. Those predawn walks were one of my most effective coping skills.

I typically spent evenings alone in my hotel room, trying to shake off the buzz from my day's interactions. Coworkers would sometimes urge me to join them for dinner, but my need for quiet was much greater than my need for more relating. It was in solitude that I felt restored and refilled. Many weekends I would simply lie on my hotel bed, reading a book and relishing the quietude. Sometimes I went out to explore the area surrounding a base. I was always in areas that were new to me, and when I started working on bases, I thought seeing new sights would be refreshing. I couldn't have been more wrong.

One weekend early in my new work, I went for a hike in some nearby mountains. Since hiking had been a real pleasure throughout my adult life, I thought I'd enjoy exploring new trails. As I walked along the dusty path that twisted and turned upward, I tried my best to enjoy the rock formations jutting into the sky and the deep ravines with creeks pouring through them. But I realized I was making an effort to enjoy the scenery when what I really wanted was just to rest. I turned around and went back to the hotel. As the months of military work unfolded, I learned I needed to shut down and savor stillness more than I needed to explore.

Someone once asked me how many soldiers I talked to during a day. I guessed that number could sometimes be a hundred or more, including very brief exchanges or simple greetings. Although it might be brief or casual, each encounter was crucial and merited my best attention, because even the most casual conversation might be an avenue for a soldier asking for my support.

I sat next to Kathy, a commander's wife, while she smoked a cigarette at the concrete picnic table outside the base convenience store. The sun was a little too bright and a little too hot for comfort, but since it was the only table around, we squinted at each other through the blazing sunlight. A soldier's wife had recently been harshly critical of Kathy's attempts to reach out and support spouses, so she wanted my input on her efforts.

When I got up from the table to walk back to the battalion building, I ran into a pudgy, reserved private who was new to the base. We talked for less than three minutes about how his day was going, but he showed up at my office the next day, asking for help. As I continued down the hallway to get back to my office, I came across a corporal who smiled and said her young daughter was doing well. The previous week, we'd talked about her daughter's struggle with the corporal's recent divorce. I was tracking literally hundreds of stories, far more than I would have been tracking in private practice.

At a different base, I attended a lunch meeting where I tried to help spouses iron out some difficulties in their support group. I walked back to my office, closed the door, and sat at my desk for a while. Snow was falling outside, and the warmth of the room felt embracing and comforting. I pushed my chair close to the desk, rested my head on my arms, and savored the few minutes of solitude before I pushed through the remaining hours of my day. I still had ahead of me a meeting with a commander to discuss some changes to the battalion calendar, three challenging sessions with couples who were struggling, and a briefing to give to about two hundred returning soldiers. I loved the variety and swirl of activities in my day. It also took its toll.

All of the calming things I did helped, but as the months went by, I realized the stress was piling up no matter how hard I tried to release it. The work was simply overwhelming. During my third assignment, I recognized I had to do more to get my heart fed, so I found a nearby animal shelter and volunteered to walk the shelter's dogs after work. Three times a week I'd finish work, change my clothes in my car, then drive to the small shelter that was tucked behind old warehouses on the busy highway.

Walking into the yipping, jumping, wagging scene of about twenty dogs in their runs was the highlight of my day. I picked Boomer on the first day, a black and white pit bull mix whose skinny tailed whipped back and forth like a crazy metronome. When we walked to the fenced field across the dirt road, Boomer looked back at me every couple of steps as if she wanted to make sure she was going the right way. As soon as she was off her leash, she'd tear off across the grass, racing the entire fence line of the field at full speed. She always put a big grin on my face.

Tiggs, an Australian shepherd mix with white, black, and gray fur and sky-blue eyes, wanted nothing more than to be chased. I thought of Tiggs as the shelter clown. After we romped for a while, I went back for KJ, a medium-sized, tawny-brown mutt with one ear that stayed cocked upright while the other flopped over toward her face. The dogs were elated to get outside, and their unbridled enthusiasm made me laugh every time. For my part, it meant companionship free of further conversation and the need to track verbal details.

The reality of my work was that for months on end, I saw no one who was personally familiar to me, no one asked me how I was doing (other than as a pleasantry), and no one truly *knew* me. I sometimes fell into long, yawning stretches of loneliness while doing the work I had come to love so much. While working at one base that bordered a wilderness area, I heard there was going to be a spectacular full moon one night, a supermoon, which meant that the moon would look enormous because of its closeness to the earth.

As the sun set and the sky began to darken, I drove around nearby neighborhoods to find a high, open spot where I could park my car and watch the moon rise over the mountains. I wound up one street and down another, and finally found a street that meandered along a high ridge with a clear view to the eastern horizon. I pulled over just as the sky darkened into a deep indigo blue.

A few moments later, a beautiful soft-yellow glow seeped into the eastern sky, lighting up the edge of the mountain range I faced. No moon showed yet, but I felt my anticipation grow as the shimmering glow intensified. A blazing white slip of light appeared at the top edge of the mountains, and the moon slid upward. As I took in the beauty of this luminous sight, I sunk into great sadness to be viewing it by myself; I didn't have a friend within five hundred miles of where I sat. Bleakness enveloped me and I stared at the moon with tearful eyes. I wondered if soldiers sometimes felt like this, far from home, looking up at a beautiful moon, their hearts tinged with lonely sadness.

All of the emotional and relational energy in my life was pouring into my work, and there was very little coming in to refill me. Once, a couple of friends drove several hours to have dinner with me, and they spent the night at a local hotel. The next day, we toured the little town next to the base, exploring museums and finding a great Thai café where we talked for a few hours. I took them on a tour of the base, showing them the building where my office was located. I was elated. For those couple of days, I was infused with a quiet contentment, soaking up their company and savoring what it felt like to be around friends again. But after they left, I fell back into loneliness. I felt profound nourishment from the work I was doing, but that was not the same as feeling a friend's hug or spending hours with someone familiar and comforting.

"Tell me about the base," my dad said, during one of our phone conversations. My dad was in his late eighties, and he *loved* talking about my job. He had been in the Army Air Corp during WWII and still remembered the texture of military life.

I was sitting in my hotel room, in an uncomfortably rigid chair, with my feet propped up on the window sill, the windows wide open to catch the evening's breeze. I looked out across the parking lot to the line of sad, scraggly little pine trees that separated the hotel property from the building behind it. My dad wanted to know what the base looked like, how the commanders ran things, and whether the troops were behaving themselves. (He always asked this last part with a teasing smile in his voice).

"I met the colonel today, Dad. He's been leading this brigade for two years; really great guy. We talked for about an hour."

"You met with a colonel for an hour? He must like what you're doing. Not too many colonels have that kind of free time."

I could picture my dad in his easy chair, with a blanket across his knees, pressing the phone tightly to his ear with a shaky hand, straining against his fading hearing.

"Well, actually, he wanted to talk about his concerns with his soldiers. Very savvy guy, Dad. Very alert to what his troops are struggling with."

Every week when I called my dad, I told him about things like the candy bowl episode and other funny exchanges I had with soldiers. His quiet chuckle on the other end of the phone was a great reward for the stories. While I couldn't tell him about particular soldiers I was working with, I told him lots of stories about the bases, different commanders, and the situations that I found myself in while doing my work.

"I'm proud of what you're doing," he kept telling me. He couldn't wait to hear the next story or listen to the next challenge I had run into.

These weekly conversations with my dad were something I treasured long after he had passed away.

The acknowledgment of my work and of soldiers' needs was something I frequently heard from people. Once, in between base assignments, I flew to South Carolina for a break. On the flight, I sat next to a middle-aged business executive, and we talked about his work designing containers for different kinds of beverages. He told me he'd gotten into that line of work after training as an architect, and we laughed when he said it must be the most unusual career path he'd ever heard of. After a while, he casually asked what I did for work.

"I'm a counselor. I work with soldiers on military bases, soldiers getting ready to deploy or just coming back from deployment."

He set down his soft drink, pushed it gently to the back of his tray table, and said, "Thank you for what you're doing."

"Well, it's a privilege, to tell you the truth. I really love it, and I feel like I'm doing something worthwhile." We went on to have a long conversation about his concerns for the troops.

"What do you do for work?" a smiling clerk asked in another encounter, as she rang up my purchases at the clothing store where I was buying a jacket and some warm socks for the winter chill that was starting to settle in outside. She was middle-aged, friendly, and genuinely eager to chat up her customers. Her charm bracelet jangled and clattered as she removed tags and refolded the jacket so she could slide it into the bag standing next to her on the counter.

"I'm a counselor. I work with soldiers," I replied.

Her hands stopped in midair. She placed the jacket back on the countertop. She tucked a lock of brunette hair behind her ear and looked thoughtful for a moment. Her face lost the look of chatty friendliness as she peered at me intently. "My nephew's in Afghanistan right now. I'm so worried about him. Darlin', I just want to thank you for helping those soldiers. I hope someone's there to help him when he comes back."

Once, I ran into a soldier in a grocery store who was wearing his uniform. I was used to seeing soldiers in uniform in all the stores near bases, but we were at least two hundred miles from any base. I asked him where he was stationed, and he said he was on orders to do some work with the National Guard troops nearby. We stood near the frozen food freezers and talked shop for a few minutes, talking about his work and discussing how long he had been in the military.

"So, you in?" he asked when he realized I was using military terms and referencing various bases.

"Nah. I work on bases all over the country. I'm a counselor."

"Oh man. Thank you for that. We sure need people like you around."

Another time, I was on a short trip in between assignments. I stopped to eat lunch at a local park and wound up watching a woman walk an adorable chocolate Lab puppy across a large grassy expanse. The pup was all tumbling gawkiness as he loped over to greet me. His owner was tall and thin, with bleached-blond hair and heavy makeup. She wore a bright-red Windbreaker over a dark T-shirt and worn jeans, and she laughed as the puppy stumbled over his own feet.

We started talking about her dog, and she asked me if I was from the neighborhood. When I told her I was on a break from working with soldiers, she mentioned her husband would be deploying soon from a base a couple of states away. It was the first time he had deployed, and she admitted she was really nervous about what it would be like for both of them. I asked if she knew of the counseling available to them through the program I worked with. She didn't, so I found a little scrap of paper in my pocket and wrote down information she could use to find the program on her local base.

It was consistently clear that *many* people worried about soldiers, wanted them to have support, and wanted to know that their needs were getting addressed. Yet it could feel awkward to be thanked for doing the work I felt so blessed to do. Soldiers often told me they felt unsure how to respond when someone thanked them for their service, and I felt something similar in moments when I was thanked for doing work I felt privileged and honored to do.

BALANCE

If I had asked soldiers what they did to keep their lives in balance, I imagine they would have burst out laughing. The question would have struck them as psychobabble, not connected in any way to the pressures and structure they lived in. Even posing such a question would have been a ridiculous faux pas, and the conversation would have died out right there.

But if I had asked them how they coped with being under a lot of pressure, I would have gotten responses that pointed directly at the issue of balance.

Soldiers have very little control over their lives, and the stress of that can throw things out of balance. Their work can be unpredictable and demanding, suddenly requiring them to leave for weeks of training, to work intensively alongside folks they don't necessarily get along with, or to show up before dawn for exercises. In a system that left him little recourse, one soldier told me that after he had upset his sergeant, he'd been assigned to the duty desk every weekend, even during a visit from his in-laws, who were visiting from another country after the birth of his first child. The harsh edge of frustration in his voice was unmistakable.

Another soldier told me deployment wasn't so hard to handle, but he described the strain of ramping up for deployment: training for long weeks out in the field, coming home for just a day or two, then heading back out for more training. "I gotta tell you, I'd prefer deployment to this schedule." The scenarios soldiers shared about having no control over their days were endless, and I'd find no semblance of balance in their descriptions.

Juggling a sense of responsibility to their families while being involved with their work duties was also highly stressful. So many soldiers I spoke with—both men and women—told me they never felt like they were available enough to their families. They worked long days, dealt with complicated work schedules, and often struggled with moving between the hard-edged tenor of the military work to the softer emotional needs of their family life. Accustomed to giving or taking direct orders, to being handed clearly defined tasks and operating in a strictly structured environment, it could be hard for them to gather a needy child into an embrace, have the patience for a tantrum or meltdown, or respond gently to a spouse feeling weary and overwhelmed.

While working on the bases, I watched many soldiers struggling to cope, trying to recalibrate their internal pressure gauges. Partying hard every weekend was how some endured the week. The base gym was usually full to capacity as soldiers worked out to work off stress. Target practice with high-powered rifles at the shooting range; outdoor sports like soccer, softball, or football; and avidly following favorite sports teams were popular ways to blow off stress. Numerous family activities were offered by services on every base, and each base had a mix of recreational facilities: movie theaters, golf courses, libraries, playgrounds, ball parks and football fields, bowling alleys, and arcades. Organizations for single soldiers offered specially planned recreational activities and trips.

The need to "find balance" is practically a cliché in American culture, but for the military personnel I worked with, this cliché was inherently paradoxical. Soldiers' highly structured, high-pressure environment makes a balanced state essential—even as it makes achieving such a state extremely difficult.

I Want to Come Home

The man and woman sitting in front me are strained, tense, looking anywhere but at each other. Both glance toward me with tight, pain-filled eyes. I notice in them that strange combination that sometimes presents itself under extreme tension: a bristly twitchiness combined with studied stillness. My office is very small, so they have to sit in chairs that are right next to each other. I'm guessing they'd be more comfortable with several feet of space between them.

Amy sits on the edge of her seat, her hands holding on to the arms of the chair, as if to anchor herself during the earthquake she's afraid might be rolling through. She's an athletic-looking woman with strawberry-blond hair pulled back in a girlish ponytail. Her shorts and tank top make it look like going to the gym is on her to-do list for the day. Paul, who's just returned from Afghanistan, is in uniform. He's slouching in his chair, his relaxed posture belying the tension I see between them. He's flipping his sunglasses open and closed, open and closed with his left hand, then resting them on his leg, not even looking at his hand's movements. When I ask what brings them in, Paul motions for Amy to start talking.

Amy starts by describing how hard it was to have Paul gone for so long. "I only got through the year by promising myself things would be fine once he got home. It was so hard raising Stefan by myself—he's a teenager, for Pete's sake! And managing the house and working and everything. Some days it felt like too much, so I just told myself, 'Wait 'til Paul gets home. Just make it 'til Paul gets home.' I mean, I was clinging to that to get myself through. I got so lonely I thought I was going to fall apart. I really did. I felt a little panicky sometimes. But I kept telling myself it would all get better when he got home."

"Sounds like it didn't turn out the way you thought," I say.

"Well, to be honest with you, he's not been warm and supportive at all. He's kind of distant. Like, distracted. I don't feel close to him, and I'm thinking he must not like being home. He doesn't act like he's glad to be back. I don't know what he feels. I wonder if he even loves me anymore. Maybe he's thinking about a divorce. We've been together seventeen years, but maybe he's thinking about leaving. I mean, maybe he even got interested in someone else while he was gone, one of the women in the battalion. I don't know. I can't tell. All I know is, it sure hasn't been what I expected."

Paul studies Amy very carefully as she talks. His manner is subdued, but sharply attentive. Occasionally, his eyes scan toward me to gauge how I'm reacting to Amy's account. I meet his eyes, but keep my face neutral: *I'm just gathering information.*

When Amy finishes, I ask Paul how he sees things. He quickly states he agrees with everything Amy's said.

"I know I'm distant. I know I'm not really as involved as I should be. I don't really know what's going on. I just feel like I'm behind a glass window or something. Everything feels surreal, and I can't really relate to anything."

I ask him how long he's been home.

"Five days, ma'am."

Our conversation then takes a turn. His description of his state and his recent return tell me we're dealing with something more than a simple communication issue between the two of them. I begin to ask him about his work during deployment.

"I worked with the battalion's communication system. I had to focus on tons of details, and most days I worked by myself. I hated that at first, but after a while I got used to it. And then I got to where I preferred it. It was a lot easier than dealing with a bunch of personalities.

So, pretty much, it was a year's worth of isolation. I kind of liked it, I guess."

When I ask him how it's been, being home, he sputters and has a difficult time articulating the experience of the past few days.

"I don't know how to describe it, ma'am. Everything feels confusing. I listen to conversations, and I feel like I can't quite track what's going on. I can't keep up with anything, can't figure out how to respond. I want to connect with Amy, but right now I don't know how. I feel sort of lost, I guess."

"I think I understand. Sounds like you're kind of disoriented. As you know, it takes time to adjust to being home. You'll have to give yourself more time. Ease into being here. Let your nervous system figure out what just happened."

Amy is listening to the exchange with rapt attention. As soon as I finish talking, her words slice through the room: "What about me? What am *I* supposed to do?"

She's upset, bordering on angry. "I've waited for a whole year. Am I supposed to just keep *waiting*? What if he's never going to feel like relating to me? What are we going to *do*?"

I let her talk for a while about her overwhelming fear. She's scared he won't find a way back to the feelings of closeness she's counted on in their marriage. I let her show me the unbearable pressure she feels to reconnect with Paul, so that her fear, sometimes panic, will calm down. We talk about the way she keeps turning that same pressure toward Paul, frantically pushing him to talk to her, be close to her—she's desperate for things to seem OK *now*.

"Is it working to pressure Paul? Does it make the two of you feel closer?"

I can hardly hear the "no" she says in response.

Amy's face now streams with tears, little rivers coursing down the broad expanse of her face. She's sitting in her worst fears. I glance at Paul and see helpless worry etched on his face.

"I honestly don't know what to do. I love her, but I don't *feel* anything. I don't want things to be bad between us, but I don't want to pretend with her. I sure don't want us to split up. I'm not thinking about leaving, but she doesn't believe me."

"I just wanted him to come home so everything would be OK," says Amy, her voice plaintive and defeated.

I look over at Paul, slouched even lower, looking sad and emptied. "I have a weird question for you, Paul. Do you actually *feel* like you're home?"

He shakes his head slowly.

"So, your body's here, but somehow you're not really home yet, right?"

He nods and then glances up at me. With tears in his eyes, Paul says, "I want to come home."

This is the moment where they finally start to meet. It's the moment when Amy understands Paul isn't withholding; he's doing his very best to *arrive*. It's the moment when Paul stops his struggle long enough to let Amy know how very much he wants to be with her.

I work with them a few more times, and each time they come to my office, they are lighter, happier, more connected. Amy's able to slow down, to wait for Paul to truly return home, and Paul finds himself more and more able to bring himself back home, back into his marriage.

Battles Back Home

CPT Grant tells me that when she came home from her year in Afghanistan, her house was trashed—holes in the walls, lamps broken, junk all over the floor. There was no food in the house and her young children—then five and six—seemed skittish and wild. The whole house smelled like cigarettes and beer. She found other women's clothes on the floor. Her husband swore up and down nothing had happened, but the neighbors told a different story: parties every night, the kids going hungry, him running wild while she was overseas fighting and sending checks home.

She found her car in the garage with dents in it. He had been driving her car since his got repossessed. When she left home, she had money in the bank; when she returned, she discovered she was thirteen thousand dollars in debt.

One night shortly after she got back, her husband got drunk, stole her car, and headed for Tennessee, where his family lives. He got picked up for DUI just across the state line. When the sheriff's office called at 3 a.m. to tell her he was in jail, she hung up on them.

Enough.

She's scared to be alone with two kids and a job that overwhelms her every day. But something in her isn't willing to fight battles back home after all the battles she's been fighting overseas. "I did my part downrange and I'm proud of it, but I didn't spend a year over there just so I could come home to someone who doesn't even respect me. My life here needs to feel balanced. He can leave. I'll figure it out."

You Wanted to See Me?

SFC (Sergeant First Class) Turner is one tough son of a gun. He's a big, gregarious guy who can often be heard telling his newest joke, but he's all business when it comes to battalion work: focused, sharp, and infinitely attentive to detail. He's glad I'm there to counsel and support his soldiers, but he's the kind of soldier who would never, *ever* consider coming to a counseling session himself. He wears his role and his rank with great pride, and sees himself as someone who can handle just about anything because "that's what a soldier does."

But lately I've watched him spend weeks and weeks navigating endless planning details, basically chained to his desk, day after day. He's in charge of logistics for several hundred soldiers returning from Afghanistan, sorting out transportation, housing, job assignments, and communications. Every time he gets things set up, the schedule changes and he has to start all over again. He's looking stressed and serious, his typical jokes and smiles have disappeared, and it's clear he's lost his usual balanced outlook. These days, if he speaks at all, it's down to one- or two-word exchanges.

I decide I should come up with a way to lower his stress level and help him regain that balance, even if he won't come in for a session. So the next morning, I walk into his office, take a seat in the chair right next to his desk, and wait for his attention. He's absorbed at his computer screen, so it's a few moments before he looks up.

"Yes?" He's busy and just wants to know what I need from him.

"Morning, Sergeant. You wanted to see me?"

"What?" He's totally thrown off.

"I understand you wanted to talk to me."

"Me? *I* want to talk to you? Not me!" he starts to sputter. He looks around to see if anyone's watching or has overheard.

"Well, Sergeant. I'm just saying, I heard that you really needed to talk. I just wanted to stop by so you could tell me what's on your mind."

Turner starts getting more and more flustered. He pushes his chair back and turns it at an angle, as if to get as far as possible from someone who might want him to share his feelings. His face is registering disbelief, and I can almost see his mind racing, trying to come up with an explanation for what's happening.

Before he can say anything, I talk to him in a soothing "therapist" voice. "It's OK, Sarge. You can talk to me. Just let yourself say what's bothering you. You'll feel better."

Now there are a few soldiers standing at Turner's doorway, listening to the exchange and starting to chuckle at his discomfort.

"You got something wrong here, ma'am," he protests. "It ain't me. No way. I'm telling you, I'm good. I promise. I don't need to talk!"

I keep a straight face. "Well, you know, I was surprised myself. But word got back to me you were hoping I'd stop by and you just didn't know how to reach out. I understand it's hard to reach out when you're struggling. I figured I'd make it easier. We can talk right here if that works for you."

The poor guy is nearly panicked. The soldiers in the doorway are slapping each other on the shoulder and holding their hands to their mouths to hide big grins. SFC Turner turns to them. "Montief, did you set this up? Baker?"

They're grinning like crazy. "No, Sar'nt, no way. Wasn't me."

He looks back at me, his eyes just a little wild. "Ma'am, I promise you, I'm good. I'm real good. I'm always good. Yeah, ol' Sarge is just fine. Don't need to be talking to a therapist. Honest."

Finally, I start smiling at him. "I know, Sergeant. You've just been looking so stressed, and I figured I needed to punk you a little bit."

He breaks into a wide, sheepish grin. "Oh. Oh goddamn. There for a minute I thought you were going to make me do *counseling* or something!"

He starts laughing and shrugging his shoulders, as if to reset himself after the frightening notion of a counseling session. The guys in the doorway are gleeful as they move on.

He looks at me and growls, "Now get the hell out of my damn office," but he's smiling, and he gives me a fist bump as I leave.

CHAPTER 14

At the end of each assignment, there was always a heart-twisting moment: going from deep, daily involvement with people I'd come to truly care about to an empty highway, all alone. This huge emotional gap made it difficult to adjust to my time off. I was always ready for a break and needed some deep rest. But when I was between assignments, I thought about all the soldiers who were also going from lives of intensity and daily sense of purpose and mission to the sagging emptiness of normal daily life. It was tough.

When I left one of my last assignments, I didn't realize how overwhelmed I had become by the work I had been doing. I knew I was tired, but weariness was typical when I got to the end of an assignment. Similarly to the way soldiers in a tense combat zone hyperfocus, I had been concentrated on the situations and immediate needs in front of me every day, offering support and steadiness where I could. I hadn't really taken the time to realize that I'd listened to innumerable stories of trauma and unrelenting sadness. But it wasn't the tragic stories that burdened me. Over the course of my career, I'd learned how to listen to heartbreaking stories in a way that kept them from getting "stuck" in my psyche and heart.

I realized instead that the constrictions of the job were creating a burden that was too heavy for me. The directive to do only brief, solution-oriented work was too stifling; the growing awareness that soldiers simply weren't getting enough help was torturous; the endless moves to places where I knew no one left me empty. Without knowing it was happening, my heart and my nervous system had gotten overwhelmed by helpless grief. It wasn't until I stepped out of the swirl of activity that the holes in my functioning—the rips in my inner fabric—opened up and the grief began to hit hard.

A few days after finishing an assignment at one particularly busy facility, I sat on a bench chatting with a dear friend I had traveled to visit. We sat next to a lovely little stream, talking about recent events in her life. After a few minutes, I realized I couldn't follow the conversation. I tried harder to focus on what she was saying, imagining I needed to listen more carefully. She was talking about things I was interested in, but it was as if she was speaking Hindi. The harder I tried, the scarier it felt: I couldn't follow her words. Instead, my mind was absorbed in remembering people, conversations, moments, experiences I'd had during my last assignment. It was as if some inner cup was finally full to overflowing and not one more drop of conversation was going to be wedged in.

I commented on it, and she kindly said she understood how tired I must be. I figured I just needed time to process the recent barrage of experiences, and then I'd be back on track. I went to a retreat center to rest, a place with little cabins tucked into dense woods. I thought the quietude would be restorative. Instead, my symptoms worsened. It felt like a cascading blackout was moving through my neurological system. The circuits had been overwhelmed, and now physical, psychological, and emotional grids were crashing, one after another.

I found that being around people was far too overstimulating. Trying to follow their conversation made me feel as if I was on speed or some terrible drug that rendered their words an incomprehensible word salad. But being alone was frightening and left me too aware of my inner state. I began to wake up several times a night with panic attacks, gasping for breath and trembling with terror. I told a friend I kept waking up "as if a gun had just gone off right next to my head," the jolt of panic dramatic and sudden. These awakenings left me shaking with adrenaline and unable to fall back asleep, my nervous system throbbing with amorphous fear. There was absolutely no apparent reason for the panic. Often, I could remember a pleasant dream I had been dreaming, but the moment of awakening was drenched in terror.

Although I had strong self-soothing skills, they were useless against this level of anxiety. The terror would sometimes ignite at completely random moments, and then I couldn't calm my system down. Day or night, the anxiety would suddenly wash through like a tidal wave, and I'd be pulled under until the wave passed through; it might take an hour or it might take a few days. Of course, then I lived in constant fear of the next wave, because I never knew when it might occur.

My raw and frayed nerve endings jangled with every sound, movement, light, touch, and thought, as if I had no skin to protect them. I struggled to shut down as much stimulus as possible, staying holed up in the retreat cabin and keeping to myself, trying to keep my days as quiet and as simple as possible. My whole nervous system was so dysregulated, not one single moment felt safe or tolerable.

Up to this point, I didn't have a name for what was happening. Although I'd worked with people with PTSD, I'd been so washed under by my symptoms that I didn't have enough awareness to put two and two together. One night, when the dreaded anxiety was starting to ratchet up again, I called Linda, a therapist friend who was also working in the military counseling program. Linda, who specialized in working with PTSD and trauma, knew the intensity of the assignments.

After talking with me for about ten minutes, Linda asked, "Are you aware you have secondary PTSD?"

"No. What do you mean?"

"Well, folks who work closely with trauma often get overwhelmed by the stories they've heard and the grief and helplessness they feel. They fall into a kind of PTSD; the trauma didn't happen directly *to* them, but they are affected by it. It happens a lot to first responders—police, firefighters, emergency room staff."

Yes, I actually knew about secondary PTSD, but since I was already in the throes of it, I wasn't coherent enough to recognize that's what was happening.

Linda began to suggest ways to help my system regulate again: slowing my breathing, looking around my environment to find something to focus on—a plant, a painting, a pitcher on the table—and small doses of interactions with trusted friends.

To ease my stress level, I asked Carrie, another dear friend, if I could stay at her house. I didn't feel like I could manage daily life by myself right then. Carrie graciously agreed, and I drove a few hours to stay with her.

During my next conversation with Linda, she told me, "Make your world as small as possible. Make sure there are no surprises. Keep everything—your thoughts, your focus—in the immediate present."

My world immediately shrank down to the size of Carrie's couch.

For the next few weeks I stayed as close to the present moment as possible. Anything more than that, and my anxiety would skyrocket. I only allowed myself to think about how I was doing in that present moment—no thoughts of how I was going to get through this, no musings about future assignments or the months ahead, nothing but how to manage my present state. Bit by bit. *Feed myself, get dressed, reach out to friends, ride the waves of anxiety.* Anxiety management. Period.

I spoke with Linda every couple of days and followed her suggestions religiously. I was so scared about what was happening, I clung to the recommendations she offered as if they were a life raft for my desperate psyche: I took long showers, lay on the bare ground, ate frequent small meals, reeled in my thoughts, paid attention to anything that helped soothe the dread.

One day Linda asked, "Are you able to run? I mean, are you physically able to run?" Yes, I could run.

"OK. Then just take off and run anytime you feel your system starting to ratchet up. When you feel the anxiety starting to rise, get up and run, even if it's only for a half block. Give in to the 'fight or flight' your system is cuing you into."

So I ran.

Anytime I felt a wave of panic start, I put on my sneakers, headed outside, and I ran. If it was nighttime and not safe to run outside, I sat in a chair and pumped my arms and legs, tears streaming down my face, until the anxiety began to ebb slightly. It felt as if I were bleeding off a tremendous, threatening pressure.

I stayed with Carrie for a few weeks, and then settled into my own place to try to address the ongoing inner struggle. I took long walks, started doing therapy with a therapist who specialized in trauma, and kept my world small and manageable, all in the hopes it would help me resettle my system. I had to face how much grief I'd sat with while listening to soldiers, how utterly helpless and hopeless I'd felt when I realized they weren't getting enough help. I faced the loneliness of working so hard while having no one familiar nearby. I let myself remember all the sad and heartbreaking moments in my work. I looked back at my own history and remembered times when overwhelming heartbreak and helplessness had crossed my path before. It was like laying broken pieces of my heart on a table and finding the ways to put them all back together into a whole.

It took months. In fact, it took well over a year of coping and struggling and doing intensive therapy before my nervous system began to quiet down.

During those long months, my world felt like it was constantly tilting on the edge of cracking. The stress and fear was enormous, but I slowly began to gain ground. Bit by bit, I taught my nervous system that life was manageable, that I didn't have to be on high alert all the time, fearing the overwhelming feelings would flood back through me. I had to shift down to a much slower pace of daily living, and I had to bow to the fragility I sometimes felt. It took some dedicated attention and a good deal of help from others, but I eventually got my system to calm down.

After I felt better and had resumed my work with soldiers, one aspect of my bout with PTSD made me profoundly grateful: I now knew even *more* organically what soldiers were talking about when they faced that particular struggle. Before I encountered this specific struggle in my own psyche, I knew PTSD only theoretically. I knew the textbook explanation, the list of symptoms and the recommended ways to address it. Now, I understood it on a cellular level. I was vastly more attuned when a soldier said, "I'm not sleeping too well," or "I feel kind of anxious," or the hundred other versions of "I can't cope" I heard while talking with soldiers.

The PTSD turned me inside out, but it also lit up in me a whole new world of understanding and compassion. I could recognize a certain look in a soldier's eyes. I could see the immense strain of trying to hold it together.

"How are you doing?" I'd ask.

And he'd invariably say, "I'm good."

But I knew he wasn't. And I'd slow down. And we'd chat. And bit by bit we'd wade into the inner world that was so hard to acknowledge.

PTSD AND MORAL INJURY

When soldiers deploy, there are theoretically three possibilities: (1) they come home, (2) they come home changed, or (3) they don't make it home at all. But in reality, only the last two options occur.

The "self" I was when I began the long journey of counseling soldiers by driving down an Arizona highway was long gone. The men and women I had spoken with, the stories they shared, the ways I'd come to care about them and the burdens they carried—these had changed me irrevocably. And they had made me much more acutely aware of how much change, trauma, and disabling stress soldiers (and their families) tolerate in their journeys down war's highways.

As of September 2014, there were approximately 2.7 million American veterans of the Iraq and Afghanistan wars.[11] According to RAND, a global policy think tank that was originally formed to conduct research and provide analysis to the United States Armed Forces, almost 20 percent of those veterans have documented PTSD and/or depression. Only 50 percent of those with PTSD seek treatment, and out of the half that seek treatment, only half of those get "minimally adequate" treatment.[12] Interviewed by *The Sun Magazine*, Edward Tick stated that the Disabled American Veterans organization puts the PTSD rate in modern wars at 100 percent.[13] In their view, the question isn't *whether* you get PTSD, it's how severe your case is.

By those unfamiliar with it, PTSD is sometimes mistakenly thought of as an emotional or psychological reaction to trauma. But although PTSD does have emotional and psychological impact, it is at its core a neurological reaction: one in which the nervous system gets stuck in—or is too easily triggered into—a hyperalert fear of impending danger. Without intervention, that heightened state of fear can last for decades—as it has with many Vietnam-era veterans. PTSD can interrupt sleep, muddle thinking, make raging outbursts common, and can make life seem utterly unbearable. PTSD can mean memory problems, depression, emotional numbing, loss of appetite, a feeling of being socially disconnected to a profound degree, and other devastating symptoms that vary widely from one veteran to the next.

There are effective treatments for PTSD, but the effectiveness of those treatments—and understanding this is crucial—varies widely from one person to the next. In other words, what works for one combat veteran might be completely useless to another.

I've talked with soldiers who found recounting their battle traumas to be relieving and helpful; other veterans have told me that retelling their traumas only made their symptoms much worse. One veteran told me he got a lot of relief from CBT (cognitive behavioral therapy), which focused on the fact that his thoughts and fears were irrational since he was no longer in combat. Another veteran felt CBT was so useless, he quit therapy and then felt hesitant to reach out for help again.

Related to PTSD—but distinctly separate—is the issue of *moral injury*, which has been defined as "perpetrating, failing to prevent, bearing witness to, or learning about acts that transgress deeply held moral beliefs and expectations."[14] Veterans who suffer from moral injury feel they participated in—or witnessed—something that violated their sense of morality deeply. As a result they lose their footing in a spiritual or soul sense. They no longer feel like they are worthy of solace. They cannot forgive themselves for these transgressions, and they are not able to recover their sense of belonging to a world that has clear boundaries about what is morally right and wrong. Through their combat experiences, they have walked into a tangled spiritual/psychological web that has damaged their sense of self. They are often left with irresolvable guilt, debilitating shame, and spiritual confusion—all of which make life feel like it's no longer worth living.

As with PTSD, there are ways to treat moral injury, but what works for one veteran will not necessarily work for the next. Helping our veterans heal means tending to them not as a homogeneous group but as individuals who have suffered and are suffering still, each in his or her own way.

Feeling Something

Over the course of a few weeks, I notice that when SPC DeLeon hangs around with soldiers from his company, he never takes part in the ongoing banter. In the training rooms and company offices where they work, there's a good deal of laughing and horsing around, but DeLeon always stands slightly off to the side looking somber and detached.

Now, he sits across from me in my office, clearly unsure how to begin talking about what's troubling him. I ask him some general questions to help put him at ease.

"So, where are you from?"

"Des Moines."

"How long have you been in?"

"Eight years."

"Been deployed?"

"Just once. Early on. Iraq."

"How'd that go for you?"

There's a slight pause. "It went."

"Something about that bringing you in to see me?"

He thinks about this for a moment. "I don't feel anything."

"Tell me what you mean. Help me understand."

His eyes are flat and his face is expressionless. He fidgets a little. "I don't know what else to tell you. I don't feel anything. Nothing at all. I *guess* it's from being over there. Since I've been back, I just feel numb or whatever. You could tell me your mom just died, and I'd just shrug and say 'sorry,' but I wouldn't really care."

"And being downrange, that's when you started not feeling things?"

DeLeon studies me carefully for a while. I see him stare hard into my eyes, sizing up whether or not I'll flinch or falter if he brings up whatever it is that has him jammed up inside. His stare doesn't waver as he tries to explain.

"OK. I'll tell you straight up. Here's what went down: over there, all the killing bothered me. When I got there, I was scared to death and I was shaking all the time, and I was just totally freaked out. The first few days, I thought my heart was going to jump out of my chest. I mean, I was a nineteen-year-old kid. I prayed—like, a *lot*. And I wondered what the hell was going to happen to me. I'd had a lot of training, but this was for real. Combat for fucking real. Every day, I was getting shot at and every day, I could get blown up. Every day, I had to kill people—or they were going to kill me. Every single day.

"I was scared out of my damn mind. But after a few missions I didn't feel anything at all. Everything went quiet inside. I was like a machine. I just did what I had to do. I did my job. Period. I didn't question it or think about it. Everything seemed perfectly clear. It was me or them, and I just had to make sure it was them. I was walking through all that fucking insanity, and all I had to do was keep shooting, so for the whole fourteen months that's exactly what I did. My weapon became my best friend, more important to me than anything else on the planet. As long as I had my weapon, I was good. Like, 'I got this.'"

"By the time I came home, I was dead inside. I was like a robot. My wife kept on me all the time about it. She said I was different, told me her funny, happy husband was gone. I used to be kind of a happy-go-lucky guy, always talking shit and punking people. She liked that in me, she did. But when I got home, I was tense, angry. I kept to myself. I stayed out in the garage all the time, working on my truck. It was like I was a million miles away. Pretty soon, she said she couldn't take it anymore. She took my kids and left."

DeLeon pauses. He's still staring at me with laserlike focus, holding my gaze and gauging my reaction to what he's saying. He waits a while before continuing, and the rest of the session passes, infused with his anguish and loss.

We keep meeting, and the war stories pour out of him. He continues to speak in a flat monotone about everything he saw and did while in combat. His voice never falters, never wavers. It never lifts with any kind of intonation or inflection. I lose count of the times he states, "I don't feel anything," as he talks about buddies who were killed or firefights that raged for hours upon hours. Trying to help him is like trying to thaw an enormous iceberg, melting the barrier he had to build around his heart, his humanity.

One day, he speaks about his family. He talks about his three kids and how hard it was to leave them for the fourteen months he was overseas. He tells me that when he came back, he didn't know them anymore. And they didn't know him, either. He remembers trying to do things with them. He went to the playground with them and took them to McDonald's, but everything felt awkward and "off." He had been home for only three months when his wife decided to walk away.

I ask DeLeon how old his kids are now, and he stops talking altogether. He stares at me as if I've asked him how many miles it is to the edge of the galaxy.

"They're seven, nine, and ten," he says curtly.

"Do you ever see them?"

He shrugs. "Not since they left."

"Do you *wish* you could see them?"

He glares at me. "What the fuck difference does it make if I *wish* I could see them? They're five states away with their mother."

His eyes are flashing and his voice is tight with warning, like a wounded animal growling to keep a hand away from a jagged bleeding gash. Since it's the only topic where he's shown any emotion, I decide to press.

"Did you enjoy being a dad? I mean, before you were deployed?"

"I always wanted to be a dad," he says, his anger replaced with sad wistfulness.

"Must have been hard, coming back and feeling like they didn't know you. Kind of like you'd lost them, too, on top of everything else—your buddies, yourself. Must've been tough."

He nods, but won't look at me.

"Maybe you were looking forward to getting back home, back to being a dad again. Maybe being around your kids, being a dad again was going to help make things OK. Even though you weren't feeling anything over there, maybe there was some hope that seeing them would turn things around."

I say all this tentatively, not wanting to spell out what's been going on inside him, but trying to give him puzzle pieces to sort through, so he can see if they fit as he's trying to make things whole again.

DeLeon has tears in his eyes now. He stares at the floor as if he could bore right through it.

"Well, it wouldn't do them any good to have a dad that can't feel anything, anyway. I'm no good to them," he spits out bitterly, his last defense against oceans of grief.

"Seems to me, they have a dad who misses them so much he can't let himself feel a goddamn thing."

DeLeon slowly doubles over like I just knocked the wind out of him.

He hides his face in his hands and half turns his body away from me. A torrent of grief pours through him. The sobs carry raw and broken shards of unbearable loss, loss that he'll never truly be able to tally up. DeLeon continues to sob, far past the time when our meeting is supposed to end. Finally, the torrent begins to subside and he straightens back up on the couch. He won't look at me. He pulls on the seam of his pant leg, rubs his finger along the crease, smooths the fabric with the edge of his hand until the crease disappears, then bunches the crease back into it and smooths it out again.

"You OK?"

"I think so. Yeah. I think so."

Thermostats

The thermostat in my counseling office cycles on, making a very distinct but barely audible *click*. Instantly, SGT Hubbard's gray eyes narrow and flick toward the thermostat, scanning the wall next to the door. His hands grip the arms of the chair, and his legs are so tense that he's almost lifted himself off the seat. His breathing stops as every cell in his body catapults into high alert. If you were standing behind him, you wouldn't have seen a single movement, but watching him carefully, I see each flicker and flare of trauma coursing through him in the milliseconds after the thermostat's click.

"It's the air conditioner," I say softly. "It's going to click on from time to time."

I try to get him to look at me, to anchor himself right here, right now. Staring at some mid-distant point between himself and the floor, he tugs on the cuffs of his uniform and shudders. "Thank you, ma'am." His eyes move to my face for just a moment, then back to the thermostat again, then back to me.

I nod in response: *We're in this together.*

It takes a few minutes for his breathing to settle down and for his eyes to stop flicking in that direction. He's been home two days.

Hubbard's talking to me about the stress of trying to keep his men safe while downrange. Bringing all of them back home was a task he took supremely seriously. Although he returned home with his unit intact, he's still struggling with the hyperalert state he kept himself in during the long months they were in combat. His mind goes over and over decisions he made that might have been dangerous. He examines again and again the hours when his soldiers were on patrol. He can't stop considering and reconsidering the situations, the responses, the choices.

I let him go over and over the hundreds of choices he faced as a leader. These are not things he would dream of discussing with his soldiers. He knows his role: being clear, decisive, and steady. But he got so acclimated to the enormous responsibility and the hypervigilance it required that he doesn't know how to shut it off.

During one session, he talks about a night he's mentioned before: "Then there was the time we were on night patrol. We were up on a ridge, like sitting ducks. I couldn't see everyone and the radios weren't working. I was pretty sure we were OK, but I couldn't confirm. Until everyone was all accounted for, I . . . well, I . . . I felt kind of edgy and worried."

Edgy and worried. For any other person, those words probably mean a slight uptick in anxiety. For him, they indicate a roaring sense of dread that scorched his insides like wildfire and left his nerve endings charred with fear. Any event he tells me about is just one out of hundreds he tolerated during the past year that left his nervous system scrambled and seared. Now, a slight movement out of the corner of his eye seems like a dire threat. An unfamiliar person might be a deadly enemy; the click of a thermostat could mean sudden death. Normal little flickers of life get translated by his wary system into crazed fears of survival.

He's desperate to find ways to calm down, but his nervous system refuses. It might be logical to relax now, but the nervous system that kept him and his men safe is entirely unconvinced the danger has passed.

"I've always been pretty laid-back, but I'm on edge 24-7. Even when I sleep, I feel like my system is on high alert. Sometimes I wake up in the night with my heart racing and adrenaline running through me, but I don't even know what woke me up. And I feel jumbled a lot in my head, like I can't quite sort things out clearly."

He's describing PTSD symptoms more clearly than any textbook. He says it feels like being on a bad drug trip that he can't get off of. He's now at the mercy of a ragged, tortured nervous system that got lost along the way to keeping him safe.

"I can't stop replaying things. You know, those moments are over, but I can't stop reviewing them and thinking about them. Sometimes, I can't even track what folks are saying, I'm so busy in my head with what I'm remembering."

His mind's like a machine stuck on replay, his ability to attend to present moments greatly impaired. Without intervention, his whole system could stay in this mode for years to come. I reassure him his symptoms are familiar, even predictable. We work together for many weeks, me listening to the stories that need to be told, him learning to focus deeply on his body, tracking the spikes of energy that tell him when something needs to be released, discharged, calmed. It's slow going, but little by little he starts to function in his familiar zone again.

I know we've gained some ground when he chuckles one day during a session, something I've not heard him do the whole time I've been working with him. I think his inner thermostat might be finding the right setting again—not the setting for the blast furnace of war, but the more comfortable, cooler setting for home.

The One Left Behind

We've chatted for nearly an hour before SGT Devereaux feels comfortable enough to say, "Hey, I've got a funny story for you."

I'd been working with soldiers long enough to know their "funny" stories often mask a tinge of underlying pain.

Devereaux and I are standing close, facing each other in his tight closet of an office. He's a large, solidly built guy, and although his shaved head and tattooed body lend a tough-guy quality to his look, his voice often has a soft thoughtfulness threaded through it. We chat when I make my rounds through the battalion offices where he works, but we've never had a longer conversation. Until today.

"So, yesterday I was walking across the parking lot over at the PX when a car backfired, really, really close. Before I know it, I hit the deck, crouching down behind a car in the parking lot and looking for incoming rounds. My heart's pounding and I'm freaking out. I'm feeling like I'm about to get blasted into nowhere.

"Then I realize, *Oh, that's a car.* So I stood up and brushed myself off. There was a civilian walking by. She looked at me *really* strangely and said, 'Are you OK?' I told her I was fine. But I must have been shaking for the next half hour."

His chuckle at the end of the story is strained and a little off-key.

"I never know when something like that's going to happen. I've been back almost six years now, and . . . you know . . . I still take cover like that."

He shrugs his shoulders as if it's no big deal, but the look in his eyes has just enough pleading in them to let me know he wonders if he's a little weird, doing something like that.

"What else?" I ask evenly.

"What else, what?" Devereaux shifts nervously on his feet. His shoulders are suddenly completely still. Any sense of joking around and telling funny stories has disappeared.

"What else do you do that's like that?" I keep my voice casual, with a thin veneer of chatting in it, but I'm opening the door as wide as possible, wanting him to feel free to tell me anything—no matter how weird or embarrassing or confusing.

Devereaux's blue eyes are suddenly skittish, flickering around. His chest heaves with a big breath, and he blows the air out of his mouth like he's pumping up a life raft.

"OK. Um, I sleep with my gun on my nightstand. I can't sleep if it's not there. I finally got myself to stop keeping it loaded. But the magazine has to be right next to it. If I wake up in the middle of the night, I have to check and make sure it's still there, or I feel like I'm going to go crazy."

He looks over at me to gauge my reaction. I look back at him with pure patience and steadiness. *Tell me the rest,* my look says.

He takes another deep breath.

"Everyone sees me here at work, smiling and happy. They all think I'm fine. Yeah . . . they . . . they think I'm fine."

Since he repeats this, I take it as a clue: *please don't think I'm fine.*

"I drive a different route to work every day. I can't shake the feeling that someone might be tracking me, gunning for me."

His words start to tumble out faster now.

"I look over my shoulder all the time. I mean, *all the time*. I never relax. I can barely stand to go into stores, and I catch myself checking the roofs of buildings for snipers. I drive close to the center of the road when I can, so I don't take a chance on something being hidden near the side. My wife says the church bells near our house are a real soothing sound to wake up to in the middle of the night. But when I wake up, I'm panicked. It's the only way I ever wake up—so damn terrified, wondering what's wrong. Like I'm locked and loaded before I'm even awake.

"I never leave the house except to go to work. I just can't. A buddy invited me over to his house for dinner a couple of weeks ago. I told him I'd come, and I *wanted* to go. But when the time came to head over there, I just couldn't do it. I freaked out, had to stay home. I didn't even call to let him know I wasn't coming. It's just too weird."

I keep nodding, wanting him to just let the words, the stories, the pain, spill out freely. Every part of me communicating: *tell me more*.

Devereaux stops for a long time. I can tell there's a story he doesn't want to speak. Several more deep breaths come and go. His voice softens and drops into a pained quiet. "You see, over in Iraq there was one kid in my company that I'll never forget. He was just nineteen, full of life. A joyful kind of kid, you know? Skinny black dude from the Deep South—real intense Southern. I mean, that guy had a drawl and a half.

"He'd gotten into some trouble with the commanders, just being a punk, really. I pulled him aside and talked to him, told him to settle down and let the Army work for him. We talked about him making a career out of it. Every so often, he'd get these care packages from home, and he'd act like a little kid at Christmas. He'd get excited and dance all around and show everyone what he got. Goofy, but sweet, you know? We got real close, and I felt like I was kind of watching out for him."

Devereaux's eyes are watery now. His breath is ragged and his voice sounds choked.

"He went out on patrol one day, and he never came back. Roadside bomb just blew his unit's truck right out from under him. The guys who were with him were hurt, but . . . he was gone. I remember feeling like something in me went dead. Not a kid like that. Not a kid who was funny and goofy and so alive. And so goddamn young. It just isn't right. I could never make sense of anything after that."

When Devereaux looks up at me next, his eyes have gone flat, as if any bit of coping he'd cobbled together since then has suddenly left him, and he's now stranded in a searing desert of grief. He shakes his head, keeps looking at me, can't continue talking. We stare at each other and let the moments just open up in silence, honoring one soldier gone too soon, and honoring the one left behind.

CHAPTER 15

At one base, a base where soldiers would soon return from a year's deployment, I started an assignment that took me deeper into the heart of the military spouses' world. For a couple of months, I worked primarily with the spouses who were anxiously awaiting their loved one's return. While I'd worked with spouses before, this assignment immersed me fully in their concerns: aching loneliness, tremendous reunion anxiety, and fierce, illumined dedication to those who were fighting on the other side of the world.

Shortly after I arrived at the base, I helped staff a weekend spouses' retreat, where the wives attended workshops designed to help them get ready for the soldiers' return. Many bases have a number of male spouses and many dual military families, but at this small base the spouses were exclusively female. The retreat took place at a hotel near the ocean, a relaxing setting for discussing anxieties and challenges. The beach's gentle curve arced outside the vast windows of the conference room, and most of the rooms had balconies that looked out over the ocean's expanse. The wives sat in small groups to discuss topics and share insights.

During the workshops, the chaplain offered exercises that helped the wives identify the things that made their marriages strong. They took notes on what might help them communicate better. The chaplain outlined suggestions from a workbook on improving relationships, but I noticed the atmosphere got much livelier when there was open discussion and the wives got to talk about the concerns that were most pressing for them.

"When should I tell my two-year-old that her daddy's coming home? How much lead time should I give her? And what do I do when the schedule changes and he doesn't arrive on the day I promised her he would?"

"I'm nervous about seeing my husband. When we talk on the phone, he sounds . . . different."

"I don't know how he's going to fit into our family. The kids and I have pretty much gotten used to our own rhythm."

"I've changed so much, being on my own this year. I don't feel as needy as I used to. I kind of like it, but it's kind of scary, too."

"We were only married a few months before he left. I'm scared we won't even remember each other."

The chaplain and I offered suggestions, and they eagerly offered each other ideas for managing the challenges. Some of the wives had been through several deployments and had accumulated a lot of experience in dealing with the tensions of reuniting marriages and families. As I listened, I faced my ignorance of what it meant to be married to a soldier. The complexity and dedication they embraced for the love of their soldiers was impressive, a rare and unique challenge.

During lunch in the dining hall, sunlight flooded in through the soaring windows overlooking the beach. We passed big bowls of salad and spaghetti, and talked more about how to face all the changes and decisions looming in the next few weeks. I could barely eat with all the conversations that were happening, but I was grateful to get a better sense of what they were grappling with.

"How do you manage?" I asked Trina, a captain's wife who had two kids under the age of four. She was a perky, delightful person to talk to, and she seemed well liked by the other spouses. Her husband had been deployed five times.

"I love him," Trina replied, as the bowls were passed for a second round. "I'm so proud of him and what he does, and it means the world to him. Chris absolutely loves being a soldier, so I'd never ask him to do anything different. Do I wish he could stay at home? Of course. But if doing what he loves means he has to leave sometimes, then we're going to deal with that."

Delores, a rather quiet Hispanic woman with many years as a military spouse, leaned in from across the table. "I know what you mean, Trina. It's so hard, but if you love them, why in the world would you want them to quit? I'd support Dave until the end of time if this is what makes him happy."

"It's a lot to put up with, though." This was Rachel, a pretty young wife who had been married to her soldier-husband for four years. "It's not like the Army really thinks of the family. It seems he's 'on call' for them, and we come second. I'm glad he's doing what he wants, but I sure resent it sometimes."

The conversation continued through lunch, with everyone around the table talking about how they managed the loneliness and the worry. As we started stacking our empty plates and reached for dessert, Cathy chimed in. "I'm sorry, but I don't think civilians can ever really understand it. I think they figure we shouldn't put ourselves through this. But being in the military is a really good life. Jack and I both love the Army. It provides for our kids, we get to see the world, and it paves the way for them to have a good life. We're well taken care of. Even when he's away, there's support for me and the kids. I couldn't imagine doing it any differently."

"I could imagine doing it differently!" said Theresa. "I'd love to feel like he's married to *me* and not to the Army! Most of the time, I feel like I don't have his full attention. He's always thinking about his job and which training he has to do next. We don't have kids yet, and sometimes I'm not sure I want kids if they'd end up feeling like their dad's not there for them." There were understanding nods in response.

Noni was a young wife, in her early twenties, who had been married for three years. She was struggling through her first deployment. "The hardest thing for me is just not knowing if he's OK. I try my best not to think about it too much, but there are days where I feel like I can't stand it one more minute. I just want him to be here and be safe. I can't help worrying. Sometimes I know when he's out on a mission, and until I hear from him again, it eats me up."

"Me, too!" said Serena. "I try to keep myself busy. That's my one big coping skill. But I don't think I can ever explain what it's like to have to go through that over and over again. It's really the worst part, isn't it?"

I saw lots of nodding as I looked around the table. It was time to go back into the afternoon workshop, but I left that lunch table with a different heart. In my private practice, I'd worked extensively with couples, but I began to understand—very clearly—the level of courage these women sustained during their husbands' deployment. It occurred to me that few civilians knew what it might be like to manage the intricacies of a marriage and a family while on their own for a year. These spouses weren't simply separated; they were separated while one of them faced life-threatening situations, every day, far across the world. Some of them had been, for all intents and purposes, single parents of five or six children during their husbands' deployments. Other spouses were as young as nineteen or twenty. They didn't have a lot of tools for managing relational stress. Some were from rough backgrounds and had been raised in unstable homes, without any examples of how to work through difficulties in a marriage.

Through all the exchanges I had that weekend, I saw that these complicated layers of stress, courage, and heartache were all a part of the reality of being a soldier's wife. Rather than talking with one soldier or spouse or couple, as I usually did, the weekend gave me the chance to be fully immersed in the spouses' side of the story, and their side of the story landed in my heart with great impact. I had a lot to think about as I drove back to my hotel room near the base.

I put my things away and went out for a long walk through a nearby neighborhood, up one street and down the next, as the sun went down, thinking about all I had heard over the weekend. In my work with soldiers and spouses, it took time to integrate what I came to know each time an experience broadened my understanding or further opened my heart. With an experience like the spouses' retreat, I wanted to absorb the spouses' perspectives and experiences, so those would inform my work going forward. I had a better grasp now on the dedication it took to endure deployment, the loyalty and pride the spouses felt for their soldiers, the toll it took even when they understood the sacrifices.

As I walked that evening, I felt grateful to the military spouses who had carried the burden of having their beloved partners sent off to war and who had shared so much with me about their lives.

As part of my work to prepare spouses for their soldiers' return to this base, I had been asked to give a workshop at a base's reunion fair. The fair was scheduled to take place just a couple of weeks before the soldiers returned, and the spouses were wired with excitement. When I asked the organizers which workshop they wanted me to offer, they looked at the list of topics they could choose from.

"What about this one?" Ms. Kennedy, the lead organizer, pointed to a workshop on "Reigniting Sexual Intimacy." I agreed. While working intensively with couples over the years, I'd gotten very comfortable discussing the intimate aspects of their relationships, so the workshop would be well within my scope of expertise.

On the day of the fair, I spent the morning in various workshops helping other presenters. In the afternoon, when it was time for my workshop, I walked into the large classroom where it would take place and was surprised to see that there wasn't an empty chair in the room. In fact, wives had squeezed into the room and were standing along the back wall. We spent the workshop discussing their greatest fears about feeling like strangers with their spouses, and we talked about the best ways to get through feeling out of sync in their intimacy (patience, and lots of tolerance for awkwardness). The spouses were frank and open, and they joined in with ready laughter as they spoke about their concerns.

I admired the way they discussed the vulnerabilities they faced. I couldn't help wishing the soldiers were there, too. I was sure they carried their own anxieties about the intimate aspects of their relationships. Repeatedly, I'd seen that spouses were hungry for help and support, and I was glad they had workshops, retreats, fairs, and classes for the marriages burdened by deployment separation.

Just a couple of days later, I walked past the battalion's conference room and heard the chattering noise of multiple conversations coming from inside. I was curious about what was happening, so I stuck my head in the door. All the conference tables that usually formed a large U-shape in the middle of the room for command meetings had been pushed together end to end to form one long line that ran the length of the room. A line of eight or nine battalion wives filled small paper bags with travel-sized bottles of shampoos, lotions, shaving cream, and soap. They walked along the long row of tables piled high with hundreds of bags lined up on the tabletops, working like a well-oiled machine as they filled the bags with razors, face towels, energy drink powder, and coupons for discounts at movie theaters and restaurants.

"What the heck are you all doing?" I asked.

"We're getting the welcome-home bags ready," Sadie said. Sadie was the leader of one of the family support groups, and she worked tirelessly to reach out to help the soldiers and spouses. She'd been married to an officer for nearly twenty years, had lived on several bases, and easily assumed leadership of the spouses when things needed to get accomplished. Her wild red hair and wilder, colorful manner of dressing stood in contrast to the "all business" attitude Sadie adopted for projects. "We've got three hundred bags done, and only two hundred and fifty more to go. We're on a roll!"

I laughed, and stayed to help out. Denise, another take-charge wife, told me they'd spent the morning making up the beds in the barracks for the single soldiers. I knew Denise's five children kept her endlessly busy at home, but she was so willing to help others.

"How many beds did you make?" I asked.

"Oh, I think it was just under three hundred," she said with a tired grin on her face.

"You all just made three hundred beds!" I stared at her in amazement.

"Oh, that's nothing," said Renata, who was standing next to Denise. Her soft-green eyes danced with an impish flicker. "Think about it. We had to launder all those sheets—and the towels, too. We left towels in each room for them. You know, they won't have access to their bags for a day or two when they get back, so we just want to make sure they have the necessities for those first few days."

I was stunned. I simply hadn't been aware of how much work it took behind the scenes to make sure soldiers had soap and clean sheets and razors. The women chatted and laughed as they worked. They wanted their soldiers to feel welcomed and embraced upon their return and were glad to do the grunt work of making that happen.

From spousal retreats to assembly-line work in a conference room, my grasp on the basics of military life kept expanding. I imagined some people wouldn't *want* to know all this, but I did. I wanted to know as much as I could about their lives. The passion I felt for my work grew as my compassion expanded.

SPOUSES

Military spouses have a unique and complex position in the military culture. They are relied on for support and patience while their spouses work, train, deploy, and return. They often function as single parents, most of them will move many times over the course of a military career, and many will look on their contribution to their military spouses' work with great pride. Indeed, the military spouse also serves. In light of all this, it's clear that the spouses' need for support is unique. To respond to this, there are family support groups on every base, spouse support groups on many, and most spouses in the command structure take a special interest in supporting the spouses in their unit, battalion, or brigade.

Since civilians have so little access to the insights and perspectives available only to those who have walked in the spouses' shoes, military spouses miss out on the support and compassion soldiers often receive from their fellow troops. There is a tender complexity to their position.

One spouse told me that when civilians say she "chose" the military life (implying she shouldn't get any sympathy for the burdens of it), she feels strangely blamed. "I didn't *choose* this military life—I chose my partner. I married my best friend and I'm supporting him in his career, just like other spouses do." She bristles at the implication that she knew what she was getting into when she married him, believing that none of us *really* knows what we're getting into when we marry.

Rather than being one homogenous group, the military community (and the spouses' community) is incredibly diverse—religiously, politically, ideologically, professionally, and ethnically. Just like any other small community, bases have their fair share of gossip, backbiting, and rumors. On some bases, the spouse support network functions beautifully with a tight, inclusive group of husbands and wives; on other bases, the different factions in the community don't get along.

When there is friction between two partners, deployments can be especially difficult. Different ways of coping with the stress of separation might cause fractures in a relationship to widen, and managing households and "single parenting" in the face of that kind of divisiveness adds stress.

One wife told me that while her husband was deployed, she found reserves of resilience in herself that she never would have accessed otherwise—she took over managing the finances, home repairs, parenting, and running the household—and still managed to create very close bonds with the other spouses on the base.

"While deployment is the hardest thing imaginable—being separated and not knowing if he's safe—it's also the thing that made me into a better person. I have to remember that." She laughed and told me both she and her husband felt like they had the harder assignment during deployment. "I dealt with it all pretty well, but seeing my kids' sadness was the worst thing to deal with. They just missed their dad so much."

Diversity also runs through the political views of military members and spouses. "I think civilians have a very hard time separating the service member from politics. My husband's service isn't about politics or ideology—he just really believes in being of service to his country," one spouse stated. She felt "branded" by the assumption that she and her husband must agree with the political forces that sent him to war, when the truth was that he would have placed himself on a different end of the political spectrum.

Referring to the priority of military demands in her husband's life, even while stateside and assigned to a home base, one spouse said, "I was able to deal with this whole military thing better once I realized the military always comes first. Always." She was referring to the lack of control her husband had over his schedule, the ever-changing demands on his time and attention, and the immediate response expected if and when those demands arose. Her husband was sent for trainings, sent into the field for exercises, and sent on deployments; he was also required to report to his unit at a moment's notice, if need be.

While civilians might unconsciously picture a woman when they think of military spouses—and many of the spouses I've referenced here were women—in fact, 7.5 percent of military spouses are men,[15] and 6.5 percent of active duty service members are dual military (both husband and wife are active duty).[16] Male spouses sometimes say they feel like the "invisible minority" in military culture. At one small base I was assigned to, there was one male spouse and nearly two hundred female spouses. I met several dual military couples during my years on bases and was genuinely impressed with the juggling they did to make each career thrive at the same time. They sometimes had families to raise; those without children still juggled competing demands for their time and attention.

Military support services for spouses have grown tremendously in recent years, and groups outside of the military have also grown with online chat or support groups, newsletters, and Facebook pages. SpouseBuzz and Military Spouse are two examples of online organizations that are vital and vibrant gathering places for members to find resources, information, connection, and interaction.

Don't Leave Me with Her

Maria comes into my office looking distraught and slightly in shock. Her flowery, brightly colored summer dress is a dramatic contrast to her stern, anxious face. She drops her thin frame into the chair across from me and begins to chat about the suddenly warm weather. Although I don't know Maria, I know she's not here to talk about the weather. When she called earlier in the morning asking if I could see her as soon as possible, her voice flooded with relief when I said I would work her into my schedule.

When I prompt her to tell me what she'd like my help with, she says, "This is a little weird for me. I've never felt like I needed to come in and talk to anyone before. I don't really know where to start."

I ask her if her husband has just come home with the rest of the battalion, and she nods silently, any hint of casual ease now wiped from her countenance. Her face drops into an expression of solemn tension.

"How's it been going?"

"Well, I thought everything was fine. I mean, Arsenio's been deployed before, so we kind of know there's going to be some adjustments when he gets back. But this time isn't like before. He's totally different this time. I don't know what to do."

As Maria tells me this, her voice is markedly quieter than when she was chatting about the weather, as if someone has suddenly turned the volume down on this scene. She's holding the hem of her dress in one hand and keeps twisting it as she talks. Her eyes are slowly filling with tears, and she looks out the window as she heaves a big sigh.

"I can't really tell what's going on with him. I don't understand."

I ask her to tell me what's making things so difficult. She puts a hand in front of her mouth and coughs slightly.

"Last Saturday, we needed to go shopping, and we took our three-year-old, Cassie, with us. I found what I needed and was ready to pay for it, so I left Cassie with my husband and walked over to the cashier. Before I could even pay, I looked up, and Arsenio was coming back toward me really fast. He was pushing Cassie along in front of him, hurrying to get to me. Arsenio looked awful. I didn't know what happened. Arsenio pushed Cassie over to me, and then disappeared.

"I finished paying and went outside to find Arsenio. I saw him standing off to the side of the parking lot, and the way he looked scared me. He was shaking and teary, and he was lighting up one cigarette after another. For a long time he wouldn't even talk to me. Finally, he said, 'Don't leave me alone with her. It freaks me out. I started to have a panic attack.' I don't think he was angry, he was just freaked out. He turned away and just kept staring at the woods, smoking. He wouldn't talk to me the rest of the day."

Maria falls silent, a little lost in remembering the incident. "What happened to him? What do I do?"

I ask her if she knows anything about what happened downrange with Arsenio.

"He won't really talk about it. He just says things got pretty bad and I don't need to hear the details."

I nod and offer the possibility that he's trying his best to protect her from some horrible stories.

"But what do I *do*?" Her voice is begging for help.

"Maybe take things slower? Even though he doesn't tell you the details, you see how hard it is for him to adjust. Maybe you can stay close by when he's with Cassie. Off to the side, there if he needs you. Maybe you can do little things like hand him a toy to hand to her, or make sure to include him when you and Cassie are talking. Little things. Arsenio just needs more time to find his way back to being a dad again. Does that make sense?"

Maria nods, but she still looks rattled, uncertain.

She asks if she can come in again soon.

Going to Work

As we stand in the hallway outside the conference room, SSG Henderson and I start chatting about the reintegration briefings we're attending. In the midst of our conversation, her cell phone rings. She glances at it and says, "It's my son's school." She turns away slightly as she speaks into the phone.

"Everything OK?" I ask, as she closes her phone and slips it back into her pocket.

"Well, it's my boy, Trey. He's five and they tell me he just hauled off and hit a kid in his class. I have to go meet with the principal and his teacher after lunch." She shakes her head in frustration, and rolls her eyes. Henderson's tall and thin, with beautifully rich ebony skin and dark eyes that are very expressive. She had told me she was a track star in high school, and I can still see the lithe, strong confidence in her movements. Her smile flashes brilliantly when she's joking around, but as she speaks now, there's a definite line of worry etched across her forehead.

"Sorry to hear it—is that typical for Trey?"

"Not at all, not at all. But you know, I just got back last week, and it seems like he's kind of out of control. I hate to say it, but this is the second time in a week he's hit one of his little friends. My husband and I try to talk to him. We tell him he has to use his words, but I think he's just kind of wound up or something. I really don't know what to do."

A bell rings, indicating it's time to go back into the conference room.

"Hey, listen, next time I see you, let me know what happened, OK?"

We part ways and head back to our seats.

Two days later, I run into Henderson in the hallway of the battalion building.

"Got a minute?" I ask her.

She nods and grins, knowing the question I'm going to ask.

"How did it go with your son the other day?"

Henderson bursts out laughing. "It went great. Well, not the meeting at the school. That was super intense. But you'll never guess what was *really* happening with Trey. The morning after that school meeting, I got ready to leave for work, and I told him, 'OK, buddy, Mommy's going to work.'

"I say that every morning, just before I head out the door. Anyway, I was holding him when I said it, and I noticed his face changed—a *lot*. He looked away from me, and I knew he was upset. I could tell. I put him down and sat on the floor with him and asked him what was wrong.

"That little guy started crying and saying he didn't want me to 'go to work.' It took me about fifteen minutes to get it out of him, but it turns out that when I was downrange, me and my husband would tell him I couldn't be at home with him because 'Mommy has to be at work.' So now, every morning when I'm telling him I'm going to 'work,' he's freaking out. He thinks I'm leaving for a whole year."

At this point, Henderson laughs again and shakes her head, her close-cut dark curls bouncing a bit and her grin spreading wide. She drops one hand into the other for emphasis. "I felt *terrible*. I had no idea he was going through that every single day. No wonder he was hitting kids and acting out. Poor little guy. So we talked about it, and now I say, 'Mommy's going to her *office*.' I'm going to bring him down here this weekend so he can see my office, and he'll know I'm not so far away."

If a Pillar Falls

Deborah and I sit on a bench overlooking the pond on the far side of the base. Although it's too chilly to be sitting outside, it's clear Deborah would rather talk to me where there's little chance of being seen by others. Deborah has the clipped and efficient bearing of someone who's been living in the military her whole life. She was raised in a military family, and her two older brothers joined the service right out of high school. After working as a dental assistant for a few years, Deborah became an officer's wife and then later, began raising their children. At this moment, however, her eyes are telling me a different story—one that is contained just below all that practiced containment and efficiency.

Deborah begins by talking about her ten- and eleven-year-old daughters who started having problems in school during her husband's fifth yearlong deployment. She's concerned Sophie and Katie have never gotten over all the upheaval of moving to six different bases during the years their dad was coming and going on his combat tours. I offer ways to help the girls talk about their frustrations, as we reflect on how disappointed a child might feel when life tumbles through too many changes they can't predict or control.

As we discuss the girls, I wait for what I know Deborah is actually wanting to talk about: how difficult all those upheavals were for *her*. Sure enough, Deborah tightens and smooths the ponytail on the back of her head, and starts to talk about herself.

"The last deployment was the worst. There were so many casualties in David's command; I literally couldn't even keep track of them all. It seemed like there was bad news every single day."

She pauses for a long time, and I watch her face change from a look of tight concern to a raw vulnerability that surprises me.

Her voice is barely a whisper when she speaks again. "I've been to ninety-three memorial services."

That last sentence hangs between us. We both stare at the pond and feel our way through an immense silence as the reality of ninety-three memorial services ricochets through both our hearts. I know she's just walked out on a thin sheet of ice that covers deep, dark waters. Minutes pass, and I wait for her to speak.

She finally glances over at me. "It was absolutely terrible. I knew I had to stay strong, no matter what. You know how it is. I'm the commander's wife. All these casualties are piling up, and everyone—especially the soldiers' wives—they're looking at me to see if we're going to be all right.

"I'm sitting there at the memorial services, in chapel after chapel, with the widows—some of them only nineteen or twenty. I'm hugging the parents who just lost their child. I'm sitting in pews, just across the aisle from soldiers whose friend isn't coming back. I felt like a nurse who couldn't stop the bleeding. Sometimes I went to two services a day. It was"—and here Deborah falters—"*crushing.*"

Her lip quivers and she slumps as she continues without even looking at me.

"When things are so bad, it can feel like the entire outfit is sliding into chaos. I couldn't let that happen."

Tears are rolling down her cheeks and her breathing is shallow and jagged. The cost of staying strong through so many hellish moments shows on her face.

"You see, it's like having a big structure, with a pillar on each corner holding up the whole place. If a pillar falls, you're in trouble—the whole thing is coming down. I just wanted to make sure they didn't see a pillar start to fall."

Deborah can hardly get her breath now. This is the very spot where she's been making sure not to feel things, for years. A short while ago, she was holding herself upright. Now, she's slack against the back of the bench, letting the wooden slats hold her weight.

"I'm so sorry."

She nods a little. She's looking at her hands, tightly clasped in her lap. "I can't even go into a church anymore. I try to step inside, but I just can't."

We sit in silence for another ten minutes or so.

Eventually, she reaches over and squeezes my hand. "Thank you so much. I just needed to say all that."

Deborah stands up, pulls the collar of her coat tight around her neck. She touches the top button to make sure it's secured, tugs downward on the bottom of her jacket with both hands, then runs a hand over the front, straightening and smoothing it into place before she walks away.

Check My Ride

Former SSG Dominguez is one of the largest human beings I've ever seen, big like a mountain—six and a half feet tall and wrapped with solid muscle. He's so big, he walks with a swagger that comes from the mechanics of moving such a large mass of a body through space. He fought in Vietnam, put in his twenty years, and now works as a civilian manager in the facilities maintenance department on the base. Several times a week I pass by his office, where he checks ledgers and orders supplies, and I usually stop to chat. He often thanks me for helping "his" soldiers. He feels an abiding bond with anyone in uniform. Dominguez never speaks about his own experiences, but sometimes expresses concern about "the kids" who are currently in combat.

"Hey, you ever seen my bike?" he asks one day.

I reply that I haven't, and he chuckles. "Well, come on outside, then. Come check my ride."

Dominquez leads me out the back doorway of the building and down a long straight stretch of sidewalk leading to the parking area. When we get near the end of the sidewalk, he points to a monstrous black and chrome motorcycle parked at a slant in one of the tiny edge spaces reserved for motorcycles. The bike looks as big as a Volkswagen.

"What do you think of it?" he asks, his chest puffed out with obvious pride.

It has been customized in a hundred different ways. The seat, the saddlebags, the lights, the handlebars—all are custom-designed. Chrome details swirl and glint from every surface and strut. Perfectly polished, the swirls on the struts match the swirls on the handlebars. The saddlebags are custom-stitched leather with the same swirls repeated.

"Well, it's remarkable, really. I've never seen anything like it."

"Yeah, it's cool, huh?"

We talk about the bike for a good twenty minutes, as he points out different details he designed or added. He mentions bike weekends he goes to in nearby beach towns, where he can ride with others, and tells me about solo rides he takes out into the countryside, where he rides for hours just to clear his head. Dominguez confesses his wife isn't crazy about riding it with him, but he hasn't given up hope of getting her more interested. His hands dart and flutter as he talks. His body moves in a sweet dance around the bike while he describes the fun he has on it, his eyes more animated than I've ever seen them. We laugh as Dominguez describes his multiple plans for tricking his wife into going on Sunday rides with him.

After a while, the words stop and we stand quietly admiring the bike. His voice is surprisingly somber when he speaks again. "When I got back from 'Nam, I couldn't get my head clear. I wasn't in good shape. Kind of depressed, real nervous. Angry a lot. I didn't know what to do, and I'm not really the counseling type. But this dude I knew from my platoon said he'd gotten a bike, and something just clicked. I thought I'd give it a try. So I went down to the dealership and took one for a test drive. I gotta tell you: from the very first moment I got on it and headed down the road, I felt free. Man, I felt *peace*. The bike still does that for me. It still clears my head. I don't know what I would have done without it, to be honest with you."

I reach over and shake his hand. "Nice ride."

CHAPTER 16

By the time I arrived at my fifth assignment, the *arriving* part of my nomad life was second nature: check in at the hotel, unpack and redo the hotel room to make it "home," find a route for my morning walks, withstand the deluge of the first two weeks, then slowly find my way into the rhythm of the new assignment.

This time, I wasn't working with deploying or returning soldiers; I wasn't working with military spouses; and I wasn't working with multiple battalions scattered across a sprawling base. I was assigned to a facility where two hundred soldiers and civilians worked side by side, processing the belongings of service members who had been killed or wounded in combat. I'd been working with soldiers returning from combat. Now I was working in the service of those who would never return.

I'd never known such a facility existed. I suppose I'd never given any thought to what happened to soldiers' belongings if they were killed or wounded. When I got my contract for the assignment, I searched online for information about the facility but didn't find much. I spoke with a close colleague and told her where I would be working. She said, "Oh gosh. I'd give anything to get that assignment!"

"Why?"

"I've known a couple of the other counselors who got that assignment in the past. They said it changed their lives. They loved the mission and said it was an incredibly special place to work. See what you think."

I don't remember much about my first weeks there. I'm sure I was acclimating to the place and the people. I imagine I was figuring out the best way to make my rounds through the work areas, trying to become familiar with employees and their jobs, starting that long (now familiar) road of reaching out so they could come to know me. I joked with them, asked them about their families, and spent long stretches of time standing next to them while they worked.

The facility was located in a nondescript building off to the side of the base. The sign out front noted the building number and the title of the facility, but it didn't specify the remarkable work occurring inside. It was set away from the bustle of the base, alongside a small airstrip where planes carrying soldiers' remains and belongings landed and took off with sad regularity.

The building itself was cavernous—a high, vast warehouse. Large skylights in the distant ceilings brightly lit the workspaces down below. The administrative offices were tucked away at one end of the building, taking up only about a third of the space, and the rest of the huge building housed numerous work areas where belongings were processed.

The first work area was dedicated to receiving footlockers shipped from downrange. It consisted of a loading dock, detailed check-in protocols, and big storage areas where the footlockers were held until they were processed. At times, those footlockers were stacked high over my head; when there was a lull in the fighting, the stacks of footlockers shrank accordingly.

The rest of the building contained work areas set apart from each other with heavy wire screen. They looked like room-sized cages, lined up next to each other down the sides of the building and set in squares at the center of the space. These areas were designed so that once a soldier's belongings were taken into a work area, no other belongings were allowed into that area until the belongings were fully processed, repacked, and ready for shipment. There was no risk whatsoever that one soldier's belongings would get mixed up with any other soldier's belongings.

On the far side of the building, there was an area reserved for shipping footlockers off to service members' families, offices for making contact with family members, and areas for processing military-issued equipment that would be returned to the military.

I often asked the workers what it meant to them to be working in a place with such a special mission. Many of the employees said they'd waited years for a position to open up at the facility because they felt drawn to the work, and many of them were retired military.

A few days after I started, I found myself standing next to Mark, a retired Air Force pilot who had worked there for a few years. He'd waited more than a year to be hired. "These folks made the ultimate sacrifice, and I have the chance to honor that. I can do something for their families. Means a lot to me."

Some of the employees were civilians, some were reservists or active duty, some were mortuary specialists. With that as their designated military job, they had worked in morgues in Iraq or Afghanistan before being ordered here. They had been involved in the removal of bodies from the Pentagon after 9/11. They were used to grim, dedicated service to fellow soldiers. Their stories were some of the most touching I would ever encounter.

SGT McGuire spoke somberly about preparing an Afghan baby's body for burial after the tiny boy was killed by a raging firefight in the family's village. "I did my best to show the family we cared. We washed his clothes and put them back on him. He had come in with a little toy tucked in his blanket. I guess the family had done that. I made sure that little toy was tucked in next to him before we returned him to his family. I wanted to show them that we were not just soldiers with bullets, but we were Americans who took care with their baby."

As I stood next to Sammi, a civilian employee, while she carefully sorted a soldier's T-shirts so they could be washed and folded, I asked her how long she'd been working at the facility.

"Gosh, I guess it's been seven years. I was in the Army for a little while, and now I feel like I'm doing something really important. I can't imagine working anyplace else."

"What's the hardest part about working here?"

Sammi thought for a little while before answering. "It's not one thing. It's the fact that this is endless. I mean, the belongings just keep coming. I get upset with some of the details; some of the belongings I see are so sweet. The soldiers take goofy toys with them downrange or funny drawings or books. Some of them have Bibles that are so well-worn and underlined and everything. Sometimes there are photos of them clowning around with their buddies, and you can see something about who they were just by looking at the photos. It's like you come to know them."

Jonathan was standing next to Sammi. "Listen, no way you can do this job and not feel it. You really do get a sense of them, a little glimpse of who they were."

One young captain told me she didn't sleep well for a few days while she wrestled with how to best preserve one soldier's family photos, which had been badly damaged in an explosion. Another officer asked me to check in with his staff after they opened a footlocker with belongings that were riddled with shrapnel. The stunned look on their faces told me how hard the sight of those damaged items had hit them. One retired service member talked about various soldiers whose stories had stayed with him long after the belongings had been shipped out. He remembered one because of how young he was, another because her work as a military engineer was exactly the same as his had been. He recalled one soldier who was from the small town just a few miles down the road from where he—the employee—had grown up in Arkansas. Even after working here for years, their hearts were still wide open to the impact of the belongings they encountered.

One moment showed me just how much these folks appreciated support. I had started to leave a processing area one day, and a service member working at a table behind me said, "Don't go too far—I may need you."

"No worries. I got you."

That's exactly how I felt toward these folks who were doing such magnificent work: *I got you. I'm right here.*

Previous assignments had opened my heart bit by bit as I encountered different aspects of military life. But this assignment blew the doors of my heart wide open in a way I never expected. The atmosphere in this facility was so full of reverence and respect, I felt like I was working in a church.

Sometimes the work took place in utter silence as the workers focused on the belongings in front of them. Sometimes there were hushed conversations about the materials they were sorting through—a quiet comment about this soldier's love of model cars, a smile when one worker noticed the soldier loved the same NFL team she loved, sweetly exchanged smiles when they saw a soldier's photos from his recent wedding. Items were cataloged, checked, and re-checked, with meticulous attention to detail, the staff supremely aware of the families' trust in this process.

Employees laughed and joked and had their differences, but not while they were focused on the belongings in front of them. While working with those, they kept their attention fully on their task, mindful of each story behind the belongings they were handling and honoring. Their goal was to work diligently so the families would get the footlockers as soon as possible; to present the belongings so beautifully the family might take solace in the way someone had cared for their loved one's items.

After working at the facility for a few days, I stood next to Damian while he began sorting through a soldier's effects. I saw him set aside a crumpled gum wrapper he'd found in the pocket of the soldier's uniform.

"What will you do with that?"

"It'll be cataloged and photographed, just like everything else. Then we'll put it in a ziplock bag and send it back with the rest of the belongings."

"A *gum wrapper*?"

"Absolutely. You never know. This wrapper could mean something to a wife or cousin or father. Maybe it was his favorite kind of gum. Maybe every time they got together they shared a piece of this exact same brand of gum. Maybe this soldier had been trying to quit smoking and this gum was something his best friend back home suggested as a way to stop. I mean, you just never know the story, right? So we make sure that every single item gets returned," Damian said. He gazed at me until he was sure I got his point, then looked back down at the items he was sorting through. Pens, scraps of paper, CDs, letters from home, bottle caps, or pull tabs—each item sent back home.

In the course of their work, the staff sometimes read the files that accompanied the footlocker to understand the soldier's story: this soldier killed by shrapnel; this one by an IED; this one wounded in a firefight. They handled the soldier's journal, his books, his photos, and mementos. They washed her uniform, her boots, the personal clothes she wore on her days off. They sorted through his music, his computer, her cell phone, the family heirlooms they might have carried into war to bring them solace. One day I watched as CPT Shimano placed a mother-of-pearl rosary into its delicate scarlet pouch. "There's a note in this little bag saying the rosary belonged to this soldier's great-grandmother. It's great this family is going to get it back. I love that, I really do."

Inside a work area—basically, a room-sized cage—each piece of the soldier's life was laid out on the long tables. The list of items created by his unit downrange was checked against every item on the tables to make sure everything was accounted for. Each item was cleaned with infinite attention to detail. I saw staff members using toothpicks to clean small parts of a cell phone or using a toothbrush to clean dirt off a belt buckle before it was polished to a like-new shine. Every item was bagged and labeled or folded carefully, then stacked and rechecked against the list, before being placed back in the footlocker for the journey home.

One morning I noticed a commander making his way through the work areas, shaking hands with the employees and thanking them for the work they did. I turned to Stephanie, a secretary who was standing next to me. "What's he doing?"

"Oh, he does that every morning," she said.

"Every morning?"

"Yes, every morning he walks through the work areas, shaking their hands and letting them know how much he appreciates the work they do. Amazing, huh?"

I nodded. Since beginning my work at the facility, I had noticed the commanders' dedication and passion. They understood the need for respect and honor in everything the facility did, and I soon felt infused with their passion. I was proud to support these folks. Their hearts got worn down at times, but they shouldered a holy trust in their responsibilities, and they handled it beautifully.

Another afternoon I stood in the grassy area behind the building, chatting with employees during their afternoon break. People clumped together in small groups or sat at a couple of picnic tables, talking and laughing. The airstrip just beyond the fence next to us was empty, and the atmosphere was lighthearted. I was in the middle of a conversation when suddenly the area went completely silent—all talk abruptly stopped.

I looked around to see what was going on. Jake, on my left, carefully put his cigarette on the edge of the picnic table and turned toward the fence. Deborah, at the next table, set down her soda and also turned toward the fence. A few feet beyond Deborah, I saw 2LT Battley tug his cap onto his head as he faced the fence. All around me, people were setting things down, turning toward the fence, standing in silence. I was baffled. They were completely in sync in their behaviors, yet I had no clue what they were doing.

Katie, who I'd just been chatting with about her rebellious teenager, leaned close to me and quietly said, "A plane is going down the runway. When they take off from here, they usually have a soldier's casket on board. They're flying the remains home to the family, and this is how we show our respect."

I looked off to the left to see a small jet rolling down the taxiway next to the back of the facility, aiming for the end of the runway, where it would turn and take off. Nobody moved. It was as if I was standing in a crowd of statues, everyone's attention focused silently on the plane.

A commander who had been standing nearby hurried toward the rear door of the building. I looked over at him with a puzzled expression as he passed, and he said, "I don't have my hat on. It's disrespectful to be without my hat when they pass by."

I was moved by the absolute sincerity of his stance. It was intolerable to him to witness a fallen brother or sister passing by if he wasn't saluting in full uniform.

The plane taxied past. Military members saluted, and no one moved or spoke until it turned, picked up speed, and lifted off. It was one of the most heart-stirring moments I'd ever been a part of in my time with the military.

As the workers got to know me and began to open up, I became extremely busy. I was essentially on call from the moment I walked into the building to the time I left at the end of the day. I bounced from numerous individual sessions to long conversations at the soldiers' work stations. One day I was in the middle of a session with a soldier when a sergeant knocked on my door and asked if she could talk to me. I told her I would come and find her as soon as I was finished with the session I was in the midst of. As I finished the session and walked through the facility to find the sergeant, another staff member stopped me and asked for some support. I told him I would find him as soon as I finished with the session I was about to have with the sergeant. Staff members and soldiers asked for support regarding the way their work affected their hearts, and they wanted support for their personal lives, too, like folks at any other base.

I actually loved being so busy. It filled my days, and I felt that now-familiar sense of purpose and being of service. Working with the same two hundred people day in and day out for months was very different from working with two or three battalions—a couple thousand soldiers, plus their spouses. The smaller number, the close quarters, the ongoing contact, and the poignant nature of the soldiers' work meant our exchanges became deeply personal.

Sometimes, I knew which ones were expecting babies before any of their coworkers knew, which ones were in the midst of painful divorces (something they might be keeping private from others), which one had lost his childhood friend to cancer the week before, and which one felt painfully out of sync with her team members. While chatting with the commander one day, I mentioned that a particular employee was leaving the job in the next couple of days. He joked that I was tracking the staff more closely than he was. (I didn't believe it—he was deeply attuned to his troops.) I spoke regularly with the team leaders who worked tirelessly to make sure every footlocker was handled with pristine care. I worked as much as I knew how to do, and there were still more stories and more threads to follow among all these hearts.

"Gosh," said one officer, "I'm amazed at what you've accomplished here. I feel like you've lifted this place up on your back and carried us."

I was so proud he felt that way. It was exactly how I wanted them to feel.

As beautiful and sacred as the facility felt, there was no ignoring the fact that it also held oceanic grief. Day after day, the atmosphere was saturated with loss. The months flew by, and although the commanders wanted me to extend my contract, it wasn't possible—a contract had already been signed with my replacement. On my last day, an announcement was made: staff members wanting to say good-bye to me should gather in the common area. This was a typical farewell moment that happened at each base, so I knew what to expect: a few folks would show up and I'd get a certificate of appreciation or a coin from the commander. It was often a small, awkward affair, but a very nice gesture on the part of the base or facility where I had worked.

After the announcement, I glanced down the hall to see streams of people heading for the common area. A second announcement notified everyone that the farewell would be moved to the (much larger) cafeteria. I was astounded. This was nothing like anything I'd ever seen at previous assignments. All the tables in the cafeteria were full, people lined the walls, and soon they began to stand two deep all around the sides of the room; almost all of the facility's workers had shown up. Seeing all of the people I'd come to know and love, whose work I respected so very much, was overwhelming. I was given time to speak, but I felt incapable of putting my feelings into words. I stumbled through a farewell and hugged one worker after another.

As my colleague had promised, my life was changed by working in this facility. I felt more compassion than ever for those who served, knowing they might not return from war. I had developed a much deeper sensitivity to the grief families face when they receive one of these footlockers instead of experiencing their loved one's safe return. I reached a level of giving, response, and attentiveness in myself that was beyond any I'd reached before; because of my respect for the sacred work they were doing, I wanted to give even more. I was profoundly moved, day after day. I drew deeply on my spiritual heart in supporting these workers, and I saw them draw deeply on theirs as they did the difficult and important work that filled their days.

GRACE

Over the years, I watched soldiers act with extraordinary grace, especially around the death of their fellow soldiers: preparing a uniform for burial, standing silently in grief during memorial services, talking quietly with tearful eyes while remembering their fallen friend. Perhaps the most astounding examples of witnessing grace came while I was watching the soldiers and staff who processed the belongings of soldiers who were killed or wounded in battle.

It's hard to separate the word "grace" from a religious context, but the grace I encountered while watching soldiers and staff handle belongings was more akin to the definition of grace as doing honor or credit to someone by one's presence, or to honor or dignify. It was both a spiritual and a humanistic grace—a grace that expressed the deepest humility, respect for, and dignifying of the soldier who had been killed as well as the soldier's loved ones who would soon receive the belongings.

I watched them fold a soldier's T-shirt with patient, practiced care; lay out all the small belongings—bobby pins, bookmarks, coins, pencil stubs—with meticulous attention and focus; and repack the foot locker with precision and a careful eye to how it would look when the soldier's family opened it on the other end of a long journey home. Every day, I saw the grace they brought to their work, honoring and dignifying it through their dedicated sense of presence as they worked.

I witnessed other kinds of grace as well.

I witnessed grace in the way enlisted soldiers fought fiercely for those standing next to them. I saw it in the way they slogged through endless trainings, knowing they were headed into battle. I saw it in their faces as they returned from war.

I witnessed grace, too, in the stories of those who had been sent around the world in response to natural disasters and other incidents of massive need. They brought forward enormous capabilities, pride in their ability to offer aid, and deep compassion for those who were suffering.

I witnessed grace in leaders who inspired their troops (whether the leader was a high-ranking officer or a newly minted platoon sergeant). These leaders were authentic, willing to show both vulnerability and strength, compassion and steely expectations. I watched the men and women under these commanders rise up in response to the courage and clarity they saw in their leaders.

There was grace in that, too.

Visiting Hours

"Good morning, sir," I call out as CPT Eratch passes by my office door. I hadn't seen him at the office the day before, which was highly unusual.

Eratch grins and waves as he walks by. "Good to see you, counselor!" He's one of my favorite soldiers at this base. Extremely efficient in his work, he's always got an upbeat manner and a ready smile. Although enlisted soldiers often have little positive to say about officers, soldiers in this battalion seem to gravitate to him for conversation and support. Eratch's thin, muscled body moves fluidly through the daily drills and tasks, and he seems to easily keep track of each and every soldier in his command.

Later in the day, I poke my head in his office. "Mind if I have a seat?" He beckons me into a chair and I sit down. "I didn't see you yesterday. Everything OK?"

"Oh yeah. Everything's fine. I just got back from a trip to the hospital, that's all. Went to visit Esposito. I try to get over there every few weeks. It's the least we can do."

Esposito had been severely injured in combat. He was stabilized in Iraq, sent to Germany for several surgeries, and then flown to a hospital about five hours from the battalion's home base for further treatment. While he recovers from his injuries, Eratch and other battalion commanders take turns making the drive to the hospital and spending the day with Esposito and his family, keeping him company and encouraging him to get better soon. Even the highest ranking officers on the base make the hospital trips. Eratch works these visits into his prodigiously busy schedule by making the long drive after a full day's work, spending the next day at the hospital, then driving back home afterward.

"Do battalions typically do that? Do they usually make it a point to visit their wounded troops?"

Eratch shrugs and then shakes his head. "I don't really know how it 'typically' goes. This is something that's important to us. He's part of our family, and we want him to know we're here for him, and we'll be here for him all the way. I know some of the soldiers in the hospital never have visitors. Their families live too far away, and their command doesn't visit. I'm not sure what's going on there. I just know it's too important to let there be any slack. We trained with him, we fought with him, and now we're going to be there for him while he gets better. He made a huge sacrifice. We're going to make sure he knows we know that, and we honor it."

"I can't tell you how much I respect that, Captain."

"Well, that's a nice thing to say," he tells me. "But I respect Esposito and the sacrifice he made."

Escort

SFC Lin's face is like a placid lake as he speaks of escorting a fellow soldier's body back home to the soldier's family. His dark eyes take on a faraway serenity, his body relaxes, his voice soft and steady. It's as if he's telling a tale from long ago, but it's only been two days since he returned from his journey.

Leaning on the thick wooden countertop that divides his small work area from the front of the office, Lin tells me he's been in Mortuary Affairs for a few years but usually works in a morgue or is assigned to other facilities. His thin, compact body is just tall enough for him to lean on the counter without slouching. He puts his forearms on the counter, clasps his hands together, and settles into the position as he talks. The broad plains of his boyish face seem relaxed as he repeatedly flicks his head to the side so that his straight black hair slides out of his eyes. But I also notice tension in the tight, small lines etched near the corners of his eyes.

"I'd never done anything like that before—escorting a soldier's body home—but I asked my commander to give me the assignment. I wanted to serve in that way. I wanted to help a family. The soldier's name was Wilson. He was from a little town in rural Nebraska. You've never seen such flat, wide-open country, ma'am. Pretty amazing for a city boy like me.

"Anyway, the whole time I was flying there, I was in a strange mood. All I could think about was Specialist Wilson. His body was in the hold of the plane, and of course I was riding in a seat above the cargo area. But it felt like I was riding right next to him. When we had a layover, I went down to the tarmac and escorted the body to the next plane. It was so powerful—I felt like I was in a trance."

Lin stops his story and drifts off into that faraway look he still has in his eyes. Then he continues. "When we got to Nebraska, I met CPT

Bohannon, the Casualty Assistance Officer (CAO) for that region. We escorted the casket to the funeral home, then he and I headed way out into the countryside to Wilson's family home. We didn't talk much on the way out there. It just seemed kind of weird to chat about the weather or whatever. He told me he had been the one to notify Wilson's family when he was killed. When we pulled up in the driveway, I got pretty nervous. I hadn't done this kind of thing before, and I guess Bohannon was a little more used to it. He looks over at me and says, 'Ready, soldier?'

"We got out and walked up the sidewalk. Nice house. Brick. Little flower beds on both sides of the front steps. He knocked on the door, and to be honest with you, I felt my body stand a little taller while we waited for someone to answer. You know: *this is it, be your best.*

"When Wilson's mom opened the door, all of a sudden I felt like I was terribly inadequate for the task. Just, well . . . seeing a mother's face.

"She was all dressed up like she was going to church. I bet she had been sitting there in her best dress all day long, waiting for us. She invited us inside and offered us coffee. I guess she wanted company. Who could blame her? Wilson's dad had already passed, and he didn't have any brothers or sisters, so now she was all alone.

"I just kept telling her how sorry we were for her loss, and that we appreciated the sacrifice her son had made. She was teary, but gracious. She had a little area set up in the living room with Wilson's picture and his medals. Kind of like a shrine."

Here, Lin takes another long break in telling his story, remembering a mother's shrine to her only son. He stands up straight for a moment and rolls his shoulders, as if wanting to shrug off the heaviness of the story he's telling. He leans forward on the counter again.

"She asked us where we were from and if we'd been overseas. And then she insisted that we stay for dinner. Can you believe that? She's going to her son's funeral tomorrow, and she wants to cook us a meal.

We stayed and I tried my best to chat with her, to let her know we appreciated her and her son.

"Gosh, the next day was such a perfect summer day, crazy-blue sky and all that land all around us. Me and the CAO at the church early. We were in our Class A's, of course. Dress Blues all the way. Wilson's mom asked if we would stand up next to the casket while they had the service. And we told her of course we would. Standing at attention for the whole service, I felt like I was going to pass out because it was so hot in that church. But I honestly felt: *I can do this. For all he gave, I can do this.* I guess I kept thinking of my parents and how they would want the same thing if something happened to me. It would mean something to them, to have soldiers standing watch like that.

"I tried to keep my eyes straight ahead, but sometimes I'd see his mom right there in the front row. I was kind of relieved when the service ended. We went back to the house and had some food that the neighbors had brought over. I felt like I didn't belong there. I mean, they *knew* him, and I was an outsider.

"It was hard to leave. The plane ride back was tough. I just wanted to do more. I wanted to be more comfort to his mom, or I really wanted some way to make it better for her. But it is what it is. I did the best I could. I hope it was a little bit of a help to her, I really do."

"Would you do it again, Sergeant Lin?"

Without hesitating, he says, "Yes, ma'am, I would. I'd leave right now if they asked me to. I sure would."

The Banner

I stand next to a short, stocky, redheaded private just off the plane after a year's deployment to Afghanistan. He's looking haggard and bleary-eyed from the forty-hour journey, yet his face shines with relief and newfound ease. He shuffles his feet with nervous pleasure and stretches his arms out a couple of times, just to get the kinks out.

We watch soldiers search for their wives, husbands, kids, parents, and sweethearts—calling out to them, and then running into each other's arms. The hangar is like an active anthill with everyone darting around and zigzagging through the crowd to find their loved ones. The private doesn't have anyone greeting him, so we stand and chat.

"You glad to be home?"

"Oh, you bet. Yeah. Yeah, I sure am."

"What are you looking forward to the most?"

His grin gets several times bigger. "Hot showers. And clean sheets."

Admitting such simple pleasures seems to make him shy—he looks sideways at me and blushes just a little bit. He pulls his shoulders way up toward his ears, then drops them with a big exhale.

"Wow, wow, wow," he says, soaking it all in.

In the next couple of weeks, the entire group of returning soldiers will be released for a monthlong block leave, so I ask him about his plans.

"Oh gosh. I'm going back to Kansas to see my mom and dad. My sister had a baby while I was over there, my first niece. I can't wait to see her. I'm going to . . ."

He falls silent in midsentence and his face freezes. I turn slightly to follow his gaze, and I see the huge banner stretched across the south wall of the hangar: "Lest we forget: CPL Madden and PFC McKinney"—two soldiers from the battalion who were killed in combat.

I watch his eyes cloud over, and his head drops as if some great weight has just landed upon him. He keeps clearing his throat and won't look up, so I put my hand on his shoulder, and we stand there in the sea of happy greetings, remembering his combat brothers.

Footlocker

Natalie cleans the tube of a small flashlight disassembled on the table in front of her, rubbing the casing with a soft treated cloth until the metallic-blue finish shines like it's brand-new. She pushes a small bit of the cleaning cloth inside the tube to clean the inner surfaces—surfaces no one will ever see. Reaching for the flashlight's tiny lens, Natalie polishes it to a sparkling brilliance. Then she picks up a Q-tip and carefully swabs the threads on the flashlight, turning it around and around, intently wiping each curving ridge where the parts screw together.

When Natalie finishes cleaning the flashlight, she reassembles it, places it in a small ziplock bag, and sets it aside with other bagged belongings. She reaches for a cell phone power cord. Stretching the thin cord out to its full length, Natalie runs a cloth over it several times, making sure she gets every speck of dust or dirt. Again, she uses Q-tips to clean around the prongs and the ends. When the cord is shiny clean, Natalie wraps it into a neat coil, secures it with a rubber band, and places it into another small ziplock bag.

Natalie is cleaning the personal belongings of a soldier killed in combat. T-shirts, pants, jackets, and sweatshirts are laundered and sorted on a long stretch of tables. The clothes are folded, military-neat to the exact same size, then placed in perfect stacks. Socks, turned inward in uniform small bundles, are laid out as if they are in formation. Books, journals, photos, letters—all are sorted, packaged into ziplock bags, and placed into the boxes headed for home. The footlockers, too, are scrubbed inside and out before being refilled. Natalie and her team treat the fallen soldiers' possessions with the respect and reverence given to restoring a Renaissance masterpiece. Their gloved hands move slowly and deliberately; their attention is focused and calm.

I check on Natalie later in the afternoon and find her scrubbing the bottom of the soldier's boots with a toothbrush. At times, she uses a metal file to pry at dirt caked into the pattern of the hard rubber. When the sole is spotless, she rubs finishing oil into every nook and cranny, giving the rubber a smooth sheen. She washes the bootlaces, dries them, and gingerly weaves them back through the eyelets, making sure they cross over in the same direction all the way up the front of the boot. In a small tub next to the sink, she's soaking his Velcro name tags. She'll start scouring those with small brushes next.

As she leans over the sink, suds covering her hands, I ask if the job is difficult for her, if she ever feels too sad. She shakes her head at first. Then she admits that sometimes a particular case really touches her heart. She'll find herself thinking about a soldier for weeks after the belongings have been sent off.

"You know, my heart cries when I see photos of their little babies, or pictures of their young wives or handsome husbands back home. But I feel like I'm doing all this for the soldier. I imagine them watching over me as I work. For a few days while I'm working on their belongings, I come to know them. I feel all the grief; I do. But then I remember: I'm helping their family. I'm helping their story continue."

I watch her begin to work on the cloth name tag in her hands, and I see the almost sacred regard she brings to her work. Looking over at the clean belongings waiting for shipment, I notice the soldier's patrol cap perched next to a squared-off stack of his T-shirts. The cap's been cleaned and scrubbed. But Natalie has also taken stiff brown paper, bunched it into the right shape, and gently pressed it into the inside of the cap. Now, the cap stands straight up. With the cap placed on top of all the beautifully packed belongings, his family back home will soon lift the lid on his footlocker, and they'll see his cap, proud and tall, right next to the family photos he kept close in battle.

Natalie sees me looking at the cap, gazes at me for a moment, then returns to her work.

Little Cowboys

In the photo, they're standing on the front porch steps of a small white stucco house, squinting into the sun with wide-angle grins: two boys, maybe three and four years old, in their tiny cowboy clothes—pressed jeans, plaid shirts, big belt buckles, miniature boots, and huge tan cowboy hats that make it look like UFOs have landed on their heads. The older brother has his arm slung over the shoulder of the little one. Both boys have a hand raised, waving to the camera.

The photo was tucked inside their dad's journal. He carried it overseas with him, into whatever wild world he was facing during his months in combat. He couldn't send letters very often, so he wrote letters to his family in his journal. He wrote to his sons pretty much every day, in a neat, tight script. In his letters, he tells them again and again how much he loves them, and reminds them he wants them to be good boys and listen to their mom.

He calls them by their nicknames—the older one, Monks (a nickname that started as Monkey), and the younger one, Buster. He asks his boys if they're getting big, and wonders whether or not they're helping to feed the dog. He assures them he'll be home soon, says they'll go for ice cream or play with the big Tonka trucks he bought just before he left. He promises he'll push them "way, way high" on the swing out back.

In entries addressed to his wife, he says he misses her and wants to hug her forever when he gets home. He tells her how sad and frustrated he feels, having to be gone for so long. He grumbles about the heat and the dirt and the tight quarters, but he always ends with "My one and only, I love you so much." In one of the last entries, he writes about getting close to the end of his deployment. Two more months, and he'll be back home with them in Colorado. He's leaning toward that finish line as hard as he can.

In his last entry, written in a field medical unit, he says the bullet wound in his stomach is hurting bad. He doesn't yet know: that very wound will be the end of him, later that same day.

His unit was ambushed while escorting a supply truck to troops on the front line. He was wounded by a sniper's bullet, killed by an enemy he never saw.

He was twenty-two years old when he died.

CHAPTER 17

As time went by, the structure of my job became more and more of a challenge for me. The length of the assignments on the bases—which varied from one month to six months, as determined by the Department of Defense—meant any therapeutic relationship I established with a soldier or spouse was soon disrupted as I moved on to the next assignment. There was a logic to this that I understood: shorter stints helped soldiers remember that the counselors were outside the system, not part of the military, and therefore a safer option for disclosing troubles. The shorter stints ensured soldiers didn't get too attached to any particular person in terms of asking for help—a useful pattern in an environment where people (both military and civilians) were constantly moving all around.

But the therapeutic disruption created by the regular arrivals and leave-takings of the job was profound. When I got to a new base, it could take several weeks to make myself known to the battalion, spouses, and command with whom I worked. It might take a little longer for soldiers or spouses to get up the nerve to ask for help. Because of the time it took to build rapport, I sometimes only saw a soldier once or twice before it was time to leave that assignment.

One time, the day before I was leaving a base, I got a phone call. "Ma'am, this is Dickerson. Remember me? We talked a month or so ago?"

I remembered. The previous month, Dickerson, a high-ranking officer, had heard me give a briefing and called just a few minutes after I finished the presentation. Dickerson told me he never knew before that off-the-record counseling ("off-the-record" being the most crucial aspect of the program in which I worked) was available. He told me he had been desperate to find help but didn't know where to turn because his concerns could prove problematic to his career. From the tension in his voice, I could tell he was struggling. He asked how soon he could come to my office. He walked in five minutes later and broke down almost immediately. After sobbing and laying out all the aspects of the issue he had been afraid to speak about, he looked relieved. A thousand-pound weight was starting to lift.

Dickerson had talked with me three times before being sent to a distant base for a special project he was working on. Now that he had returned to his home base, calling me to set up an appointment was one of his top priorities. His call came the morning before the end of my assignment.

"I'm so sorry, sir, but my time here at the base ends tomorrow. There's a counselor who'll be replacing me."

I heard a sharp intake of air on the other end of the phone.

"You're leaving?"

"Yes, sir. You can talk to—"

"But I don't want to start over. You already know my story and how complicated it is. I want to keep talking to *you*."

I could hear his voice starting to shake. I hated moments like this. As a therapist, I didn't ever want to interrupt a therapeutic relationship, especially when a client felt an authentic connection to me and working together was proving helpful. Soldiers, spouses, and commanders consistently expressed complaints about the short stints. They joked about the "rotating counselors" who became something of a blur to them.

They'd tease that they wouldn't even bother to remember my name since I would be gone so soon. At one base, I heard complaints every single day of my four-month assignment. When I crossed paths with the UPS driver who delivered to that base, even he said, "Oh yeah. I see you guys around all the time. But you're always changing out." I lost count of how many soldiers told me they never asked for help because they didn't want to deal with the "rotating counselor" effect.

"How can I refer anyone to you people?" a battalion chaplain exclaimed with great frustration. "Think about it. Would you want to start therapy with someone, open up to them about difficult things, only to have them up and leave after a few sessions? I can't with good conscience refer anyone to you. I'm sorry."

A couple came to see me when they were facing a very challenging time in their marriage; a new baby had escalated the pressure and highlighted their difficulties. The husband's training schedule made it nearly impossible for them to make an appointment. We finally met, and the session was extremely useful for the couple. I was able to offer them clear, immediate suggestions for improving their relationship, and they said they felt like they had hope for the first time in months. As it happened, the soldier was headed back out into the field for three more weeks of training, and I would be gone by the time they got back. The wife got tears of frustration in her eyes when we talked about my departure.

"What are we supposed to do?"

I knew they could schedule more appointments with my replacement, but I also knew they already felt comfortable and understood by me. This same story unfolded (in different versions, with different details) with every assignment I took.

I felt helpless, and sometimes I felt like I was part of a practice that caused the soldiers and spouses considerable distress. Regardless of how well I understood the rationale for this pattern, I found it painful to gain others' trust only to walk away once they had opened up. Did

I think they could get good help with another counselor? Surely. But the disruptions were so frustrating for the soldier or spouse that I was afraid they might not reach out again. As a therapist, I held great faith in the healing power of sincere relationship. Eventually, this aspect of the program was changed and assignments were lengthened, though still limited. But this didn't help the soldiers—or me—at the time.

Despite all the limits set on my job, I worked hard to make the best of every contact I had with each person I encountered. I reminded myself that even one or two sessions was more help than they'd have if they hadn't reached out at all. I waded into deeper concerns when a soldier seemed to be crumbling under the weight of his or her burdens, or if I felt referring them would mean they'd get no help at all because it was clear that the soldier would avoid pursuing help within the military system.

Having had full control over my work throughout my career, I chafed against these restrictions, especially when I saw soldiers suffering. I felt the restrictions ruled out the responsiveness I knew it would take for them to truly heal, and staying within the restrictions increased my sense of helplessness.

In this way, a crack began to open between my values and the job. I kept working, but I felt the gap widening between what I was tasked to do and what I deeply believed was helpful, therapeutic, and sincerely responsive. As this gap grew larger, I began to feel more and more stress in doing the work I loved doing.

I moved on, heading to my next assignment whenever the last one ended. In each new town, I had to get myself oriented in the most basic ways. I had to figure out where the grocery store was, where to buy gas, where I could get a haircut or find a replacement cord for my cell phone, or any number of the tedious details required by daily life. I walked into dozens of grocery stores in dozens of new towns, and each time I had to hunt through aisles and far corners of each supermarket for the bread aisle, the dairy coolers, or the produce section. This wasn't too challenging the first few times I did it, but after I lost count of the grocery stores I'd been in, it seemed stressful and difficult. This process of reorienting was happening at least every few months. Sometimes, in between stints, I was moving around every few days.

While I had always loved traveling and seeing new places, I had finally had my fill. Figuring out the basics again and again and again eventually wore me out. Early on, I'd taken to the cycle of reorienting myself like a hiker who must figure out the complex coordinates of the new mountain range she's learning to navigate. But after a while, I'd walk into a new post office and think, *Oh, this is like the post office in Kentucky. No wait. It's like the one in Texas. Or maybe it was the one in New York?* The same jumble would happen with stores, gas stations, and stretches of highways. It was a little like having flashbacks, but without any orientation to what I was remembering. All the coordinates started to blend as the assignments and the bouncing around in between assignments stacked up. My "inner GPS" had become overwhelmed with too much new information and too many new destinations.

This constant need to figure out my surroundings, along with the pressure of being "on" all day and engaging with such large numbers of people meant that my nervous system sometimes had difficulty turning off when it was time to rest. One night just after starting a new assignment, I woke up at 3 a.m. with my mind revving, reviewing all the new people I'd met during my day and the various soldiers I'd talked to. Lying in the hotel bed, staring at the outline of the window created by the spotlights in the parking lot below, I failed to relax enough to get back to sleep. In my whole life, I'd never had any trouble sleeping; now I was so overstimulated during the day, it was common for my nervous system to keep buzzing during the night.

"I'm sorry if this sounds rude. I don't mean it to. But why do you do this kind of work? What makes it worth it to you?"

This question wasn't unusual. It was puzzling to soldiers, and to their spouses, why a civilian would work the schedule I did, moving so often, starting all over with each assignment, spending time away from friends and loved ones. This time the person asking me was a commander's wife, a very frank woman who sat across the table from me in yet another conference room as we waited for a women-in-leadership meeting to start. Her reddish-blond hair was styled close against her face, her green eyes were flashing, and she turned her chair toward me as if gearing up for a difficult discussion.

"I've asked several of you counselors that same question. And no one will really answer me. I get some 'party line' answer, but no one will say why they *really* do it."

"I can tell you why. I'm happy to talk with you about it," I replied. "It's like working in an emergency room. There's an intensity and a brilliant purpose to this work. If you could follow me around for a day, you'd understand immediately."

"Follow you around for a day?" The commander's wife chuckled, looking at the women who were sitting nearby. "I don't know if I'd want to do *that*."

I had to smile. Others had indicated they felt this way about my job.

"Oh, you'd be amazed. The way this job is set up, I get to be right there with soldiers wherever they're working, and their issues come up to be dealt with in the most unusual instances. I love that immediacy."

She gazed at me steadily, listening intently and considering my words. She was imagining the work differently now, not just endless days of listening to people's problems, but grasping the true nature of my days.

"I think I see what you mean," she said.

"I really do love this work. Honest, if you followed me around, you'd know what it's like to see a soldier's face finally relax after he admits how much he's struggling. Or how good it feels to see a spouse finally get past her anger or disappointment so she can enjoy her marriage again.

It's incredibly meaningful to me. I can't say I like the moving around, but something about helping soldiers and spouses makes it worth it."

And then I added a piece I had never verbalized before, an aspect I hadn't really understood myself until the words came out of my mouth. "I've come to feel that soldiers are making such a great sacrifice for me; this is a way I can give something back."

That was key. Now that I'd grown beyond my preconceptions of the military, now that I had come to know what it truly took for soldiers to do what they did (the time away from their families, the years of sacrifice, the endless training, discomfort, and bravery), I wanted to offer them something in return. They stood unwavering in experiences most of us would never be willing to stand in. Counseling was the one skill I could offer. As I saw into the hidden soul of their bravery—the true cost of combat to their hearts and spirits, and the price to their families in missing them—I wanted to help them with the burdens they carried.

The colonel's wife thanked me, nodded her head thoughtfully, and turned herself square to the table as the first speaker walked to the podium.

DISSONANCE

The Latin root of "dissonance" is *dis* (apart) + *sonare* (to sound): to differ in sound. We use the word "dissonance" to mean an inconsistency between beliefs one holds, or a conflict between one's actions and one's beliefs. I experienced dissonance with the work I was doing on bases because of the job's limitations and structure. Sometimes soldiers spoke with me about the dissonance they felt, fighting a war they didn't believe in, wars they couldn't see the benefit of.

These weren't casual conversations, and they didn't happen very easily. Soldiers are trained to follow orders and fulfill the mission. They aren't meant to question command about the finer points of the mission, the overarching purpose, or the deeper costs. But in these recent wars, I kept encountering soldiers who wondered what the purpose was in the fighting they were doing. One soldier had tears running down his face when he told me he just didn't believe in the mission anymore. He was getting ready to deploy for the fourth time. He told me he believed in the mission at first. The first time he deployed to Iraq, he sincerely hoped US intervention would help the local population. But after two deployments to Iraq and one to Afghanistan (and with Afghanistan coming up again), he no longer saw the point.

Whether the wars were right or wrong, useful or misguided, I felt sympathy for the dissonance these soldiers were feeling and for the fact that they worked within a system where they couldn't openly struggle with that dissonance; could only whisper about it among themselves and sometimes to me.

I noticed these questioning, disbelieving conversations happened more often with lower-ranking soldiers. I wondered if the dissonance went up through the ranks, but higher ranks just didn't speak of it—or if higher-ranking soldiers felt more aligned with the fighting. I wasn't sure.

I wondered what it was costing soldiers to tolerate the dissonance in themselves as they left for deployment. I wondered what it cost them in the midst of the fighting—or when friends lost their lives. Only one soldier braved that conversation with me. He told me he felt his friend's life was wasted in a war that didn't really make any sense. He said he didn't think he could ever square the loss of his friend with the fighting that seemed to be someone else's war. His voice was full of searing bitterness.

Typically, when we feel dissonance in ourselves we have ways of navigating it. We bargain with ourselves (*just this once*), or we make some trade-off (*I'll make it up to them later*), or we perhaps go into deep denial, blocking out one side or the other if we can't tolerate the tension between the two sides of our dissonant beliefs. But with lives being lost, bodies being maimed, and dissonance silenced or shamed, there's a great cost. As the United States has more recently pulled back from Iraq and Afghanistan, and watched cities fall into the hands of extremists, soldiers are left wondering what their friends died for, and the question seems unanswerable.

Of course, civilians are engaged with these wars differently than those who are fighting it. Peter Feaver, a political scientist at Duke University who studies the military, posits that these wars came to matter more to the military than to civilians. The civilian world might be relieved to cut the losses and move on, but for service members "those losses have names and faces attached to them."[17]

Civilians live with the dissonance of wars they might not believe in while juggling their sense of patriotism and support of the troops. Many soldiers live in the dissonance of fighting and sometimes paying the ultimate price for a war some feel is not "the right fight"—but they can't speak freely about it. Perhaps the place we want to aim for is that where dissonance is not only lived, but spoken, processed, and—eventually—brought into harmony.

AFTERWORD

While I was working my last assignment, I came to realize that the structure of the job was simply not sustainable for me. Living in hotel rooms far away from any close emotional connections while doing such intensively consuming work day after day created an imbalance that was not tolerable long-term.

I couldn't bring myself to work less intensively when I saw great pain in the eyes of combat veterans and spouses. But repeatedly breaking the crucial emotional attachments I'd developed with them whenever I moved on to a new assignment seemed too coldhearted a way to treat those who wanted help.

During my years of working on the bases, I came across many soldiers who seemed to be stumbling off the edge of some abyss—their inner worlds ravaged by repeated deployments or experiences their psyches simply couldn't integrate. I reached for them as hard as I could, trying to help them right themselves just enough to allow them to stabilize, to reorganize, so they could walk forward again. They weren't crazy, although they felt like it; they weren't broken, although they felt this, too. They were simply far past what their natural capacities could tolerate.

I had come to love the spouses and families I got to know. I was deeply, deeply moved by their dedication and sacrifice. I loved the days when I had the chance to joke around and laugh with soldiers. I loved the days when I sat next to heaving shoulders and offered my sincere support.

Through getting to know the soldiers, I developed a clear and distinct affinity for military service members that remains with me. If I see an article in the paper about an incident involving the military in Afghanistan (or anywhere), I read it. If I walk through the airport and see someone in uniform, I make it a point to speak to them, or at least nod as they rush by. I notice brigade, battalion, or military stickers on cars now—I hadn't before. I can often tell from a sticker or hat or item of clothing what rank soldiers hold—and sometimes where they've been stationed—and can speak more familiarly with them. I can read the code now, and it is humbling to understand where they've been and what they've done. While I still don't belong to their world, the ability to grasp a small slice of it holds compelling, pristine meaning for me, and I feel I can more clearly honor their dedication and sacrifices.

I was sad to walk away from the work I had done on the bases. In my encounters with the veterans, I felt a sense of destiny, a sense that the Divine had directed me—to this soldier or that spouse, this conversation, that picnic table or that section of empty hallway—to where the next heartfelt exchange would take place.

This shimmering phenomenon didn't happen all the time, but it happened a lot.

As my time working on the bases drew to a close, I thought a lot about the similarities in our work: both the soldiers and I felt called to a particular work that cost us a great deal, emotionally and psychologically, yet was deeply fulfilling; we both were separated from loved ones for long stretches of time; and we both had experiences on a regular basis that cracked our hearts open, in ways both painful and glorious.

We both worked within the ongoing, irresolvable tension between loneliness and dedicated purpose.

While it was the hardest work I'd ever done, it was also the most fulfilling and the most meaningful. Some people—civilian and military alike—still ask, "How could you do this? How could you work in such relentless intensity?"

Sometimes I doubted I could.

But every day I felt like I was catching hearts falling through the air.

I have never been to war, but I have been in the enormous landscape surrounding war, with soldiers who were boarding planes carrying them into wild chaos, with spouses who were shuddering with fear about who would come home tomorrow—a dreadful, bruised stranger or the sweetheart they've been missing.

I wrote my first story like this: Sitting in my hotel room at the end of a very long day, I pulled out my laptop and opened it to a stark blank page. My heart felt tattered with everything I'd seen and heard, so I sat in the soft glow of the desk lamp, writing about a battalion's grief as they learned one of their soldiers had been killed in combat. There were no hardened warriors that day, just men and women who felt their loss with a raw, stunned vulnerability. I wrote to make room for the next day, which promised to hold more grief-stricken conversations.

I crafted these stories because I wanted others to see soldiers in the way that I had come to see them: as men and women who had a kind of integrity I felt was rare these days. The world I entered into was a world of honor and commitment, separation and grief, integrity and sometimes stoic loneliness. No naive Pollyanna notions here—I saw their bitterness and disillusionment and frustrations, too.

Still, I admired the dedication they brought to their daily lives. Regardless of what I thought about the fact that their job included wars and combat, I saw their humanity. Writing about our poignant conversations and moments of intense exchange helped me support them in a much more profound way.

A couple of years after leaving the work I did on military bases, I began to work with veterans and spouses again through my reestablished private practice. I discovered a remarkable nonprofit organization based in Nashville called Courage Beyond, whose mission is making sure service members, veterans, and their families get access to counseling. Their program gave me an avenue for continuing to support those who served, and I work with service members and veterans to this day.

Many of the veterans I now work with tell me they would never seek counseling from someone who hadn't been on military bases. They feel most civilian counselors—even those with the best intentions—don't really understand their lives, which makes me value my years on the bases even more.

I hope these words hold some of the grace I feel in working with soldiers and spouses.

I hope the stories awaken your heart to the courage, heartbreak, and enormous giving soldiers stand for. They are remarkable men and women, and I am eternally grateful for their service.

ACKNOWLEDGMENTS

It's daunting to look back over the process of creating this book and name the many folks who helped me. I hope every writer has the kind of friends who cheered me on: Frances Wilson, a dear friend, a fellow writer, and someone who believed in me every step of the way; Lu Rudolph, one of the best early readers one could hope for and someone I consider a buddy for life; Carrie Brown and John Gregory Brown, who pulled me aside early on to tell me I could; Hettie Johnson, Daphne and Steve Klein, Sara Pearson, and Patrik Widrig, who each grasped the times when it was getting too hard and stepped in to lift me up.

Danny Johnson deserves special mention—no words, my friend, for all your support, understanding, humor, and invaluable feedback. Thank you for serving and for your great heart.

Hugh Huntington offered me a peaceful space for writing this book, his gracious way of supporting the veterans I was writing about.

Eruch J. showed me all I know about stillness and grace; AMB, all I know about destiny and the holiness of serving others.

And there were many angels along the way who lit the path for me with immeasurable love and kindness: Trula Crosier, Jenny Zoppo,

Marna Young, Merry Thomas, Marjorie Skwara, LuAnn Keener, Maya Youngblood.

For their writing wisdom, I want to thank Nancy Linnon, my first writing mentor and very dear friend; Katey Schultz, who gave such astute help with a major revision; Barbara Moulton, who knew the book needed the narrative thread I was trying to avoid.

Much of this book was written at the Virginia Center for the Creative Arts—a rich and thriving artist community. I'm so very grateful for the time I spent there.

Erin Mooney of Grand Harbor Press has shepherded the book with a steady hand; Shari MacDonald Strong, the editor I hoped for, helped this book shine brighter and truer. Renee Fountain of Gandolfo, Helin, and Fountain Literary Management believed in this book from the start, and gave it a chance—I'm forever grateful.

Finally, my sincere thanks to the service members, veterans, and spouses who shared their lives and allowed me to see who they truly are.

ENDNOTES

1. Department of Defense, "Total Military Personnel and Dependent End Strength by Service, Regional Area, and Country," Defense Manpower Data Center, August 26, 2015, https://www.dmdc.osd.mil/appj/dwp/rest/download?fileName=DRS_54601_309_Report_P1506.xlsx&groupName=milRegionCountry.

2. Chris Adams, "Millions went to war in Iraq, Afghanistan, leaving many with lifelong scars," *McClatchy DC*, March 14, 2013, http://www.mcclatchydc.com/news/nation-world/national/article24746680.html.

3. "10 Steps to Joining the Military: Step 3: Choose the Right Path," Military.com, accessed June 7, 2016, http://www.military.com/Recruiting/Content/0,13898,rec_step03_enlisted_officer,,00.html.

4. Amy Belasco, "Troop Levels in the Afghan and Iraq Wars, FY2001-FY2012: Cost and Other Potential Issues," Congressional Research Service, July 9, 2009, http://fas.org/sgp/crs/natsec/R40682.pdf.

5. Heidi M. Peters, Moshe Schwartz, and Lawrence Kapp, "Department of Defense Contractor and Troop Levels in Iraq and Afghanistan: 2007-2015," Congressional Research Service, December 1, 2015, https://www.fas.org/sgp/crs/natsec/R44116.pdf.

6. "How Many U.S. Troops Are Still in Afghanistan?" CBS News, January 4, 2014, http://www.cbsnews.com/news/how-many-us-troops-are-still-in-afghanistan/.

7. Department of Defense, "U.S. Casualty Status," accessed June 7, 2016, www.defense.gov/casualty.pdf.

8. Tom Bowman, "Chairman of Joint Chief Warns of Disconnect with Military," National Public Radio, January 17, 2014, http://www.npr.org/2014/01/17/263333207/chairman-of-joint-chiefs-warns-of-disconnect-with-military.

9. Alexandra Alter, "National Book Award Goes to Phil Klay for His Short Story Collection," *New York Times*, November 19, 2014, http://www.nytimes.com/2014/11/20/books/national-book-award-goes-to-phil-klay-for-redeployment.html?_r=0.

10. Jeffrey Jay, "Terrible knowledge," *Family Therapy Networker*, 15 (1991): 18–29.

11. Epidemiology Program, Post-Deployment Health Group, Office of Public Health, Veterans Health Administration, Department of Veterans Affairs, "Analysis of VA Health Care Utilization among Operation Enduring Freedom, Operation Iraqi Freedom, and Operation New Dawn Veterans, from 1st Qtr FY 2002 through 4th Qtr FY 2014," January 2015, http://www.publichealth.va.gov/docs/epidemiology/healthcare-utilization-report-fy2014-qtr4.pdf.

12 Terri Tanielian and Lisa H. Jaycox, eds., *Invisible Wounds of War: Psychological and Cognitive Injuries, Their Consequences, and Services to Assist Recovery*, http://www.rand.org/content/dam/rand/pubs/monographs/2008/RAND_MG720.pdf.

13. David Kupfer, "Like Wandering Ghosts: Edward Tick on How the U.S. Fails Its Returning Soldiers," *The Sun Magazine* 390 (June 2008), http://thesunmagazine.org/issues/390/like_wandering_ghosts?page=2.

14. Brett T. Litz, et al., "Moral injury and moral repair in war veterans: A preliminary model and intervention strategy." *Clinical Psychology Review*, 29 (2009): 700, doi: 10.1016/j.cpr.2009.07.003, https://msrc.fsu.edu/system/files/Litz%20et%20al%202009%20Moral%20injury%20and%20moral%20repair%20in%20war%20veterans--%20a%20preliminary%20model%20and%20intervention%20strategy.pdf.

15. Office of the Deputy Assistant Secretary of Defense (Military Community and Family Policy), *2014 Demo-*

graphics: Profile of the Military Community, Department of Defense, http://download.militaryonesource.mil/12038/ MOS/Reports/2014-Demographics-Report.pdf.

16. Kacy Mixon, "Serving Together: Research on Dual-Military Couples," Military Families Learning Network, October 1, 2013, https://blogs.extension.org/military-families/2013/10/01/serving-together-research-on-dual-military-couples/.

17. "America's Military: A Force Adrift: How the Nation Is Failing Today's Troops," *Military Times*, accessed June 7, 2016, http://www.militarytimes.com/ story/military/2014/12/07/americas-military-a-force-adrift/18596571/.

ABOUT THE AUTHOR

Elizabeth Heaney, MA, LPC, was a therapist for nearly thirty years before she began counseling military personnel returning from combat or preparing to deploy. She helped service members of all levels, from soldiers fresh out of boot camp to commanders. Heaney continues working in private practice and with the military community.